CW01370513

NIGEL BETTS

Blood, Sweat and Gears.

An unreliable record of a 21st century mid life crisis.

First published by Itchy Feet Overland 2022

Copyright © 2022 by Nigel Betts

All rights reserved. No part of this publication may be reproduced, stored or transmitted in any form or by any means, electronic, mechanical, photocopying, recording, scanning, or otherwise without written permission from the publisher. It is illegal to copy this book, post it to a website, or distribute it by any other means without permission.

Nigel Betts asserts the moral right to be identified as the author of this work.

Nigel Betts has no responsibility for the persistence or accuracy of URLs for external or third-party Internet Websites referred to in this publication and does not guarantee that any content on such Websites is, or will remain, accurate or appropriate.

Designations used by companies to distinguish their products are often claimed as trademarks. All brand names and product names used in this book and on its cover are trade names, service marks, trademarks and registered trademarks of their respective owners. The publishers and the book are not associated with any product or vendor mentioned in this book. None of the companies referenced within the book have endorsed the book.

First edition

ISBN: 9798842139873

This book was professionally typeset on Reedsy.
Find out more at reedsy.com

*This book is dedicated to Linda Teresa Joyce Betts.
A woman who willingly sacrificed all that she knew, for the
mystery of a life less ordinary, and in support of a man who
seldom, if ever, deserved such a towering level of devotion.*

...oh, and anyone else who knows me.

*"I have found out that there ain't no surer way to find out whether
you like people
or hate them, than to travel with them."
– Mark Twain*

"No one saves us but ourselves. No one can and no one may. We ourselves must walk the path."

— Gautama Buddha, Sayings Of Buddha

Contents

Preface   ii
Acknowledgement   vii

I   Part One

1. Avoiding misery handed down.   3
2. Life as a flightless bird.   19
3. Punishment of answered prayers.   29
4. Pain without purpose.   112

II   Part Two

5. Plans and pandemics.   141
6. Nothing behind, everything ahead.   164
7. Back to the past.   226
8. Always look a gift horse in the mouth.   244
9. Still in the Arena.   318

Conclusion   330
Notes   333
About the Author   337

Preface

*"As you get older, three things happen. The first is your memory goes,
and I can't remember the other two".*
- Norman Wisdom, comedy genius

It is October 2017.

I am 51 years old, and find myself, in the words of Dante Alighieri, *'Midway along life's journey'* and I had *'woke to find myself in a dark wood'*.

* * *

I had arrived, figuratively speaking, bloodied and bowed in that very 'dark wood'.

Mentally and physically broken, often debilitatingly anxious, and with an uncontrollable, yet undefined, yearning to do something better with my life.

I was suffering from a severe form of a midlife affliction that will, no doubt, be readily recognizable to many men, like me, of a certain age.

Not unlike when you inadvertently put on an old T-shirt back to front - on the surface it functions just fine, but actually, everything just feels wrong.

This is what my life was like, and in my case, it felt very wrong indeed.

* * *

So, that was me in 2017, at what felt like a critical tipping point in my life, desperately seeking the longed for relief. Picture yourself finally removing a pair of ill-fitting shoes after a full day of walking in the baking heat and dust.

Tradition suggests that crises, such as these, should be averted in any number of extravagant and frivolous ways, from buying shiny brand-new Harley Davidsons, to ill-fated extra marital affairs with women half my age.

Tempting though they might appear, and seldom one to be diverted by the conventional, I became determined to relieve my own personal *'itch'* by living on top of an old Land Rover as a full-time overland traveller.

That fateful decision would have a profound effect on both myself and my family, leading inexorably toward, what ultimately would become, three very long years of mayhem before we would even turn a wheel in anger.

Those years were packed full of COVID delays, near-death medical dramas, and those perpetual mechanical calamities that will be familiar to all Land Rover Defender carers.

* * *

Important though it is to fully understand the *'what'* of our unusual journey, it's maybe just as vital to understand the *'why'* of it first.

How did I get to the tipping point, where the only answer to my mental frailty was to walk away from the most lucrative job that I have ever had, and sink literally everything that we had into the rebuilding of a 1998 Land Rover Defender 130, and make it our permanent and only place of residence?

* * *

This memoir is a retelling of my life in two distinct halves.

Please forgive my indulgence, but the first part gives you, I hope, a self-critical but realistic recounting of some of those key moments in my first 50 years of life, leading up to that notorious tipping point in 2017.

A tipping point that was reached during the consumption of a bottle of Glenmorangie Whisky, late into the night at a farmhouse kitchen table in the beautiful rolling hills above Maranello Italy.

The second half is an honest account, or as near to that most elusive of targets as my memory will allow, of a period in time that has become known in our family as the *'world's longest midlife crisis'*. A period when I dragged my ever suffering wife Linda, and my beautiful son Oliver, closer, and closer to the cliff edge.

* * *

It is a chronicle of what happened after the whiskey hangover had subsided, and specifically, details the many and varied obstacles that we faced, and the immense struggles that we have had to overcome as a family, for me to fulfil my dream to be an authentic overland traveller.

That fateful night of drinking was shared with the unknowing architect of, what we shall call, the great tipping point: the legend that is Graeme Bell - one half, with Louisa his wife, of the fabled A2A Expedition.

His no nonsense southern African encouragement, washed down with much alcohol, finally tipped the scale, and led me to step away from a life spent joylessly toiling in Formula One, and directly to my attempt to live a somewhat more extraordinary life.

That night was to have profound effects, not only on my liver, but everything about our lives. It would lead us down a path that would ultimately test us, as both individuals, and as a family unit, to absolute breaking point.

* * *

The book that you are about to read, is not a traditional overlanding or travel book as such, although there are elements within it that are.

It's a kind of guidebook, but a guidebook of my mind, if you will.

So buckle up, we're going fairly deep.

When all is said and done, this book is a simple story of one man's attempt to overcome his own weaknesses, and convince himself that he has really does have what it takes - whatever that '*it*' might be.

I suspect, however, it's not me that I am really trying to convince, but perhaps, as you may judge for yourself, my late departed Father.

So buckle up, we're going fairly deep.

It all began a very, very long time ago…in a galaxy, far, far, away…..

Nigel Betts, Silverstone July 2022

Acknowledgement

As a part of the initial funding efforts for the first edition of this book, a number of people gave well above the odds and, consequently, they deserve some very special recognition.

Regardless of what drove you to do it, I sincerely thank you for your belief in me, and by extension, this book.

I salute you all, but in no particular order.

- Leigh Pettifer
- Dr. Mark Gillan
- Stefano Mucelli
- Perry Cohn
- Ron Hartvelt
- Colin McGrory & Vicky Moore
- Les & Ray Rockley
- Neil Simkins
- Chris Botting
- Ross Pinchin
- Stuart Bailey
- Mark Halleybone

Before and after.

The project that is Itchy Feet Overland, is the work of many people, both directly or indirectly. Here are just a few of the special souls that have made such a difference in our lives, and made it happen. Many of them, stepping up during our very darkest of hours.

Legends one and all.

- David Smith

- Gillian Louise Ross
- Janine Mold
- Edd Cobley
- Scott Antoniou
- Tony Hayes
- Alan Strachan and Jewels Hill
- Graeme and Luisa Bell
- Sara Garbugli
- Mauro Falcone
- Jon Norman
- Steve and Viv Middleton
- Sarah & Rob Slade
- David & Angela Bradley
- Mark & Barbara Attard
- Graeme and Laura Thompson
- Barry Selman
- David & Angela Bradley
- Elisa Casagrandi
- Andrea Rifici

The following businesses, also had the towering faith to support us in our crazy dream.

We are forever indebted to them.

- Darche – Trek Overland Ltd
- Exmoor Trim Limited
- Falken Tyres
- Terrafirma 4x4
- PWR Technology
- Portable Power Technology
- Global Telesat Communications (*GTC*)

- Equipt Expedition Outfitters
- Safety Devices International
- Maxtrax
- AT Overland
- Pakelo Oil
- Survival first aid kits
- RST Land Rovers
- LRD Security
- Stanley Europe
- Helinox Europe
- Protrax Adventures
- Ram Mounts USA
- Presson UK
- Ardent Works

I

Part One

"The first half of life is learning to be an adult - the second half is learning to be a child."
— Pablo Picasso

1

Avoiding misery handed down.

> *"If you have never been hated by your children,
> you haven't been a parent."*
> **- Bette Davis**

How often have you wondered if the universe is truly infinite[1]?

Not a trick question, but maybe one that's a tad heavier to begin with than you were expecting. As an 8-year-old child, it was the one question that I simply couldn't stop asking myself.

Those thoroughly intoxicating bouts of late night overthinking, as I lay in bed stubbornly putting off the inevitability of sleep, were a prescient indicator of my future mental health challenges.

It should be said, that I think a lot, about everything, all the time. My favourite pop song is 'Can't get it out of my head' by E.L.O. Not really, but I do like it, and it probably should be.

As a child, I simply wasn't content to gently drift off into the nothingness of sleep at night. Maybe I should have been dreaming of being, my then hero of heroes, Peter 'the Net Buster' Lorimer[2] of the mighty Leeds United, or surely some other mortal being.

Much higher notions were intent on troubling me. The concept of an infinite cosmos[3] fascinated, electrified and periodically worried me - I simply couldn't fathom that you could travel in one single direction forever, and never arrive back where you started.

My pocket-sized 8-year-old brain would fizz and pop, as I wrestled with this most fundamental cosmic conundrum, along with the equally tantalising possibility of endlessly travelling the solar system at the speed of light.

Too much Star Trek before bed maybe…

* * *

As I look back over the last 50 plus years, it's striking that the adrenalin released into my brain during these nocturnal mind-blowing periods of wonderment and awe, were seldom to be felt ever again.

Gradually, they were replaced by feelings of inadequacy, anxiety, and, more than often, impending doom.

So what, exactly, went so spectacularly wrong?

* * *

Everybody knows how to raise children, except the people who have them.

AVOIDING MISERY HANDED DOWN.

- P. J. O'Rourke

I was born in the summer of 1966 in Wellingborough, Northamptonshire, one of any number of nondescript market towns that pepper the centre of England, famous for little, and notable for little more than it's useful proximity to the London bound fast rail network.

A dormitory town, now full of what my mother, when alive, would snobbishly refer to as, 'London overspill'.

My early childhood was vanilla in the extreme. A middle class boy, in middle England - in one small bungalow, with two parents, one older sister, Jenny, and a gold fish, whose name escapes me, that stubbornly refused to die.

A life free of traumas, or even real hardship of any kind.

Boy Scouts, bike rides, church choir and windswept seaside holidays. I enjoyed all that comes as part and parcel of the English vanilla life.

Arriving as a home birth at the tail end of the baby boom, I was soon discovered to be a sickly child.

A life threatening respiratory crisis at the age of 18 months, after many weeks in an Hospital oxygen tent, was eventually diagnosed as chronic Asthma[4]. A complaint that I continue to manage to this day.

Some of the earliest memories that I hold, are of me perched on the edge of my bed, in the dark hours of the early morning, shoulder muscles on fire as I lean forward and silently fight to expel the air in my constricted lungs.

I hid my asthma then, and continue to do so, even now. I was, and inexplicably, still am, ashamed of my infirmity. It often stopped me playing sport at school, and would inevitably cast a long shadow over my early life, until, finally, it was brought under some level of therapeutic control in my late teens.

In the 1960s deaths from Asthma were not uncommon, and interestingly, one of the treatments for severe Asthma at that time, was the use of ephedrine (*adrenaline in other words*) - though I don't recall if I was ever treated with this drug, could this be connected to my aversion to the naturally occurring adrenaline ,and by extension, the circumstances that would be produce it?

It's an interesting thought, but I am no scientist, and surely lack the necessary patience for sufficiently rigorous research to prove a conclusion. Best that this intriguing theory is stored, for now at least, on the ever growing pile marked 'curious'.

I was a sensitive child, and remain a sensitive adult. I cried easily as a child, and would do anything to avoid a physical fight.

I hated the sensation of being out of control. I learnt early on in life, that when I became angry, I lost control of my faculties very quickly.

My heart rate would soar, my skin light up, and my brain turn to mush. By the time I was 15, I had learnt to largely suppress these unpredictable reactions.

* * *

My parents, both now passed, were introverted in their own unique and distinct ways, not unlike me, I suppose.

My father was an only child and, perhaps common for his WW2 generation, if he had the capacity for overt displays of affection, either verbal or physical, he hid it very well indeed.

AVOIDING MISERY HANDED DOWN.

My mother was the sole provider of affection.

When, after one of my many teenage paternal run-ins, I despairingly asked her 'Why did you marry him!?', she replied calmly and matter of factly, 'Because I love him.' No answer to that.

My mothers way of displaying additional affection was to shower myself and my sister with classic 1970s and 1980s food - in culinary terms, a very dark era, filled as it was with, what would now be regarded as life threatening quantities of starch, lard and sugar. The last thing that an asthmatic child needed.

Looking at my childhood photographs, my weight started going awry at the age of around 5 or 6 years old- for sure, not a time when I was independently managing my calorific intake.

A combination of restricted physical exercise, due to the poorly managed asthma, and over eating set me on the road to physical ruin. I neither blame nor resent anyone for this, its just another facet of my emotional makeup.

My weight would become, and remains an ongoing battle, and is inextricably linked to my emotional and psychological well-being, and by extension, my mental state. I continue to self-medicate for my anxiety, with food and alcohol.

Kathleen Margaret Betts was a quiet, calm and largely inscrutable soul. Tall, slender and strikingly raven haired in her youth, she was a natural, warm, compassionate mother, with a shy laugh never far from her lips.

A working life hunched over a typewriter reduced her stature considerably (*I now share her appalling posture*), it remained impossible to tell if my Mother was frustrated with her lot or not.

She was serene, quietly intelligent and always affectionate. She seemed happy enough, but I couldn't help feeling that she had failed to reach anywhere close to her potential - certainly not in comparison to her brother Brian, a high flyer at the MOD in London. Whether this was by choice or, more likely, social conditioning, I will never know.

Oddly, I often felt annoyingly frustrated on her behalf. At the end of her life, the recurring breast cancer was dealt with, in the only way that she knew how, with calm stoicism and quiet resignation.

Her premature passing robbed me of the twilight years that I eagerly expected to enjoy with her. F**k cancer.

* * *

It is very easy to imagine that an overweight, asthmatic child with two left feet, was considerably less than my Father had hoped for in a son and heir.

As a parent of a boy myself, I can well understand the anxiety, and surely some disappointment, felt by him as I wheezed my way though those early years - ex Royal Navy, county standard cricketer, self taught cabinet maker and precision engineer - any hopes and dreams of a sporting passion to be shared, surely violently dashed on the unforgiving rocks of my pre-adolescence.

Derrick Charles Sidney Betts was a quiet, diminutive, square jawed and powerful looking man, with strong features and a charming lopsided smile.

A resemblance, at least in chin, with Bruce Forsyth was regularly joked about in his later years. Photographs of him in his late 1940s naval uniform reminded one of a devilishly handsome 'jack the lad' character in any number of wartime propaganda 'flicks'. Though small in stature, he was definitely a catch.

Never overtly cruel, he left me in little doubt, however, about the lingering disappointment that he felt in me. In later life he became a driving instructor and, after a deeply fraught and entirely unsuccessful attempt to teach me himself, he paid for me to have driving lessons with one of his colleagues.

On the morning of my driving test, he commented to me, matter-of-factly, and without obvious malice, 'Don't worry. **When** you fail, I'll get you some more lessons.'

I passed first time. His reaction? A monotone "That's good then", an utterance devoid of both eye contact, and more importantly, emotion. Things weren't to be celebrated, until mum came home from work, that is.

She was delighted, of course.

Though not an outwardly emotional man and obviously uncomfortable and ill-equipped in some ways to be a father, he was far from being a bad man. Never, ever, physically violent, he was a hard working man who never failed to financially provide for his family, but he clearly struggled to show any emotion other than mild disappointment or outright anger.

The only exceptions being his Sunday music sessions with his huge headphones on - a way to escape the world for a while. Maybe we are not so different after all.

As he came to the end if his life, I formed the distinct impression that he had almost certainly harboured niggling feelings of unfairness about his life outcomes. These would occasionally surface in his mild resentment of the close relationship I had with my mother - for example, commenting in my early teens that I was now too old to get a loving embrace from my mother. Looking back, I can;t help thinking that he resented in some form, the disturbance that we, as children, had made in his life, but I can only speak fir myself.

Nonetheless, he played the cards he was dealt, and left the world no worse than he found it, so for that he should be applauded. Not all can say this of themselves.

It's impossible to know if our relationship would have been materially different, had I not been asthmatic, or maybe just a possessor of one left foot instead of the two, but I somehow doubt it.

Sadly, our relationship remained largely transactional, and, for whatever reason, we both lacked the necessary emotional tool kit to conduct a deeper relationship, and I lacked the initiative to really find out why. I neither blame nor resent him for that, but the void in me, where the sons love for his father should surely reside, is deep, black, and very empty.

His passing was quite sudden but not entirely unexpected. What was unexpected, was my failure to have any feelings of loss or bereavement. When the end came, he passed away quickly. Too quick, in fact, for me to get to the hospital.

I arrived in Kettering, having driven from Milton Keynes, and in the absence of any nursing staff on the ward, and knowing which bed he was in, I went and pulled back the screens surrounding his bed.

What I found was a grotesque distortion of my father - his dead body unprepared and contorted with death, mouth wide open as if he was mid way through screaming. I will die with that last image of my father in my minds eye.

I didn't complain, maybe I should have, but I understand the pressures on staff in geriatric wards, and honestly, I felt no great emotion on seeing him.

This troubled me then, and continues to trouble me know. I remain bemused and slightly jealous of those that have such a relationship with their parents, that the loss of them is an emotional fracture in their lives, a fracture that can, in some cases, take years to heal.

I have thought many times that there must be something wrong with me, as surely, the unnaturalness of my ability to emotionally detach myself from anyone or anything signals something that, maybe, needs some further attention.

* * *

I suspect that this 'emotional constipation' experienced by my father did not begin with him, and can more than likely be traced back through the generations of his family tree.

However, as in many things in life, it's possibly more important to look forward, rather than back. Breaking this poisonous chain is something that I have consciously prioritised with my own son, Oliver. Outward displays of affection are crucial in building healthy relationships, and are something that I have had to learn to give, and more importantly, Oliver understands WHY I regularly make these displays, and the significance of them for his own development.

One can only hope that he will, one day, share his unbridled affection with his own children, regardless of how many left feet they may have…

If I have a regret, it's that I never got to explore more deeply in later life, the barriers to my relationship with my Father.

If you take one lesson from this, remember, you can't ask a

dead man any questions…

*   *   *

Fat, asthmatic, and routinely reminded of my 'shyness' by those around me, my self-esteem was fully deflated as I stumbled into my teenage years.

Despite my mothers obvious love for me, both she and my father were ill-equipped to guide me out of this dark, dank, well shaft of inadequacy.

We didn't discuss emotions or feelings. It was no the Betts way.

I was a painfully anxious child. Anxious about everything, all the time. I was one of many latchkey kids in the UK - so called as, from the age of 11 years, I would walk home from school each day, on my own, to, more than often an empty house.

Only now do I understand quite what a profoundly negative affect that this has had on me psychologically. I would worry endlessly about my mother returned safely home, and left alone, rather than doing homework, or something just as productive, I would be consumed with anxiety until I could see her walking down the street towards the house.

I absolutely hated these times, but told no-one of my experience of them.

The bottling of emotions, feelings and anxiety had begun in earnest.

*   *   *

Over the last ten years, I have given much time and thought

to understanding how I have arrived where I have, mentally speaking.

During my final days of work in 2020, my state could best be described as mentally exhausted, with bouts of non-specific anxiety and occasional depression (*with a small d*).

This 'depression' manifested itself, primarily, as severe exhaustion. I would sleep a lot and wake up just as tired, I'd be unable to focus on anything, and gaining no enjoyment from things that I would normally, on these rare occasions, I wanted nothing more than to lie in bed all day.

Now I am no longer working, the depressive episodes still happen, but much less frequently, and I don't have to fake the 'flu' so often, and stay in bed for a day …

It's not unlike being a secret alcoholic, though rather than hiding bottles of booze in ever more obscure and ingenious places around the house, I am just as equally adept at obscuring and hiding all of the symptoms of my fragile mental health.

I have never sought out professional help - arrogance maybe, but I always felt that I could 'cure' myself. Despite a lifelong mistrust of psychiatry and therapy in general, the study of Buddhism has led me to understand the importance of meditation in mental balance, and this led me back round in a full circle to the power of talking therapies.

The thought of truly opening up to another person, stranger or not, fills me with absolute dread. I can rarely open up to myself. Sometimes, my mind feels so fragile, I worry that if my 'Pandoras Box' of a brain is fully opened up, the consequences could be utterly catastrophic - sometimes it's best not to know.

As a part of this long term introspection, I have come to recognize one of the primary reasons for my ongoing anxiety, is that, for much of my life, I believe that I have suffered from a mental condition called Cherophobia [5].

As a sufferer of this form of anxiety, I continue to live with an irrational belief that any satisfaction and sense of achievement that I may experience in life, will eventually be cruelly and effectively punished.

If I allow myself to be outwardly happy or excited, I irrationally fear that I will be brought crashing down to earth with a thud, realigned through a negative occurrence of equal or greater measure.

I rarely get excited, ever, about anything, only in the closed and quiet sanctuary of my mind. Trust me, you would never know, unless I told you.

This irrational belief, and the associated feeling of inadequacy, has left a severe blight on my life - it has curtailed many of the life experiences that I might have had, restricted the people that I might have met, and torpedoed the greater achievements that, just maybe, I could have realized, had I chosen a path more suited to my character.

It continues to cast a significant shadow over everything that I do, and is an ongoing daily battle.

* * *

"Character isn't something you were born with and can't change, like your fingerprints. It's something you weren't born with and must take responsibility for forming."
- Jim Rohn

Being called shy as a child, was an appalling and highly damaging misdiagnosis of my introverted personality.

I am toward the extrovert end, of the introvert spectrum, so my introversion can be quire subtle and is not always clear to people that I interact with. This can be doubling frustrating, as by the very definition, we introverts tend to keep our feelings hidden and rely on others to read us rather than listen to us.

When combined with Cherophobia, and a single sex secondary education, this personality cocktail made for a very 'interesting' adolescence.

* * *

Later in life, I would have the opportunity, more than once, to have my personality defined by something called the Myers Briggs Personality test (**MBTI**).

The test seeks to define each persons personality, through analysis of their answers to standard questions and, specifically, to which one of the 16 personalty types that occur in the general population they most closely conform.

I am defined as INFJ, someone with Introverted, Intuitive, Feeling, and Judging personality traits. It is quite disturbingly accurate, both with the good and, if I'm honest, the bad aspects of my traits.

We make up only 1% of the population and INFJ's are believed to be the rarest personality type.

INFJ's are defined as those that *"tend to approach life with deep thoughtfulness and imagination."* Whilst an *"inner vision, personal values, and a quiet, principled version of humanism guides them in all things."*

The deeper you delve into the characteristics of your personality, the more that you can learn. It may even begin to explain that many of your supposed 'weaknesses' may actually be strengths.

I find the subject fascinating and had I had this information when I was in my early 20's I could have, maybe, avoided much of the mental discomfort that I have endured over the last 30 years. Just maybe.

I thoroughly recommend these tests[6] for everyone who feels that they would benefit from knowing more about themselves. The test is just the beginning though, the trick is to use the results of the test to guide your life, work and relationships.

Self development is something that anyone can do and the benefits can be huge. Knowing that I am not shy, that I am introverted, is a vindication of what I felt inside.

The reason why I have a mission, the reason why I become emotionally drained, everything is there. They are not weaknesses, they are naturally occurring characteristics, I have been fighting them.

I had my first test around 1998. The biggest sin that a business can commit, after commissioning this expensive research, is to do nothing with the results. We should have been counselled privately, and if we had, I honestly believe that I would have left motor sport for good in 1999, and gone on to do something much more *'meaningful'* with my life.

If I have a major regret - this is it, right here. It would be 24 long years later, before I tried to do something more *'meaningful'*.

* * *

AVOIDING MISERY HANDED DOWN.

My mental escape from this swirling anxiety vortex was travel. Not physical travel, obviously, that would require some risks to be taken, and, potentially, even some happiness to ensue! A childhood in the 1970s seldom involved much travel anyway, unless you count Skegness and Cromer.

My head was my universe, and I began travelled to every corner of it, night after night. I trace my life-long wanderlust back to my vanilla flavoured childhood. Tarzan on TV, the books of Jack Higgins[7] and the epic TV travels of firstly Alan Wicker[8], and later, the incomparable travels of Michael Palin, of Monty Python fame.

They all laid the foundation of a fire, but the one thing that really turned that fire into a raging inferno, was one very short BBC TV news bulletin, one incredible man, and one rip-roaring book of old-fashioned derring-do. The man is ,the splendidly and extravagantly named, Sir Ranulph Twisleton-Wykeham-Fiennes, and his book 'To the Ends of the Earth: The Transglobe Expedition'. I own it still, and dip within it regularly for inspiration. This stirring tale of British pluck and perseverance resonated in my young mind, and filled it full of epic possibilities.

I felt convinced that one day, I too would head off into the unknown and face the hardships and privations of expedition travel. Simultaneously though, my mind was stuffed full of crippling doubt.

Surely adventure is just for those *'others'*, not for me… a chubby, middle class, asthmatic nobody, with two left feet, from the centre of England.

Some believe that the biggest influences on a child should be their teachers, but as any teacher will tell you, most children spend far more time with their parents than with their teachers.

So, in conclusion, could my parents have been more encouraging in my development? Undoubtedly. So, am I really any better at encouraging my son to take calculated risks and push himself? No.

One of the primary duties of a father is to not make the mistakes your own Father made - break the chain. I can claim only partial success in this regard, but hopefully I've done just enough to avoid Oliver having to bear his soul in writing in years to come.

Could a late 1970s British state secondary education have a part to play?

2

Life as a flightless bird.

'Youth is wasted on the young.'
— **George Bernard Shaw**

After a largely uneventful infant and junior school education, the end of summer 1977 heralded a very rude awakening indeed.

School attendance in the UK is normally defined by catchment area so, in other words, you routinely go to the secondary state school that is closest to your place of residence - in my case the somewhat notorious Westfield Boys School awaited my arrival.

However, by dint of having an older sister attend one of the 'better' schools in Wellingborough (*Wrenn School, the co-educational former Grammar School*), I had the additional option to attend there.

At the age of 10, friends can be everything and the daily ups and downs of life can take on an importance and weighty significance out of all proportion with reality.

Despite the best efforts of my mother, during many fraught kitchen table 'discussions', she finally succumbed to my pleadings to join my other Junior School friends, and reluctantly agreed that I could attend the school of my choice. I may be wrong, but I don't recall my father showing any particular interest in either outcome. So, when the dust settled, Westfield it was, complete with mythical threats of ritualized head flushing and other such potential horrors.

Despite the undoubted advantage of sustaining life long friendships with those that I have known since we played together on sit-on wooden trains at Mrs Ravens playschool in 1971, in our woollen ties and chunky v neck tank tops. I can't help thinking that this decision may have been the very first of a small number of significant ill-judgements in my life, but, looking back, it's very hard to determine just how much it might have negatively shaped my life experience, or even blunted my future prospects.

Undoubtedly, I would have lost touch with people, and lost friendships that I now highly value, but if I am honest, the doubts remain.

*　*　*

"My school days were the happiest days of my life; which should give you some indication of the misery I've endured over the past twenty-five years".
- **Paul Merton**

My arrival at Westfield Boys School in the summer of 1977,

was stark, jarring and violent, almost from the outset.

As my mother knew full well, and I was beginning to discover, Westfield was a school that enjoyed some significant notoriety within the county of Northamptonshire. It was termed a 'sink school' by those, including my mother, that felt the need to label and disparage it.

The 'sink' moniker refers to its perceived role as the local school of last resort (*short of something a little more 'prison-like' that is*).

It was a boys only school in a world in which single sex educational establishments were becoming far less common, certainly in the state sector. This anachronistic aspect led to a preponderance of 'old school' teachers on the staff roster, with their respective 'old school' teaching methods - some arriving at the school for no other reason than to openly perform some sort of personal protest against the co-educational system.

The threat of violence was ever present and widespread - amongst pupils and staff alike.

One of my first memories of school life was, in fact, a random act of violence, tinged with a Pythonesque touch of comedy. Leaving school one afternoon amongst a teeming mass of fellow students, I felt something roughly connect with the small of my back - swinging around, I'm confronted with a boy some years older than I, brandishing an open craft knife.

Frozen in shock and confusion, I heard these calm and matter of fact words…

'Oh, sorry mate, I thought you were my cousin', he said.

This introduction to Westfield life left me scared, confused, and with a 12-inch-long cut in my brand-new Parka jacket - something that would take some serious explaining when I got home.

Corporal punishment was still enthusiastically employed during my time at secondary school (*not being outlawed until 1986, just after I had left*), and the anxiety caused by its ever present threat of use, often for the most arbitrary of reasons, cannot be underestimated.

Whilst I was too meek to ever get into enough trouble to actually receive the cane or its junior weapon, the slipper, I was, on a number of occasions, trusted by the teacher to collect the cane and punishment book from the headmasters' office.

Looking back now, the widespread use of violence as the primary tool to control the misbehaviour and violence of the students, is ironic at best.

As a deterrent, it was seriously flawed, as it only worked on those that never intended to be violent in the first place - and those that did, often revelled in the notoriety of their punishment record.

Still notorious amongst my school cohort, the legendary mass caning in Mister Ginns French class. It still lives on, in a memory as fresh as if it was yesterday. Around half the class caned at the front of the class, in a mass beating that now, looking back, is incomprehensible, immoral and more than likely illegal.

The older I get, the more I believe that the current educational blueprint is outmoded and not fit for purpose. A system, created for the needs of the industrial revolution, that only rewards people that retain information like a sponge - largely discarding those right-brained[9] amongst us who have other, less obvious yet distinct talents, is failing a huge number of young people.

Like many of my contemporaries, I suspect that I was only able to become fully engaged with educational subjects that really fired a passionate interest in me.

English mostly. Words, stories, poems. The emotion and escapism of language.

I remain in awe of what was then referred to by us *'could do betters'* as the *'swots'* - those golden children that have the ability, focus and self discipline, to learn, retain and regurgitate any and all sorts of information, particularly for those subjects for which they have no interest in, or indeed significant aptitude for. Mind boggling and frustrating.

For me, a charismatic teacher, though important, only went so far.

English Literature and Language came to me quite effortlessly, and a wonderful History Teacher enabled me to enjoy a delicious side order of Film Studies. This alone was enough to justify the many privations of school life - the endless bullying because of my weight, my introversion, my hair, the music I liked, and the friends that I kept. Bill Lanning created in me, a lifelong love of the moving image - books and films are, of course, the natural home of the introvert, but you still need a guide to get you there sometimes.

The more I reflect back on these times, I realise that I have spent the rest of my life trying to recapture those tiny and specific excitements of my early youth.

As a teenager, walking down to the Arndale centre and buying record albums in 'Revolver' on the basis of the cover alone.

Watching French art films on BBC2 in the early hours and feeling completely and utterly immersed in otherness. Nothing else existed for those 2 hours - maybe its pure nostalgia, but I long to feel these same emotions more regularly than I do.

Aspirations for an artistic life however, without the family role models, nor encouragement, were never likely to materialize.

People like me did not go on adventures, they went to school, college and joined the wage slave army. That was to be my fate… and sadly, I dutifully drifted inexorably towards the wage slave army of worker drones. All dreams of riding the Green Tortoise Bus across the USA drifting further and further back in my mind, until they were completely and utterly sublimated.

The received wisdom is that it is good to have dreams, some would say vital, but dreams can have a heft to them, a weight that can become overwhelming, and unbearable, if not very tightly controlled.

The management of my mental health has always involved a wild oscillation between the suppression of my dreams, and the warm solace of their fluffy embrace.

From my earliest school days, dreams were a way of coping with the bullying, with the betrayals of childhood friendships. Like a Beirut hostage in their 1000th day of solitary imprisonment, dreams can be a mental life raft to cling to in the oceans of pain , but in my experience, they can equally become painful reminders of inadequacy and failure.

You can guess which end of the spectrum where I spend most of my time.

By some strange superpower, despite minimal effort and even less motivation, I managed to spend my whole secondary education in the top performing cohort of students - the expectation being that I would achieve great things . Equally

LIFE AS A FLIGHTLESS BIRD.

impressively, but somewhat less mysteriously, I managed to fail all but a few of my Ordinary level examinations.

It was obviously casual Friday that day. Yes, I had hair once.

By my early teens, I had a deep seated love of all Motor Sport, and harboured a modest dream to be a car mechanic.

I loved cars, they were all that I thought about, but my father, a man that spent much of his working life dirty, working in mining engineering, wanted something *'better'* for his son and wouldn't support me in trying to find an apprenticeship. This was a crushing blow.

Lacking the gumption to do anything about my dream, unaided, I drifted into the 6th Form for an extra year to retake just enough subjects to enable me to blindly slide further towards the local technical college, and the inglorious prospect of 'Business Studies'.

I wanted to study Business about as much as slamming my head in a car door.

* * *

Ever one to follow the path of least resistance, I kept plugged along with a further course in Business Studies at the local university. In a small concession to the notion that sometimes, things happen for a reason, the absolute highlight of this period of my life was membership of the Nene College Motor Sport club - including a truly unforgettable trip to the 1985 European Grand Prix to witness Nigel Mansell's first victory in Formula One. I would never have gone on my own.

Our battered Ford Transit minibus got us to the circuit with just minutes to spare on race day. Rushing across the car parks, we muscled our way through the crowds, just in time to witness the spine tingling cacophony of over 20000 BHP being let loose in a chest pounding roar.

The sound, the smell, the overwhelming euphoria of the

crowd, it felt like a birth of sorts within me - with my nose pressed up against the catch fencing opposite the start line, I knew where I wanted to be. Where I needed to be. I needed to get on the other side.

All I could think about was working in Motor sport.

Mentally, I could not take any more learning, and soon after that, I finally abandoned the realms of academe.

It was time to get a job, any job… and then, get into racing!

* * *

Dropping out of a HND in Business Studies midway through the course, without anything as complex as a plan, was, on the face of it, yet another poor decision, and served only to continue the theme of directionless decision making, that characterised my formative years.

As for a job, the dream of Formula One was clearly out of reach, but instead of kicking doors in until someone gave me a mechanics apprenticeship, I meekly scoured the local newspapers, searching for anything remotely suitable for my 'Business Studies' background. No vision again, no purpose, no plan..

In short time, I found work in the credit control office of a local Telecoms rental business. My first experience of the corporate environment was a strange affair, to say the least.

The female boss of the credit control office, excitedly gave me the job on the spot, citing my sex as the primary reason for my recruitment. Seemingly, an office full of women was less than desirable, at least for this female boss.

Puzzled, but grateful, I was about to find out why…

The credit control office of GPT Reliance was a veritable

hotbed of gossip and bitchiness - an alien and astonishing world to me, as a highly inexperienced young man whose character and education left him completely ill-equipped to deal with such a daunting and confusing world.

Around this time, early 1987 or thereabouts, through a friend of my father, I was received a second hand copy of Autosport Magazine each week.

In a world before the Internet, the 15 minute film packages in BBC Grandstand and ITV World of Sport was never enough.

I devoured every page of them, soaking us everything about motor sport that I could. It was a delicious treat, and this generosity would ultimately lead to the first of a number of incredible opportunities that I have been lucky enough to have received.

In my wildest dreams, as I sat in a stuffy and dingy office in Wellingborough, threatening drunken care home owners with the forceable removal of their telephone and fire control systems due to non payment of fees, I could never imagine being given the opportunity to join the reigning Formula One World Champions for the 1989 season.

Amazingly, that is exactly what happened.

3

Punishment of answered prayers.

"When the gods wish to punish us they answer our prayers."
- Oscar Wilde

As far as I recall, the summer of 1988 was not particularly exceptional.

That is, unless you were amongst those perpetually thirsty souls who enthusiastically celebrated the much debated arrival of all day drinking in the UK[10], or maybe a long-suffering supporter of those legendary Bedfordshire giant killers, Luton Town Football club.[11]

For me, 1988 will forever be remembered for a chance sighting of an advertisement in the jobs section of Autosport magazine.

It is important to remember that, in those halcyon pre-internet days, the small classified section of this weekly specialist magazine was pretty much the only way to discover job opportunities in motor sport, and Formula One in particular. Unless, that is, you were amongst those precious few that were lucky enough to already be working within the sport, or knew someone in that tight nit community.

As a youth, consumed with dreams of working in Formula One, it was this section of the magazine that I habitually, and hungrily, read first.

I excitedly studied the pages, in the unlikely event that, amongst the adverts for aerodynamicists, fabricators, race mechanics and HGV Drivers, there would be a magical opportunity that would allow my dream to be realized,.

Anything that could herald my entry into that most rarefied atmosphere of Formula One motor racing. Anything.

* * *

It's worth noting that growing up with the small group of friends that I did - with many of that handful of friendships still going strong today, some as much as 50 years later - was a definite silver lining from the dark cloud of attending Westfield.

I don't think that I made a very good friend at the time. I cared far too much about what others thought about me, and often lost my way in selfishness and negativity.

Introverts seldom cope with more than one close relationship at a time, and my fear of rejection often prevented me from developing the types of friendships that I saw others eagerly enjoying. That has never changed.

* * *

PUNISHMENT OF ANSWERED PRAYERS.

A year before that fateful advertisement, driving around Wellingborough in his very cool 5 series BMW's, I excitedly declared to my oldest of friends, Dave Smith, that *'I will do absolutely **ANYTHING** to work in Formula One'*. I would happily sweep the floors, if only I could get the chance!'

Well, that chance would come, unexpectedly, dreamlike, but sadly, in the full and blinding glare of hindsight, it was fatally premature.

* * *

In 1988, Formula One was enjoying a golden era. It was the year in which Ayrton Senna, perhaps the greatest driver ever to have sat behind the wheel, would win the first of his World Championships at the wheel of the legendary, and incomparable, McLaren-Honda MP4/4.

Victorious against such iconic opponents as; Alain Prost, Gerhard Berger, Nigel Mansell, Rene Arnoux and Michele Alboreto, the McLaren duo of Senna and Prost dominated the season, save only for a 'timely' and emotional Monza win for Berger, at the wheel of the Ferrari.

This unexpected event, serving as a fitting tribute to the memory of the recently deceased Enzo Ferrari, somewhat unsurprisingly, pleased Bernie Ecclestone greatly.

* * *

The life changing advertisement that I saw in the magazine that day, was for the position of *'Junior Marketing Assistant'*, an entry level position, working for McLaren International in Woking.

Yes, that McLaren... Senna, Prost, Lauda, James Hunt!

At the time, the reigning world champions were midway through what would become the most dominant period of success by a single team in F1 history, until the Mercedes' period of dominance in the modern hybrid era.

I cannot tell you what made me do it. For once, my miserable lack of self-worth was put to one side, and I allowed the dream to seem, for once, entirely real and tangible.

My written application was duly posted, without a single expectation of a reply, let alone any form of positive outcome.

If, like me, you can remember back far enough to the days before email, WhatsApp, and the rest – the pent-up excitement of receiving a real life letter through the post, that wasn't a bill, was truly electrifying. I carried on sending solicitors letters to impoverished care home owners, and waited.

Days went by, and then days soon turned into weeks.

The inevitable conclusion was clear. I wouldn't be moving to Woking any tome soon, and it was hardy surprising - what prospect had I got?

But amazingly, some 4 weeks after posting my application, a letter duly arrived.

A beautiful crisp white envelope, with the unmistakable logo of McLaren International in the top left corner.

Inside, instead of the much anticipated *'Thanks, but no thanks.'* formulaic rejection, it contained a typed letter that would change the trajectory of my life forever. Later, I would learn that this was but one of 50 or so letters, each sent to a possible candidate, inviting them to visit the team headquarters in Woking for an interview in the days to come. The sense of astonishment, excitement and, not surprisingly, anxious dread, was palpable. Dare I dream?

A week or so later, after a fitful night of sleep, I drove the 2 hours from Wellingborough in my beloved 1983 Caspian Blue Ford Escort XR3i, nervously arriving at the McLaren facility in Albert Drive, Woking a full two hours before my 11 am interview.

As I sat in my car, apprehensively sweating, in what passed for my Sunday best clothes, it was immediately clear to me that I was entering another world entirely.

The world of, McLaren boss, Ron Dennis was a world full of perfection, and an image of imposing permanence and superiority – huge glass fronted buildings, polished floors, smartly dressed receptionists and luxurious leather sofas. Sombre colours everywhere - a sea of grey, white and black. I would soon learn the full extent of his strive for perfection - the impeccable car park and reception area was just the beginning.

The contrast to the dishevelled mess of the office I was currently working in, was stark and in some ways, reassuring. It spoke of an organization that, unlike my current employer, valued the aesthetic, as well as the functional - somewhere where perfection was not an ambition, but an achievable standard to be maintained, flawlessly and timelessly.

When seated in the voluminous sofas, your eyes were inevitably, and intentionally, drawn to a huge glass cabinet surrounding two sides of the waiting area.

Dramatically lit and full of the lustrous golden glow of race and championship trophies past, this was a clear, unmistakable statement – *'You are amongst winners, if you're **not** a winner, get out now!'* Resisting the urge to let a little bit of wee out, and run screaming back through the glass doors, I concentrated on controlling my blood pressure, and waited for my name to be called…

By now, I was not alone in my leather clad hell, and it was becoming clear that I had joined the end of a recruitment conveyor belt of other applicants, who were now surrounded me in the comfy sofas, coming and going as their allotted interview times arrived.

Unlike the Apprentice TV Show, we eyed each other nervously, even suspiciously, but didn't discuss our relative prospects as, for one thing, there was far too much breath and bowel control going on.

We all knew what was at stake - it was golden ticket time, and this Charlie only had **ONE** ticket to the chocolate factory.

*　*　*

Inevitably, the impeccably structured conveyor belt process suffered some delays and, as in the doctor's waiting room, delays seldom engender positive thoughts in those that are waiting.

Finally, the excruciating wait was over, and I was ushered upstairs into a small and brightly lit room.

The rest is a total blur, save to recall that, to the best of my knowledge, Claude Littner[12] was **NOT** amongst the interview panel. I can't convey to you how the interview went, as my mind went into some sort of hypersonic 'fight or flight' mode.

All that remains is the sensation of an almost 'out of body' experience as I was answering questions, without even seeming to consciously form the answers in my mind.

Once the interview concluded, I sat in my car and basked in the feelings of utter relief and elation, as I unbuttoned my collar and loosened my tie. The release of this, previously pent-up, cocktail of feelings was overwhelming - I was physically shaking with the release of adrenalin. Had I done enough?

**

In 34 years of employment, I have only had to endure a handful of job interviews but, with one notable and ultimately fortunate exception when I was interviewed at the ill-fated Footwork Arrows F1 team in 1996, my success rate has been, quite frankly, astounding.

I don't claim to be very good at much at all, but the evidence suggests that my interview technique is, at the least, fairly effective.

As I have come to understand, having been on both sides of the recruitment process for over 30 years, the process can be long, complicated and often fraught with unexpected bureaucratic delays.

These bumps in the roads can result in recruitment decisions taking weeks and, in some cases, months to be communicated to candidates. Sadly, back in 1988, my inexperience led me to expect that the decision would be as swift as my hero, Ayrton Senna, lapping the Monaco circuit, but it turned out to be as slow as poor old Oscar Larrauri in the tortoise-like and luckless Eurobrun...

**

Eventually a letter came, and in all respects, not the one that I was expecting.

The letter containing an offer of employment, specifically an offer to join McLaren International as part of the marketing team of the Honda Marlboro McLaren Formula One team.

The stunning emotional impact of this letter is, even 30 plus years later, acutely fresh in the memory. At that time, I wanted nothing more than the opportunity to join 'the circus' of Formula One - to be able to bask in the reflected glory of my involvement in the sport; a sport so beloved by so many people, all over the world.

Dreams, in my vanilla world, were not supposed to come true, but unbelievably, the planets had aligned to give me the opportunity of an absolute lifetime.

The fact that the role was in a field of activity that was, in hindsight, wholly unsuited to my introvert personality type, and re-enumerated at a rate that was barely sufficient to sustain a vegan church mouse, mattered not in the slightest.

This was Formula One, and that's all that mattered to me.

I was about to step behind the curtain!

I was IN!

* * *

*'They've promised that dreams can come true -
but forgot to mention that nightmares are dreams, too.'*
- Oscar Wilde

A first day in a new job is very often daunting, and this was no exception.

In only my second full-time working role, I found myself

in a large, dynamic and fast moving business, full of huge characters, from mullet haired mechanics, to smartly dressed executives.

It was completely and thoroughly overwhelming.

What I didn't know at the time, is that whilst Formula One was going through an epic period on the track in the late 1980s, with some of the most magnificent racing in its history, it was simultaneously coming to the end of its golden era in the culture of the team factories.

It was still an era of tattooed truckies, smashed hire cars, pit lane 'poo' related pranks, and apparently, nicknames for all.

My job, it transpired, was junior dogsbody with special responsibility for team clothing.

McLaren took their clothing, like most things, very seriously. Since 1981, they had been enjoying a commercial partnership with HUGO BOSS A.G, a German fashion house, notorious for their manufacture of Nazi uniforms both prior to, and during WW2. Despite this unfortunate past, the iconic Boss tailoring perfectly fitted Ron's clean cut, crisp and business like style.

My 'office' was to be the team clothing store - in effect, a large cupboard containing the clothing supplies with a small desk at the entrance to greet my many 'customers'.

It was located on the ground floor, next to the office of Leo Wybrott, long time McLaren employee and at that time, the factory manager.

Opposite was the impeccably managed stores department, ruled with a iron first by the legendary McLaren old boy, the ferocious, Ray 'Razor' Grant. Legendary for more than just his epic 1970s hair cuts, he was a part of the glorious class of

1976, being a part of the pit crew that helped James Hunt win the world championship at a rain soaked Suzuka that year, in one of the that most unforgettable finishes to a seasons racing.

'There is a white line buddy, and your shit stays on that side.'
Yes, Razor. He wasn't that ferocious really.

Appearance was absolutely everything to Ron Dennis and it showed.

Corridors were to be free of clutter of any kind, at all times. The team members, particularly when in public, must look smart, and most importantly, identical in every respect.

McLaren were one of the first teams to introduce complete travel clothing for the race staff - the consequential volume of clothing was vast, and not helped by McLaren having one of the biggest travelling teams in the paddock.

∗ ∗ ∗

My first introduction to the culture of McLaren arrived almost as soon as I did, with an early morning arrival in my *'cupboard'*.

David Bradley, tall, tanned and moustachioed, breezily appeared around the corner of the door, and greeted me with a cheerfully North London *'Alright mate?'*.

I was, as it happened, sort of.

He enthusiastically informed me that whilst his name was Dave, *'everyone calls me Woody'*[13].

Little did I know at the time, that this brief encounter, would signify the start of the most profound, complex and frustratingly challenging friendship of my life.

After shaking hands, he informed me in a mock serious

tone, that it was vital that my nickname was established, and shared to the rest of the factory without further delay.

It was evident from our chat, that 'Woody' was the self proclaimed controller of nicknames and after looking me up and down, and engaging in some cartoonish chin rubbing, the official deliberation was finally complete.

I was to be christened Fat Body, or F.B. for short.

Hardly original considering my rotund exterior, but the obvious affection with which I was named added to the perception, already forming, that I was being ushered into an exclusive world.

The initiation had begun.

I was intoxicated. *'Yea, sure'*, I lied, not wishing to appear stupid, *'I've seen the film 'An Officer and a Gentleman'*". It would be a few months later when I got to see *'myself'* in all my glory... it wasn't flattering, but then it wasn't supposed to be I guess...

He laughed loudly as he went off for a day of van driving, resplendent in his crisp white Boss McLaren T shirt and bright Marlboro Red Boss shorts.

Nicknames were de rigour at McLaren, particularly if you were on the workshop floor - and as my cupboard was situated on the ground floor, it was obviously decided that I was 'one of them'.

It was akin to being back at school (*but without the endless bullying, thankfully*). The banter was non-stop but overwhelmingly affectionate. The likes of Shaky, Fondle (*don't ask*), Tex, Teardrop, Spike, Beaker, Forklift, Tats, Woody and the rest, created an atmosphere that was both very foreign to me, but at the same time, comforting, inclusive and heart-warmingly welcoming. War without bullets.

By way of illustration, and not long into my tenure, any feeling of comfortable superiority was well and truly punctured by 'Shaky'.

As I strode purposefully through the race bays on my way to the refuse bins, he looked up from working on the chassis, and shouted, *'Oi, need any jam, mate?'*

Looking puzzled, he happily clarify my confusion.

Chuckling, he said, *'You could spread some jam on your shoes, and invite your f*cking trousers down for tea'* - the workshop erupted, along with my cheeks.

All the mechanics were now transfixed by the sizeable gap between my shoes and my ill-fitting trousers.

Despite my utter embarrassment, I couldn't help but laugh at the quality of the wisecrack. The mode in which I took the joke maybe also served to set me apart from the other *'suits'* - those on the second floor and not involved in the mechanical activities - they were mostly, though not all, seen as aloof by many on the shop floor.

Over the weeks and months that followed, I spent more and more time with the mechanics, and technicians building the cars, rather than, and at the detriment to, the work that I was supposed to be doing.

My head was turned, and my focus blunted.

They shook their heads in bafflement, as I stayed all night, perched like an owl on the Lista cabinets, while the first new chassis was fired up.

'Go home Fat Body, what's the matter with you?'.

* * *

Throughout school and college, I perennially felt like the 'the outsider'.

At McLaren, I felt for the first time in my life, that I was 'in the club'.

As I came from north of the Watford Gap, I was inexplicably declared *'Northern'* for the first time in my life, but I was accepted..

Some years later, working for Peugeot Sport in Coventry, and despite living less than an hour from Coventry, It would be deemed, by my colleagues, that I was Southern. That's what you get for being born in the centre of England - truly a country of two halves, yet I seem to have been a product of both, occasionally simultaneously.

My role at McLaren was overseen by the late Stuart Wingham, a member of the Marketing Department who previously had responsibility for, among other things, the team clothing. Stuart was a McLaren man through and through, clothed in Boss from head to foot, and resplendently bearded.

He informed me, early on and with great seriousness, that facial hair represented a sign of superiority and ensured that you commanded respect from others. I just thought he looked like a Merchant Ship captain of the Atlantic Convoys. Anyway, back in those days, it would take me months to grow a beard.

He was always professional and business like with me, and what I immaturely interpreted as his resentment at my socializing with workshop employees, was in fact his attempt to guide me on the path to a life in Marketing. My resistance to his mentoring and the subsequent inability to manage this relationship was to spell disaster for my first foray into Formula One.

With a take-home wage of around £80 per week, my accommodation options were somewhat restricted, to say the least. I begin by renting a very grim bedsit in Boundary Road, Woking. Coincidently, the same road that was originally home to the historic first iteration of McLaren International.

The house was slightly reminiscent of the *'Young Ones'*[14] in the classic BBC TV comedy show, shared as it was, by an often absent and slightly odd young landlord, and a pair of highly strung Scots - a flame haired lass by the name of Marie-Clare, notable for her eccentrically restricted diet of Mars bars and Coca Cola, and her on/off boyfriend, the remarkable and unforgettable Donald Mackenzie from Stornoway, in the Scottish Highlands.

Donald was as unique a character, as I think I have ever met. Though we shared a house for only a few months, in that first part of 1989, he left a strong and lasting impression on me, and as it turns out, many others around the world.

Donald was a complex character, full of humour, but given to bouts of anger and depression. An enthusiastic drinker and highly skilled story teller, life was never dull in his company. Donald was a man of great passions, and he let you know about them, at every opportunity.

I liked him a lot.

When I left the house in mid 1989, regrettably, I failed to keep in touch with him.

Many years later, I was saddened to learn that, after developing a strong and evangelical Christian Faith, he dedicated his life to searching for Noah's Ark on Mount Ararat, Turkey.

He was reported missing in October of 2010 and has not be heard of since. Whilst his disappearance remains profoundly shocking to me, the nature of his endeavours were not. Donald was 100% passion, and if he had a strong

Christian faith, he would have had no hesitation in sharing that faith with anyone, whether they were interested or not.

Tales of his distributing bibles in western Turkey, and his opinions on Islam may go some way to understanding his fate, but whatever has befallen him, he would have not gone without a strong fight.

Occasionality, I am asked 'Who is the most famous person you have ever met?'. In response, I instantly think of Ayrton Senna.

A genuine hero of mine. In 1994, I cried in disbelief as I watched the live TV coverage as he lay dead in his Williams after hitting that Imola concrete wall. S

From that precise moment I have never felt the same about a driver, or indeed the sport itself.

5 years prior to his untimely and tragic demise, in early February of 1989, Senna came to the factory in Woking to begin preparations for the forthcoming season, and with testing due to begin in Rio in March, it was time to check the driver kit and make the necessary adjustments.

When Ayrton toured the factory, it was akin to a royal visit - we each stood in the corridor outside our respective working areas awaiting his escorted arrival, reminiscent of a scene from 'Downton Abbey', but without the obsequious bowing, thankfully.

I heard him, long before I saw him, chatting quietly in perfect English, chuckling along with the banter from the legendary *'Razor'* Grant, in the store room opposite my 'cupboard'.

Now it was my turn.

I was in a daze.

Mouth dry and palms wet, we shook hands. He expressed

pleasure to meet me, and following my introduction, he grinned, '*Nigel, is it? I will **NOT** forget that name!*', he said.

I laughed nervously at the reference to his long running and fractious relationship with fellow driver, Nigel Mansell.

To be in his presence was stunning, and utterly unnerving at the same time.

The most surreal experience of my life. I've met many drivers since, but there was something very special about Ayrton - he exuded a calmness and authority that was almost ethereal.

Its impossible to adequately describe, but as pleasant as Alain Prost was, whilst in the presence of Ayrton, it was impossible to ignore the feeling that you were in the presence of, what I clumsily describe as, '*otherworldliness*' - his death was a tragic blow to the sport and the wider world, a world he would have undoubtedly gone on to change for the better, had he not succumbed to his appalling injuries on 1st may 1994.

As my role included the maintenance, storage and transportation of the driver kit, it was periodically necessary for each driver to spend some time in my 'cupboard', and try on all their clothing - flameproof underwear, driver suit and gloves etcetera.

This has given rise to the ultimate '*top trump card*' in terms of motor sport anecdotes, when I casually throw into the conversation that I have seen Ayrton Senna in his underpants. Striped briefs if you were wondering, which you were. Alain Prost in his boxers does not quite have the same impact for some reason.

As the weeks and months passed, with Stuart busy elsewhere, I was pretty much left to my own devices to fill my day with work.

It became apparent to me that this was, at best, a 0.75 man job. Lacking regular supervision, mentoring or support in any way, my inexperience and immaturity began to tell.

My mind began to wander far from the job in hand. Diversions, included wandering the factory and chatting with the mechanics, escalated to include the taking of long unapproved absences with Woody, or taking one of the company vans myself and heading off on a wild goose chase.

In converse to my working performance, my capacity to make new friends seemed to know no bounds. For an introvert, this was a very new, even intoxicating sensation.

I felt completely alive for the first time in my life.

The social life that developed was similar, I imagine, to a great life at university - too little work ethic, and too many nights spent carousing down at our version of the Junior Common Room, the Red Lion in Horsell.

My immaturity was displayed in full effect during one such, now legendary, nocturnal outing. A disco night at the Red Lion was drastically cut short for me, as my speed drinking of 5 pints of Courage Directors Ale in under an hour, rendered me incapable of pretty much anything.

I had only been in Woking for a few weeks, and my beer radar (*that vital support system that guides you home automatically after a savage intake*) had yet to be recalibrated to my new surroundings.

As my legs decided to quit on me, Woody stepped in and kindly guided me out of the pub, into the car park and propped me up against the wall.

My answer to the question of where I lived, seemed to baffle him. Later, when I was told the story, it baffled me too, as I have never even lived in Northampton.

Over the next days, the memory of my epic journey home, would slowly reappear through the mists of my memory. When Woody returned, after inquiring about my address inside the pub, I had gone, but not to worry, turn left out of the car park and its only a one and a half mile walk to where I was living.

What could go wrong?

Plenty, it would seem, as I turned **RIGHT** and headed off on a 6+ hour stagger around Woking - various flashbacks later reminding me of climbing garden fences, clambering through roadside bushes, and the absolute *pièce de résistance,* believing myself to be blind in one eye, only to find that I was lying in the centre of the road, with one eye looking at the white line, and the other at the black tarmac!

How I managed not to die, or at the very least get scooped up by the local constabulary, remains a considerable mystery to this day.

My last recollection of the night, was crouching unsteadily at the front door of my home, focusing intently on guiding the key into the lock, and finally with the door open, slowly crawling up the stairs on my bloodied hands and knees, and sliding into a bed that seemed intent on spinning me in increasing violent circles until I lost consciousness.

* * *

The morning after the night before, the full extent of my 'adventures' were starkly and painfully apparent - from the stiff and bruised limbs, to the the torn jeans, blooded knees and massive gravel rash down the side of my face.

The picture was very clear. I had just about got away with this, but at least it taught me a vitally important lesson, and consequently, I have never put myself in such a vulnerable position ever again. Either that, or my resistance to the effects of alcohol has improved considerably.

Less than a year in to my dream job, my worsening relationship with Stuart Wingham and my generally lack lustre performance, was such that it was clear to all that I was not able to rise above my disinterest in my work, and singularly failed to see the bigger picture of what this job could become, if I knuckled down and made it my own.

This was just the first example of what would become one of my signature failings - plodding along in a job that I hated, and refusing the mentorship of those around me.

The potential for this role was absolutely vast, but in hindsight, was totally unsuitable for someone of my introverted personality. I should have walked away and put it down to experience, but stubbornness or more likely inertia, forced to wait to be pushed.

The push finally came from Ekrem Sami, the boss of McLaren Marketing, in a brief but painful meeting, made all the briefer by my complete acceptance of my unsuitability for the role, and my offer to resign quietly and leave. He seemed relieved and we agreed that I would work until the end of the month and then leave.

It seemed the right thing to do.

The pill was sweetened ever so slightly by Gordon Murray[15], who remarked to me on my final day, that this could be *'The very best decision that I never made'*.

I do not wholly agree, but I get his point.

Gordon was then but one member of Ron Dennis's engineers 'zoo' - my term for a collection of Technical Director standard engineers who were employed by McLaren but not involved directly in the design of the current F1 cars.

Ron collected them like rare postage stamps, paying them handsomely I'm sure, to ensure that the other teams in the paddock could not make use of them. Just another example of Ron's ruthless push for success.

Looking back to those times, from over 30 years of experience, it is clear that I let myself down, and I let Stuart down, during my time at McLaren.

Just looking at the success that my replacement continues to make of his career in marketing, its clear that I blew a massive opportunity. However, I truly believe that the emotional cost of operating in a environment that is wholly unsuitable for me, would have been significant.

As you will see, this would become an evolving theme throughout my 30+ years of work, as I continued to push myself, somewhat masochistically, into high stress job roles, wholly unsuitable for introverted characters such as myself.

I met some fantastic people in my short time in McLaren, and I have many memories, some fond, some more bittersweet.

I created friendships that last until this day, got to spend some time with a woman whose smile routinely lit up my world, although I patently failed to light up hers. Discovered weed, the blues. But lets face it, most importantly, I got to wear the full Marlboro Kit at Silverstone for the British Grand Prix.

Following my last day at work, I went home, packed my bags and feeling a little ashamed, and defeated, I slid away and headed north, driving forlornly up the M1 back to

Northamptonshire in my enormous and dilapidated Vauxhall Victor estate. A car barely alive, held together, as Kevin Hicks would say, by dog shit and tram tickets.

Back in Wellingborough, it was Friday evening. I sat in my old familiar space at the family kitchen table. It was 6.30 in the evening, and as I forlornly ate the comfort food provided by my mother, the phone in the hall jarringly rang.

For introverts, telephones are like Kryptonite for Superman.

'Can't be for me, its never for me.', I thought.

It was Woody, but who else could it be...

"What the fuck are you doing there?' he screamed down the phone.

It became very clear, very quickly, that my attempt to lick my wounds by disappearing in the night was, to put it politely, very unhelpful.

Very soon the great and the good of McLaren International would be assembling at the Ship Hotel in Weybridge, to raucously wish me farewell.

The band had been booked, the beer was waiting - the only problem was, the guest of honour was over 80 miles away.

My only means of transport was still a derelict and highly unreliable Vauxhall. Nevertheless, to my mothers confusion, I threw my belongings back in the car, and set course back to the M1 and the south.

Just under 90 minutes later, I arrived in a huge cloud of foul smelling oil and brake dust outside the Ship Hotel, entering to find a very relieved Woody and and an already well lubricated assortment of the teams technicians, race mechanics and marketeers.

It's for others to say what impact I had in those 12 months at

McLaren, but the experience of this party was truly humbling.

The evening was marred only by the most recent disaster to befall my already woeful car. As a consequence of my *'give it full beans'* approach to returning south, I was now minus the middle and back sections of my exhaust system, last seen in my rear view mirror bouncing down the M1 Junction 14 slip road.

I regret, that due to the urgency of my mission, I concluded quickly, that stopping was not an option, and ploughed on regardless in a car that now resembled a very poorly tuned race car - the noise, resonating through the body, was truly excruciating.

I cant recall what became of this classic beast after that, but its previous owner, Richard Moody, a test mechanic at McLaren, would become a colleague again some 18 years later at Honda F1 - on meeting him in Brackley for the first time, I immediately asked for my money back. He refused, the bastard.

The party was classic Woody. He was the team jester - the organizer of unofficial team activities, and never far from trouble (*with a small 't'*).

He had the capacity to pull everyone together with his infectious *'cheeky chappy'* charm but it's impossible to analyse my burgeoning friendship with Woody, without concluding that it had a detrimental effect on my career at McLaren, but the ultimate fault remains fairly and squarely at my doorstep.

We were both drifting in many respects, and I was, at that time, very easily led. When someone like myself, who feels inherently an outsider, find themselves ushered into a new world of friendship and brotherhood, it's more than just mildly intoxicating.

PUNISHMENT OF ANSWERED PRAYERS.

I went crazy for the social opportunities that presented themselves, but, in essence, let everything else go to hell in a hand cart.

Why did I learn from this pivotal year of my life? Not a lot at the time, it has to be said, but looking back with some more clarity, born of bitter experience, it was clear that my inexperience and immaturity were significant factors in my failure to maximise the opportunity.

As the title of this chapter suggests, things often do not turn out how we would like, or indeed imagine, even when our dreams become true. Most importantly, the opportunity came too early in my life.

At 23, I was emotionally still in my late teens at best , and I lacked the life experience and emotional maturity to deal with leaving home, and working in such an unsupervised and dynamic environment.

* * *

Following my first ill-fated foray into Formula One, other than the friends that I had made, the one silver lining in the dark cloud that surrounded me, was my introduction to, what would later turn out to be, a new career path back into Formula One.

A few of my former colleagues at McLaren blamed the team management for my situation. In particular, they blamed Stuart Wingham, my direct superior, for my downfall. I went along with it, but if I am brutally honest, I made my bed, and I crapped in it. No one else.

However, one of the most vociferous proponents of this flawed theory, was Ann, one of the receptionists who formed part of our tight nit social grouping.

Through one of those simple twists of fate that have peppered my life, Ann had recently begun a relationship with a man called Martin Hurcombe, the owner of a local engineering firm, and ironically, one of the largest suppliers of machined components to the McLaren team.

I got to know Martin socially whilst at McLaren and was part of an effort that supported them both during a very difficult time in their lives.

Despite this, I was still surprised when, a few weeks after leaving McLaren, I was told to report for an Interview at Tufflay Precision Engineering - a small organization, also based in Woking.

They were in the throes of expansion and were about to transfer their factory from their cramped and unsuitable premises in the centre of Woking to a new, modern, out of town factory.

This interview was very different, with Bill Tottle, the General Manager, cheerily exclaiming *'I've been told to give you a job!'*

So without further ado, I was now in charge of the tool and material stores in a precision engineering company. No clue what was expected of me, but I was beginning to get used to that.

The next 3 years were spent happily at Tufflay, as I moved from the Stores to the production office, and finally running that office.

I narrowly avoided a lifetime of precision engineering due to the recession in the early 1990s. I, along with a handful of others, who were seen as either non-productive or represented capacity that was over and above what the depressed order book could justify, were duly made redundant.

Now, at least I had some marketable skills.

I understood precision engineering, and could read technical drawings.

Surely, something any racing team would be interested in..

* * *

When people say that they can't find a job, I tend to, somewhat uncharitably you might think, scoff a little.

In the mid nineties, I found myself jobless, and living in a shared house a long way from the rest of my family.

Despite my negative experience during my time at McLaren, my passion for Motor Sport remained undimmed, and I was determined not to sign on for unemployment benefit (*something I have still yet to do*).

To find my next role, I determined to use an old marketing trick and mailshot every team that I could think of, and offer, what passed for, my '*services*'.

In the pre-internet age, finding the postal addresses of teams was only really possible through the Autosport Directory - this annually published little red book was indispensable for finding out the details of teams, suppliers and sponsors in the major motor sport categories.

Armed with the directory, I set about writing to every single seater team and manufacturer, every sports car team, every rally team, and even some Indy car teams in the USA. I forget the exact quantity, but it would not be surprising if I spent the last dregs of my redundancy money sending out over 100 CV's.

The hit rate was abysmal, with a slack handful of letters

coming back my way as responses.

As you know, you only need one arrow to hit the bullseye.

The one that did, was a letter to Mick Linford, the long time boss of Peugeot Sport UK, a factory Touring Car and Rallying team, based out of the old Humber factory in Coventry, UK.

I was about to be sent to Coventry.

* * *

Timing, they say, is everything, and as my letter to Mick Lindford landed on his desk at the historic Humber Road, Coventry offices of Peugeot Sport UK , it turned out to be the most perfect of timing.

The team manufactured their own touring cars, largely independently of their French owners, and were undertaking their 1993 season, operated a brace of Peugeot 405 Mi16 touring cars in the British Touring Car Championship[16].

At the time, Peugeot Sport UK was the last of a dying breed, it was a team embedded within the manufacturing facility of a car manufacturer. Bucking the modern trend of using small specialist engineering business, set up for the singular purpose of designing , manufacturing and operating race and rally cars, Peugeot Sport UK was manned with a hybrid workforce of time served factory employees, and a small number of *'mercenaries'*.

Crucially, the team operated in a unionised environment - an environment that offered some rather unique challenges for a racing team…

A day before my letters arrival, Fred, the purchasing and parts controller for the team, a full union worker, had incapacitated himself in a most spectacular fashion.

Whilst removing the advertisement flags from the roof of the car transporter at a blustery Oulton Park circuit, the hapless employee was caught by a particularly strong gust of wind, lifted clean off their feet, and violently propelled sideways off of the top of the articulated vehicle.

Without the training of a parachutist, he understandably froze, locking his legs solid in shock, and fell the 20 feet to the ground, landed squarely on both feet.

Despite landing on grass, the grim result, was the violent snapping of both ankles.

This unfortunate turn of events ushered in my second bite of the cherry.

I was back in the saddle.

* * *

Part way through the 1993 BTCC season, I moved back to Wellingborough, and happily joined the Peugeot Sport UK team as one of a small group of self-employed 'mercenaries' - the non-union workers employed by the team in those specialist roles that, the union deemed, could not be filled by staff within the factory.

Unions are seldom found in motor sport organizations, for a number of reason.

The unions at Peugeot still had real power and despite delicate negotiations, some very odd arrangements were necessary to avoid conflict and possible industrial action.

One of the main areas of contention was trucks, and specifically, the truck drivers who drove them.

Traditionally, a team would employ at least one person with a full heavy goods vehicle driving licence to transport the cars to and from the circuit. These *'Truckies'* were additionally experienced in, and had responsibility for, the loading and transporting of race cars and very often, the management and provision of fuel and tyres at the circuit.

Peugeot employed Bob Whitehead as their Truckie, a large jovial farming man, who I would work closely with, and come to like greatly.

In those pre *'Heath and Safety'* days, one of his favourite, and most spectacular, tricks was to put out a lit cigarette in a drip tray full of petrol. Not recommended unless you know how it's done.

When I joined the team, the Union had insisted on the ridiculous arrangement whereby, as the tractor unit was a factory vehicle, a union driver must drive it at all times. Additionally, the driver, due to union regulations, would be unable to do anything **OTHER** than drive the tractor unit. No loading, unloading, fuel or tyres - just driving from A to B.

This gave rise to the ludicrous, and expensive, practice of maintaining the wages of 2 drivers with one of them paid to spend the majority of the race weekend in a nice 3 star hotel.

For a team of such limited budget, this infuriated the management. Consequently, they eventually introduced the new practice of sending a car to the circuit along with the truck, to bring the driver immediately back to the factory, only to return them again on the Sunday night after the race. This satisfied the unions regulation, but removed all the perks.

Very soon, and somewhat unsurprising, the team was allowed to use a non union tractor unit, and drive it themselves without restriction.

This was but one of the many strange practices of the

Peugeot Sport UK team.

As time went on, the onion was peeled further. It seemed we had to 'buy' the standard components we needed, in just the same way that we would have, should we have been an independent Peugeot Dealer.

Touring cars at that time enjoyed large grids, and racing was highly competitive - for 'competitive', read 'aggressive'. In one race weekend, we could expect to damage up to 6-8 bumper assemblies across 2 cars. Having to purchase this volume of components was hugely draining on the budget.

It often felt that, despite being within the Peugeot factory, we were, in some ways at least, at war with it. War, as you may know, often gives rise to innovation and leads to unique and audacious solutions to problems.

In the case of the bumpers, it was my first introduction to *'corporate borrowing'*.

Gary Timms, the long time chief mechanic of the team at the time, was an affirmed factory man. On my arrival, he made his thoughts crystal clear about 'mercenaries' like me, but despite that, we found an understanding and eventually, somewhat grudgingly, even mutual respect.

A local Coventry boy in his late 30's, Gary was disturbingly energetic, fizzing, tightly wound as a clock spring. Capable of great humour, but often angry at someone or something, he was definitely the teams Sergeant Major.

Impeccably turned out, he was a great lover of hair cuts, seemingly enjoying them more regularly than I managed to get hot dinners. Legend had it that maybe this had more to do with who was carrying out the adjustments, rather than the necessity for them.

He was instantly notable for the most perfect set of white

teeth that you will ever see this side of a Kardashian. Workshop folklore had it that the teeth were a replacement set, provided by his employer, after he was hit squarely in the face by a whee; and tyre combination, in years gone by, whilst recovering a roof rack full of wheels from the upturned support van, in a ditch on some foreign rally.

Peugeot was a crash course in race car engineering - having an office next to the designer, Andy Thorburn, led to a great, symbiotic relationship. Andy shared this knowledge freely and every spare moment, I sat in his office watching him turn problems into ideas and then ideas into 2D drawings - drawn by hand in those pre CAD days.

Fascinating, and I think I learnt more about race car componentry, from him, than any other person.

In the weeks that followed my arrival in Coventry, I got to know one of the mechanics better than most, and through him, the next stage of the long journey back to F1 would ultimately begin.

Alan Strachan, a tall, wiry Scotsman, almost identical in age to me, and clearly a man that had plans. A mercenary like me, he was often found caked in dirt. He was a doer, but happy with *spannering* cars he was not.

He was demonstrably ambitious and, it was obvious that he was not going to be satisfied with scrapping around at the back of the grid with a second rate touring car team.

In tandem with ambition came opinions, and lots of them. He had opinions like a beekeeper has bees. He wont mind me saying that he was more than happy to share the resulting 'honey' of opinions far and wide, but not everyone had such a sweet tooth.

Soon enough, he saw his opportunity, and he headed a few

miles across Coventry to an arch rival - the, by then, legendary team of Andy Rouse Engineering (**ARE**).

I plugged away at Peugeot for what remained of the season and well into the next, being an unwitting witness to what, in hindsight, was the beginning of the the slow death of Peugeot Sport UK as a Touring Car entrant.

It baffled me that the French company were bank rolling the manufacture of an identical car at their headquarters in France and would campaign it in their own championship.

From what I could see, there was precious little to no meaningful collaboration between the two teams, and not for the last time, the politics of racing would leave me scratching my head in bewilderment.

A small team of plucky and enthusiastic individuals, was no match for the mighty names, drawn towards the bright light of the mid-nineties British Touring car scene.

What is widely regarded as the golden era of British Tin Top racing was now the target of large, specialist race teams from across Europe, and with the professionalism and sophistication of the likes of Schnitzer BMW, TWR Volvo, and Alfa Corse brought to the championship, an underfunded *'old school'* factory outfit like Peugeot was always going to struggle to compete.

Peugeot UK finally left the British Touring Car Championship in 1998, after 6 long winless years.

* * *

In the summer of 1994, to illustrate the old phrase *'It's not what you know, its who you know',* my brick of a mobile phone rang one morning, and on the other end of the line was my old grumpy Glaswegian friend, Alan Strachan.

Having jumped ship the previous year to our rivals on the other side of Coventry, he was now junior engineer for the legendary Andy Rouse.

Andy Rouse was legendary in the sport of Touring cars, accumulating 9 class wins in the British Saloon and Touring car championships in a 21 year driving career. His experience was unparalleled - he designed, he built, he engineered, he drove. There was no one quite like him.

From his tiny factory unit in Binley, he took on all comers, becoming synonymous with Ford, in particular with his giant killing exploits with the Group A Ford Sierra XR4Ti and RS500, and later the manufacturer supported supertouring Mondeos.

Along with his former Broadspeed colleague, and ARE partner, Vic Drake, he had reputably built some of the most powerful RS500 engines ever constructed. Unlike Peugeot Sport UK, Rouse found a way to compete at the very highest level whilst maintaining, by comparison with his competitors, a small and modestly funded team. But the world was beginning to change around him.

In my first experience of the old boy network, Alan alerted me to an upcoming vacancy at ARE. The Parts Manager was leaving, and by the sound if it, the job was mine if I wanted it.

The opportunity to join a front of the grid team, was a no-brainer. At the time, I had not met Andy Rouse before and, not for the last time in my career, the man, though undoubtedly a legend, was far from what I expected.

Tall, wiry and surprisingly nervous when we first met, Andy greeted me with a clumsy handshake, and told me a little about his history.

PUNISHMENT OF ANSWERED PRAYERS.

I asked him about the future, and It seemed that I was arriving at a pivotal time for the team. At the end of the season 1994 season, Andy would finally hang up his professional driving gloves, and assume the singular role of Team Principle.

As it turned out, this transition would be bumpy to say the least. Despite expectations, born of outward appearances, as I settled into my new role, and got to know the team, the parallels with Peugeot were worrisomely obvious.

Rouse was a tiny team. So tiny, that for the first time in my career, I would be a part of the race team, travelling to the majority of events. The Parts manager role was all encompassing - cradle to grave - I bought it, stored it, packing it into the truck, managed it at the race circuit, and tossed it in the bin when it was done with.

Whilst undoubtedly a great opportunity to learn about racing, I would come to learn that most other teams achieved the same result with up to 3 people sharing these duties.

Right there, I should have known, but hey, I'm going RACING!

Those 2 years with Andy Rouse Engineering were amongst the happiest of my whole career. Travelling the length and breadth of the UK, being the other side of the safety fencing, living the dream.

* * *

I would find out much later that it was her first night working behind the bar of the Queens head in Wellingborough.

She was tiny, slim as a racing snake, with long blond curly hair.

She was absolutely stunning in her tight fitting dress.

Thankfully she was too busy working to notice the psychopath staring at her from the corner of the bar all evening. I could not take my eyes away from her.

I was hypnotized.

As the night drew on, the pub emptied and the usual Friday night remnants, including my brother-in-law John Kelly, would be *'locked in'* by Sean, the gregarious Irish landlord, for our usual private session of beer and political debate.

The barmaids now retired to the drinking side of the bar, and before long, I wound myself sat next to a giggling, slightly tipsy, Linda Ashley.

As 2.30 approached, it was clear that Linda had reached and possibly exceeded her alcoholic capacity.

Sean beckoned me over, 'You'll need to walk her home, but any funny business, and I'll f*cking kill ya'. Understand?'. I Understood. Apparently she was having a very rough time, and she needed looking after. I promised, no funny business.

Equipped with a vague understanding of where she lived, unhelpfully about as far away from where I lived and still be in Wellingborough, we set off.

Progress was painfully slow, and came to a grinding halt when we entered the deserted market square.

She plonked herself down on the kerb stone, head bowed, and declared emphatically. 'I'm going to sleep, just leave me.'.

With Sean's threats still fresh in my ears, I tried to reason with her, and eventually, after a great deal of cajoling, we were on the the move again, but now the full horrifying effects of her Diamond White intake was kicking in.

She hobbled, and staggered her way across Wellingborough and finally were at a front door of a small terraced house.

Hopefully it was her door.

I felt like I was in the middle of an amateur production of a romantic comedy.

Finally inside the house, I follow her down the narrow corridor, blocking the doorway to the sitting room, is a dog. A very big black dog. A Rottweiler no less.

'That's Zara', Linda drawled, 'whatever you do, don't look her in the eye'. I looked in her eyes. I couldn't help it.

As I am trying to process this new,and possibly dangerous, information, Linda stumbles over a full size bicycle, propped up against the sofa, looks down at a sleeping teenager and says, 'Oh, and that's my Son, Matthew, or Andrew'.

I passed on the coffee, and made my exit.

At the time of writing we have been married for 23 years and going strong.

***

Back in Coventry, if my time at Rouse were a buddy movie, my buddy was Derek White.

A laconic and lugubrious young man. He appeared to perform most of the tasks that no one else wanted to do, he was one of the hardest working people I have ever met. As I got to know him better, he opened up to display a rare and precious dead-pan humour.

With his thick Coventry accent and a strong nasal drawl, he would often have me in fits of hysterics, as he would share his latest woes with me, with his monotonously expressionless delivery.

The conclusion is, I would always work best in small teams with fluid responsibilities, and lots of latitude to get on with the job as I saw fit - if only I had stuck with that conclusion, I could have saved a lot of pain and anxiety.

I had plenty of latitude, but despite being housed in a office that adjoined Andy's, he had lots of distractions, and the less he drove, the more he seemed to get distracted.

The team was struggling, year on year, their competitors were becoming more powerful and professional - Renault employed the Williams F1 team to build their Laguna touring cars.

The writing was on the wall for men like Rouse, and sure enough, at the end of the 1995 season, Ford withdrew the support of the Mondeo program and for 1996, we had a cobbled together program of second hand Nissans, somewhat extravagantly referred to as a 'Semi-Works' deal.

It was an ignominious end to a glorious name, and quietly over the next few years, the Rouse name would largely disappear from the pages of Autosport magazine.

* * *

"A second chance will never be able to heal the wound of the first one."
— ***Laura Chouette***

In early 1996, fate would throw another set of cards my way.

Just as the last blood was starting to drain from the corpse of ARE, yet again, the back pages of Autosport magazine offered me a possible lifeline.

Jackie Stewart, the legendary Scottish Triple Formula One world champion had somehow convinced Martin Whittaker, and the board of Ford Motor Company, to effectively bankroll a new F1 team for the 1997 season.

This was very big news - new F1 teams, even now, are rarer than the Javan Rhinoceros, and with the public backing of someone of the stature of the Ford Motor Company? Well, pretty much unheard of.

Seasoned F1 journalists were sceptical. It seemed barely credible that a team only announced to the public in January 1996, could create the entire infrastructure necessary to compete in F1 from scratch, and then launch their first car less than 12 months later.

Stewart Grand Prix Limited (**SGP**) was to be based on the northern outskirts of Milton Keynes, around 20 miles from where I was living. Well inside the 'Motor Sport Triangle' - an area of the UK that stretched from Coventry in the north, to Guildford in the south, and as far as Norwich in the east. Contained with this area were the vast majority of the worlds F1 teams, along with other minor teams, engine builders and countless supporting businesses.

I made up my best excuse for a morning away from ARE, and headed nervously to the worlds foremost proponent of the roundabout. It was time to convince someone that I was the 'Engineering Buyer' that they could only dream of.

* * *

We were testing at Silverstone in the afternoon, so I turned up, wearing my low rent Andy Rouse/Nissan team kit.

I soon found myself sat in a tiny windowless office, in a converted warehouse in Tanners Drive, Milton Keynes.

I was being quizzed by the recently appointed Engineering

Manager, Colin McGrory, and the legendary ex-Williams Team Manager, Dave Stubbs.

I felt instinctively that this was a place that I needed to be. Jackie Stewart, canny Scot that he is, apparently wanted to create a team without the negative cultural overtones of an existing Formula One outfit.

Either that, or he saw an opportunity to pay significantly less than the going rate, and save a few precious coins. Either way, it was good for me, coming from an impoverished touring car team, as I was neither tainted with the culture of F1, nor demanding the wage of a Harley Street plastic surgeon.

Whilst I thought that the interview went reasonably well, I am a perennial pessimist and, to maintain my mental balance, I continued assuming the worst. Colin, in fact, had asked me a fairly strange question. I found out much later that this was one of his *special interview techniques.*[17]

Prior to the interview, he had asked a mutual acquaintance, Mark Halleybone of Stable Fabrication, to comment on my character. Then, as part of the interview, he asked me what I thought of Mark (*to allow comparison to **HIS** experience*), and then, conversely, what I thought Mark might have said about me…

It's an interesting technique and very unsettling for the interviewee. When possible, I have used it myself. Just one of many lessons that I would take from my time working for Colin.

Despite my preference to avoid the pain of disappointment by always assuming the worst, I was surprisingly contradicted a couple of weeks later, with the arrival of a letter offering me the role of 'Engineering Buyer'.

After 6 years away, I was back in the exclusive club, the *'circus'*.

I eagerly accepted the role and informed Andy that I would be leaving his team. Impeccable timing as usual.

* * *

Formula One in 1996 was still a 'relatively' simple affair.

I say relatively, as it's never really been **that** simple, but these were the days when a competitive team had a staff of 250-300 people, not the bloated behemoths today with their 1000+ staff and factory *'wellness suites'*.

The sport was coming to the tail end of what many believe was, for spectators at least, the golden age of Grand Prix racing. When the drivers still 'drove' the cars. Before the 2000's would herald the arrival of an overwhelming array of electronic driving aids, multi million dollar wind tunnels, highly complex 7 poster shaker rigs, and the more recent space race of *'driver in the loop'* simulators.

The times were changing, and changing fast. A well balanced car and a hotshot driver were no longer enough.

In my customary 'puppy-like' eagerness to accept the role, I had neglected to question the size of the purchasing department or the scope of the responsibilities.

On arrival, it seemed that it was a purchasing department of one…me.

Despite being used to working alone throughout my Touring Car career, this turned out to be on a whole other scale.

Unlike many of the other teams, we would have no internal manufacturing capacity to begin with. This was a huge undertaking and would require an absolute attention to quality, unlike any other team.

My identity pass depicted employee number 15.
 To be a part of something from almost the very beginning, was, looking back, a great privilege. To see the team evolve from 15 of us until the 750+ or so when I left Red Bull Racing 12 years later was an incredible ride.

* * *

But back to my empty office - what amounted to a 'L' shaped corridor with desks in it. Windowless, and entered under the stairs to the mezzanine above, containing the other administrative functions and the senior management team. Despite its pokey nature and that fact that it was used as a shortcut by all and sundry to the drawing office, it was home.

* * *

In January 1996, when the team was launched at Ford Headquarters in Detroit, Jackie Stewart proudly trumpeted that his team would be the first 'digital team' - the design of the car would be entirely in Computer Aided Design (**CAD**) and not on paper drawings.
 The old Paul Stewart Racing truck bay was converted to a design office, but rather than the traditional sea of drawing boards, it contained an ocean of Visual Display Units and filled with the low humming of state of the art desk top computers.
 Sadly this digitization only went so far, and for my first days in the job, I was armed with no more than a pen, a pre-printed

order pad and an ageing, and often temperamental, facsimile machine.

* * *

My new boss, Colin McGrory, was a seasoned veteran of *'the circus'* of Formula One.

He was one of a small group of ex-employees of the Arrows Footwork F1 team who followed their renowned Chief Designer Alan Jenkins, by making the short hop across Milton Keynes to the fledgling SGP.

Six years after my stuttering start at McLaren, he would fully induct me into the exciting technical world of modern Formula One. Working together, he would introduce me to technical and manufacturing suppliers that would form the back bone of my supplier base for many years to come.

Colin though, was a man who clearly had the weight of the world on his shoulders. The size of his responsibility for this hugely complex task was mind blowing.

Increasingly grey of face and sloping of shoulder as the weeks passed, as the date if the official press launch of the SF-1 car approached, he often cut an anxious and fatigued figure.

The stress and strain of his task would make Colin seem anxious and agitated on occasion. Though sometimes appearing to be shy, he was not to be under estimated, he was razor sharp, and when things were going right, a smile was never far from his face.

I am proud to still call him a friend to this day.

* * *

The plan to launch the car to the press in December 1996 and race the first car in March 1997, was only *'just'* achievable, but extremely tight.

It's success relied entirely on the success of a new team of designers, who in large part had not worked together before, and a huge array of technical suppliers and manufactures.

Every one had to deliver in line with the plan, and just as importantly, everything needed to be right first time…we didn't have time for 'do-overs'.

The launch of a new team is a mammoth undertaking at the best of times, and when your technical leader is the notoriously *'high maintenance'* Alan Jenkins, the challenge becomes a truly unique undertaking.

* * *

Alan Jenkins, a slightly built, grey haired, bespectacled bundle of energy, had the quick witted personality, and the faint remains of an accent, that exposed his Scouse roots.

He came with the 'gold standard' heritage of working closely with, that most legendary F1 engineer and innovator, John Barnard at McLaren during the 1980s, and specifically during the introduction of the ground breaking carbon fibre composite chassis.

Ironically, carbon fibre would inadvertently ultimately contribute to his downfall… but more of that later.

Jenkins possessed the single technical vision behind the SF-1, and led with undoubted vigour, right from the front. Often quixotic in his demands though, his people skills were legendary, but not in a good way.

To be *'Jenks'd'* was not something that anyone aspired to

- interactions with him could be as ferocious as they were unpredictable. Alex Ferguson-like '*hairdryer*' dressing downs were not uncommon in the drawing office.

He demanded total commitment.

This was difficult for some, when he appeared not to have a home to go to - a situation not shared by the majority of the staff he interacted with.

He also ruthlessly used division to rule, and would show his antipathy for someone by first ignoring, and then, undermining them.

I directly experienced this when it was decided than a level of management would be inserted between Colin and myself. The arrival of Ian Prior, or someone like him, as Production Manager was inevitable as the team grew, and it had became very clear that much more than a 2-3 man band was needed to manage the purchasing and manufacturing within the team.

This seemed a natural progression to me, but not all agreed.

* * *

Don't blow off another's candle for it won't make yours shine brighter.
– Jaachynma N.E. Agu

Not unlike the Military, Motor Sport has always attracted some very '*strong*' extrovert characters.

Some of these characters might easily be termed as '*toxic*' by twenty first century standards, but, particularly back in the late 1990s days, track performance and race results were still the overriding measurements of overall success.

Senior members of staff who singularly failed to understand the vital differences between being a Boss and being a Leader, were not uncommon.

What we would now instantly recognize as *'bullying in the workplace'* was reasonably common, seemingly accepted and, in effect, encouraged and enabled by the continued upward trajectory of those that displayed the most appalling man management skills.

Success on the track was enough for the eyes to be blinded and the backs to be turned.

I would experience a fair number of these character types, right up until I left the F1 industry in 2021.

* * *

After a few weeks, Alan Jenkins, for reasons known only unto himself, took a huge and public dislike to Ian Prior.

He happily showed his complete abhorrence for him by ignoring him completely. He would only interact with me, and would spend some of his evenings in the purchasing office, late into the night, repeatedly denigrating him for reasons that weren't at all apparent to me.

Ian was a mild mannered, chirpy, scholarly looking man. A friendly Mr Chips[18], who just wanted the best for everyone, and to achieve his goals in a friendly, collaborative way.

However, rather than the groves of academe, he came from a for more relevant manufacturing background in precision hydraulic valves - a corporate environment that had ill-prepared him for anything like what he would experience at SGP.

I sensed that Jenkins saw his demeanour as a 'character

flaw' and his lack of F1 experience, as a similar obvious weakness. By contrast he would refer to me as his attack dog, his 'Rottweiler' - names I neither courted, nor deserved. I felt like a pawn in a game of chess, in which I hadn't yet learned the rules.

It can be said that trying to please everyone will always be a failure, but its something I've done through all of my working life. Trying to stay neutral was wrong and, looking back now, I regret the stance that I took.

Though Ricky Nelson said it best, when he said *'You can't please everyone so you gotta please yourself'*, I really should have stood up for Ian more vocally.

* * *

This short period of my life, by far the hardest that I have ever worked, was also, easily the most fulfilling.

Endless late nights and weekends, working with a tight-nit group of people, the vast majority of whom were heading in the same direction with a common sense of purpose - to get that new car built on time and raced.

It is, maybe naively, what I imagine war to be like, just without the bullets and the bloodshed, thankfully.

It was never easy, and there were clashes of course, but over all, it was the single most satisfying period of my working life.

The freedom to work without restriction, to be trusted to cut the corners that needed to be cut, and to be completely supported by the management was extraordinary.

Looking back, the first 2 years or so of SGP were the epitome of what I believe F1 should be.

If I knew then, what I know now, I should, and probably would, have walked away, but instead of walking away, I did what I habitually do. I stuck around, bobbing around the organisation like a disused cork atop a choppy sea.

* * *

> *'To finish first, you must first finish.'*
> **- Juan Manuel Fangio**

The 150 staff that launched that first SF1 car, and raced it in Melbourne in early 1997, were never going to be enough to achieve the lofty ambitions of Jackie and the Ford Motor Company.

Crippling reliability problems during the 1997 season, principally with the Cosworth supplied Engine, saw the SF1 finish only 8 times out of a possible 34 opportunities in its first season.

When it ran, it was a consistent midfield runner, but sadly, it seldom ran.

Over 1997, 98 and 99, the team would consistently grow in size and complexity, but save for a single glorious race win for Johnny Herbert at the Nurburgring in 1999, sustained track success never looked likely.

Jenkins nemesis would be the upcoming SF-03 gearbox - a radical carbon design for the 1999 season, that included metallic bulkheads bonded within its outer shell. A tremendously ambitious project for one of the larger, more established team. For a team barely off of the starting blocks? Engineering suicide.

In December of 1998, Jenkins would fall under the sword and would be replaced by Gary Anderson, the legendary, larger than life, Chief Designer from Jordan Grand Prix. No man was happier than Ian Prior - he would take great pride in having out lasted the wily fox.

Despite the Achilles heel of the carbon gearbox, the SF-03 chassis of 1999 was significantly more competitive than the proceeding cars, and with 10 top 6 finishes in the season, Ford were being encouraged to double down on their initial investment, and purchase the remainder of the team from Jackie.

For 2000, the team would be 100% Ford and renamed Jaguar Racing.

* * *

Throughout the 3 year Stewart period, my role had grown organically, and by the end of 1999 I was settled in the newly created position of Production Office Manager.

However, as the millennium dawned, and the planes failed to fall from the sky, the next evolution of the team began in earnest, with everything, whether nailed down or not, being painted British Racing Green, and adorned with the iconic leaping cat emblem.

We were being foolishly touted in some quarters as *'the British Ferrari'.*

This ludicrous presumption was abetted by a rampant marketing department, who turned Melbourne green in anticipation of the first race of the 2000 season, screaming **'The cat is back**!' from every Billboard, Bus and Tram in the city.

It didn't take long for those possessors of even the most rudimentary understanding of the sports history, to point out that **'The Cat'** had never been in F1, so how on earth could it be **'back'**?

This unfortunate campaign summed up the nature of the whole enterprise, largely the dream of one man, Jac Nasser, the short lived CEO and President of Ford Motor Co., who clearly bought the idea that painting a white car green somehow made it iconic, and a sure fire race winner to boot. It did not - 2 podium finishes in 5 seasons was lamentable.

The green years would grind by, but those golden days of the late 1990s SGP era would never be repeated. The Jaguar Racing team would last a woeful 5 seasons - and any one that knows F1 will be amused at the thought of the glorious 5 year plan - a plan that is often renewed each year, as yet another management team arrived to repair the damage of the outgoing one.

The team was doomed from the beginning - with Jac Nasser **'retiring'** a few months after the teams creation, the team struggled to ever find it's feet.

The team inexorably grew in size and expenditure, but better results stubbornly refused to follow. Ford could not stop interfering in the team and adjusting its structure.

Control of the team became a power struggle between the US elements of Ford and the powerful European Premier Automotive Group (**PAG**) - so for the 2001 season, Wolfgang Rietzl, boss of PAG, gave way for the very different management style of Bobby Rahal.

A hugely successful driver and businessman in the US, Bobby came armed with a very valuable friendship with Adrian Newey. Rumour had it that Bobby was appointed solely on the promise to secure the signature of Newey - then, as now, regarded as the finest Technical mind in F1 - as Jaguar Racings Chief Technical Officer.

His first gift to the team, was to gather each department together, without their leaders, and agree with them that they were working too many hours, and that that was a sign of bad management. Consequently, he was popular with the workforce, and less so with us managers. Later, he would demand that we got our staff to work longer hours to improve the lead time if development parts. A circus within a circus.

* * *

On 1st June 2001, with great fanfare, it was declared to the world that Adrian Newey had *'signed a contract to join Jaguar Racing'*.

In the following days, it soon became clear that Newey's then employer, McLaren, didn't share this view and, in a massive coup for Ron Dennis, he would remain in Woking for six more years, before finally defecting to the land of roundabouts and joining Red Bull Racing in Milton Keynes.

The whole affair was an unmitigated disaster and hugely unsettling for the team. It also serves as a fine example of the core issue with JRL - the unending obsession with the Silver Bullet.

Unlike a serial automotive environment, F1 teams thrive on continuity. Getting the right people in place and keeping that structure, allows success to flourish.

In fact, when you analyse any periods of dominance in F1, be it Williams, McLaren, Ferrari, RBR or most recently,

Mercedes GP. The single most defining characteristic for each period of prolonged success is continuity.

Continuity in Drivers, Sponsors, Team Management, Technical staff and even the race mechanics.

Change always adds risk, and risk can easily affect performance negatively.

Jaguar Racing did nothing **BUT** change things. It was as though the bosses of Ford Motor Co. were allergic to continuity. There was an endless swing door of technical staff on secondment from Ford - either a bus full of Americans, or a bus full of Germans.

Different month, different bus.

In this environment, success was always going to be difficult, and so it proved. Their next attempt to steady the ship was to helicopter Niki Lauda into the mix - when compared with Bobby, two more different characters you could not pick.

Inevitably, Bobby succumbed to the Austrians pressure and resigned.

Rumour had it later, that he would tell his friends that the compensation pay off from Ford was so bountiful, that he treated himself to a vintage Ford GT40 with the proceeds. I would not be at all surprised.

This was not the only pay off - the profligacy was astounding - with rumours that, in just one in year, around $60m was paid out in compensation for contracts either finished early, or cancelled before they even started.

Even for a team owned by the mighty Ford Motor Co - this was going to get noticed.

Sure enough, at now infamous Detroit Board meeting, William Clay Ford Jr, then CEO of FoMoCo and scion of the founding family, reviewed the salaries of senior staff, and exclaimed ' Who the **hell** is this Edmund Irvine?' - this speaks volumes, when you consider that the CEO of the parent company was so disconnected from the team, that he possessed no knowledge of one of the most famous F1 drives of his day, and the senior driver of the team that he ultimately owned.

The seemingly endless organizational changes and negative press speculation, helped to nourish my general discontent - as usual, manifesting as extreme boredom with the endless '*ground hog day*' of dealing with the same people, and the same problems in purchasing.

Looking back on my career, I have around a 3-5 year capacity to stay engaged and focused in a specific role. After those 3 years, I become emotional worn out, lose focus and lack the motivation to develop in the role that I find myself in.

I have always envied those that can work, for year after mind numbing year, doing the same thing without seemingly any detrimental effect on them.

I was never happy standing still for too long, but as the '*Peter Principle*' clearly states - '*If you perform well in your job, you will likely be promoted to the next level of your organization's hierarchy, and you will continue to rise up the ladder until you reach the point where you can no longer perform well.*'. I

n simpler terms, we all rise to our own level of incompetence, me included.

The daily grind was a familiar flow of late design releases, late part deliveries, and mysteriously lost components.

I was becoming particularly frustrated with the last one, '*lost components*'. There is nothing more frustrating than spending your day getting people to do their job, before you could do yours. I would spend many an hour scouring race bays gathering up 'lost parts' - the *'just in case'* parts that mechanics like to keep in their tool drawers.

In what I perceived to be a significant hole in our organization, I felt the team lacked a comprehensive system of management for the parts for the car. The process was disjointed, illogical and contained huge holes of responsibility.

With the last flush of youthful zest that I possessed, I set about trying to put that right.

During the Lauda era, the team made at least one solid decision, and that was to employ a chap called Guenther Steiner - he was sorely needed.

Niki Lauda was a fine figure head, but he was not a manager of people, and that was what we needed. Guenther arrived in December 2001, complete with some serious Ford heritage, having been Engineering Director at M Sport, the championship winning Ford rally team in the UK.

* * *

Guenther, a tall and imposing man, seemed to be possessed of boundless energy, and an equally boundless capacity for taking the piss.

Though Italian from the South Tyrol, it was very easy to forget his birthplace whilst trying to navigate his thick German accent, his speech always liberally peppered with swear words in 3 languages.

Finally we had someone who knew racing, understood what needed to be done, and understood how to do it.

Almost as soon as he got his huge frame comfortable in

his chair, I set about carving a new role for myself. Much badgering and brandishing of charts later, I managed to convince Guenther that the team needed a Parts Logistics department.

In one of those classic, *'careful what you wish for'* moments, I'd set himself up with a massive, and, as it would turn out, largely thankless task.

A task that crossed many team functions and had the possibility to push a lot of noses out of joint - from the race/test teams, to the manufacturing and assembly departments. This was going to be very interesting, but would ultimately keep me engaged and focused for the remaining years of Jaguar ownership.

Despite me almost getting Guenther subjected to a full body cavity search, by Brazilian customs in 2002, we seemed to get on reasonably well.

His style of humour was my style of humour. Unfortunately his fate was never in my hands, and with track success still proving highly elusive, after just one year in the role, he would succumb to yet another one of Fords *'restructuring'* plans.

Little did I know at the time, that it would be just a few short years before I would be staring at him yet again, over the self same desk, just with a different team shirt on.

In late 2002, as part of, what would become, the final Jaguar management shake up, Niki was gone along with Guenther, to be replaced by the all British PAG pairing of Tony Purnell as team principle, and Dave Pitchforth as MD. One last throw of the dice.

Dave was a no nonsense, straight talking Yorkshireman, but as it turned out, he was spread terribly thin. Managing the entire factory, and being the public face of the team at the circuit was a very tall order, and as the performance continued to show very little sign of improving, rumours soon began circulating that Ford wanted out.

* * *

It turned out that Ford were demanding redundancies, a reduced budget, and were imposing a 2 year period to turn it all around. An almost impossible task.

With Niki and 70 other employees also being made redundant in 2003, this was definitely the lowest point of my career in Milton Keynes. Having to hand letters to people, some of whom I regarded as far more than simply colleagues, was the hardest thing I have ever been asked to do.

The tragedy was that the teams headcount was never the issue, and our performance was never going to be improved by weakening our structure.

Yet further proof, if it were needed, that Ford had zero understanding of F1 racing and were treating us like a failing assembly plant - reduce cost and profit will come.

Formula one has nothing to do with profit or indeed cost.

As Ron Dennis of McLaren famously said - *'If you run out if money, go and get some more!'*.

Success bears little correlation to expenditure - you need to spend enough, but just spending more doesn't work either. Toyota proved that. Honda proved that.

* * *

As an amusing aside, in the final year, or so, of the Stewart era, I was invited for the first time, along with my middle manager colleagues, to take psychometric testing.

When the results were collated, the consultant assessor was utterly bemused by our complete lack of interest in matters of finance in general, and budget control in particular. We were not surprised.

* * *

Finally, the inevitable death knell was sounded by Ford.

In September 2004, they announced that the they would cease to enter F1 from the end of that season. An ignominious end to a grand project - with Ford's then vice-president Richard Parry-Jones, coming to Milton Keynes to inform us in person.

I give them a little credit for that, but he also used the withdrawal to criticise F1 by suggesting that *'the decision to pull Jaguar out was a warning that more needs to be done to help small manufacturers succeed in the sport'*.

This was incredible, coming from the representative of one of the largest corporations in the world, and unable to compete with organizations a tiny fraction of their size.

In the end, Ford made the same mistakes that both Honda and Toyota would make in years to come. Treating an F1 team as a corporate entity doesn't work, and never leads to success. The skills needed to make a car plant hum, are not necessarily the same for a racing team.

Cash does not equal success, and restricting the cash will often have the direct opposite effect of that which you desire (*Ferrari reputably spent $600m dollars per year in their early 2000s heyday, whilst Ford thought Jaguar could do even better with just $180m*).

In summary, Ford sent a marketing team to carry out an engineering job - they got what they deserved, zero success and a big bill.

The team would finish 2004 in 7th place in the championship, amassing a less than edifying 10 points.

The highlight of this final year, for most of us in the factory at least, was following the cheeky exploits of a blow up toy Donkey from the film 'Shrek', that was 'kidnapped' from the staff restaurant in Milton Keynes and carried around the world by the Jaguar mechanics for the final races of the season, even appearing on TV during grid walks.

Apparently Ford were not impressed.

We really didn't care. We could all be out of a job tomorrow.

* * *

The remainder of 2004 saw a parade of characters, some maybe shadier than others, coming to the factory to stake their claim as potential new owners of the team.

Allegedly, Ian Prior was instructed to give each of them their own level of tour, appropriate to their perceived standing in the suitability race for ownership.

Some left happier than others, it would seem.

Rumours were rife, Bill Gates, Carlos Slim, various Russian Oligarchs, and even some drinks company that had funny shaped cans, and apparently gave you wings.

In November, the rumours finally ended, and it was duly announced that the Drinks company had won thus particular beauty contest.

* * *

We were to be Red Bull Racing.

We stood in the race bays, and cheered, as Dietrich Mateschitz led us in a toast, as we all drank a can of the stuff, for the sake of Autosport Magazine.

Later it would transpire, that in Fords hast to divest themselves of this mill-stone around it's corporate neck, they sold the team for £1, along with some serious guarantees to not sack us all five minutes later.

Ford couldn't wait to see us in their rear-view mirror.

The frantic fire sale that included Jaguar Racing and, the historically far more significant, Cosworth Engineering, was an ungraceful end to a 30+ years involvement for Ford in Formula One.

From what little I could see, Purnell and Pitchforth had fought very hard to provide the stability and continuity that they knew was at the heart of the problems with Jaguar, and would surely become the problem for Red Bull, if they were bent on replicating the errors and omissions made by Ford.

But, for whatever reason, that wasn't apparently enough.

The axe duly fell, and on 7 January 2005, Christian Horner arrived in Milton Keynes as the latest in the long line of Team Principles.[19]

* * *

In 2005, Christian Horner was unknown to the vast majority of us in the team.

Apparently, he was a 31 yr old former racing driver, and the team owner of Arden International, a successful UK based team in the junior single seat formulas.

From the outside, it looked like an odd appointment.

Did Red Bull know something we didn't?

To this day, Christian likes to recount the story that, upon his arrival, he faced rejection by a shocked and dismissive staff, and as a protest, the factory staff cleared out early on that cold January day.

As he sat in his executive chair, still warm from them departing backside of Dave Pitchforth, what he actually saw out of his window at 5 pm, was the day shift from the manufacturing departments going home, as normal, just like any other day.

I was there, along with the remainder of the factory, working until the job was done.

If he felt that he had to overcome staff resistance, his decision to share this misconception in the specialist motor sport press during those initial days of his tenure, certainly didn't help his cause any.

Personally, I had no animosity towards Christian, he was just another arrival through the busiest swings doors in Britain, and like most others in the factory, I was not a part of a demoralised workforce. Cynical maybe, but not demoralized.

Sadly, the future looked very much like it was going to be, business as usual.

***

The initial period of Red Bull ownership, with their energetic marketing and extravagant summer parties, with hindsight, was undoubtedly the very high tide of my time if F1.

I had been, effectively, in the same team since 1996. I should have mustered the courage to leave F1 when Red Bull arrived, and do something more meaningful, yet it would by another

PUNISHMENT OF ANSWERED PRAYERS.

3 years or so before that decision was made for me.

* * *

In September 2005, Red Bull GmbH, the owner of Red Bull Racing, bought the Minardi Formula One Team, a minnow among minnows, based in Faenza, Italy.

A team that had scored just 38 championship points in 340 race starts (*with 19 of those points being earned in one race*). The team was seen variously as a sad old joke, or an inspiring and plucky underdog, depending on the charitableness of your thoughts.

This seemingly peculiar decision had all to do with long running discussions rumbling away in the back waters of the F1 piranha tank. Some of the bigger (*for bigger read* **richer**) teams were pushing the concept of *'customer cars'* - the idea that a team could sell it's chassis to another less technically adept team for a fee.

This appealed greatly to those that saw F1 as foremost a balance sheet challenge, and not a sporting or technical challenge.

For Red Bull, there were other, more pressing reasons. Much effort had been put into creating a young driver academy. A fleet of young single seater racing drivers were coming up through the ranks, and they only had 2 seats in F1 to offer them, without paying to slot them into the other teams. Four sets was better than two.

For a championship that was struggling to get participants, the FIA saw this as being a potential win/win for all concerned.

For the supplier team, YES, for the team purchasing the

copy, certainly so, but for other smaller independent teams trying to move up the grid and challenge the big boys? An emphatic and resounding *'NO, thank you'*.

Williams Grand Prix became the de facto leader of the **NO** camp.

They were the epitome of the old school of F1 but were in a lengthening performance trough, but just like their better budgeted opponents, they proudly developed and produced their entire car 'in house'.

They managed this without the benefit of a multinational corporate owner, or a friendly billionaire.

Frank Williams, eponymous founder of the team, was horrified that a new team could simply *'buy success'* and leapfrog up the grid, for much less than half of the cost of their annual efforts.

Red Bull GmbH pushed hard in the corridors of power. They were also the most proactive in their preparations, as in the hope of sharing the marketing exposure, and the manufacturing development costs, across 4 cars and not just 2, they were the only team to go as far as actually procuring another one.

Hugely tempting economies of scale were absolutely everywhere, if you were a *'bean counter'*, that is.

If you were a racer, it was anathema.

Akin to giving some of your bullets to your sworn enemy. Madness.

* * *

"Look twice before you leap."

PUNISHMENT OF ANSWERED PRAYERS.

- Charlotte Bronte

No sooner than the purchase was completed, Red Bull set about the *'Austrification'* of the team in earnest, beginning with the appointment, in January 2006, of Franz Tost as their new Team Principle.

Little known outside of F1, he was the former track operations manager for BMW during their Williams tenure.

Franz is a 'character', make no mistake. Despite his appearance of a kindly grandfather, he is a fearsome and determined competitor, and not someone to be underestimated. I think we all underestimated him a little.

Red Bull were determined to completely integrate their new toy, now dubbed **'Toro Rosso'** (*Italian for Red Bull*) without delay, and like the owner of a new puppy, they began showering toys and affection on it, at every opportunity.

The orders came from Austria that they must utilise all of the same IT systems as Red Bull Racing, including any specialist software systems used by us.

With Toro Rosso believing that they would be able to utilize the Milton Keynes manufacturing facilities in the UK to make their parts alongside those for Red Bull, reluctantly, Christian began to put in place the structures to assist Toro Rosso to prepare their new car.

Call me naive, but when the big boss asks me to do something, I saw it as a duty to try my best to do it. Such was it, when Christian asked me to leave my role as Head of Logistics, and manage the production interface between the team in UK and the new *'Toro Rosso'* team in Italy.

Not for the last time, I didn't really think twice before I leapt, or even consider the possible longer term negative implications for my career in Red Bull. I've never been political or strategic in that way.

This blind obedience was far from the whole reason though - the recurring *'Groundhog Day'* in the Parts & Logistics world was taking its toll, and my subconscious three year limit on doing the same thing, was starting to gnaw away at my soul.

In actuality, a new challenge was just what I needed to get my mojo back, and right on time.

* * *

'No man can serve two masters: for either he will hate the one, and love the other; or else he will hold to the one, and despise the other, Ye cannot serve God and mammon.'
- Matthew 6:24

I think that it is fair to say they Christian Horner was not a fan of the acquisition, feeling, not unreasonably, that it would be a huge distraction for the mother team *(his worryingly vague instructions to me included something along the lines of 'look like you're helping them, but do as little as you possible can').*

This negative view was shared by many of the Red Bull production staff, although others were more practical than philosophical, being considerably more concerned with the thought of being dumped with twice the amount of work that they thought they were going to have to manage.

Whilst I busied myself setting up a satellite office for Toro Rosso in a corner of the Milton Keynes factory and travelling to Italy regularly to help with the integration into our parts control, and lifing systems, the relationship between the two teams was deteriorating fast.

The war was over the amount of support that Red Bull was willing to provide to Toro Rosso - there was a giant chasm between the expectations of Franz and the reality of what Christian was willing to offer.

The backroom battle was coming to a head, and the winner was made clear to us in a highly memorable way, that remains unforgettable to this day.

**

The door of Christian Horners Milton Keynes office violently burst open, and an explosive Franz Tost tore into the room, interrupting our meeting.

He circled the conference table, full of us middle managers, like an enraged Bull Shark.

Flushed in the face, he slowly moved around the table directing his blackened eyes and an accusatory finger at each person in turn, spitting the same words to each of us.

'*I f*ck YOU !!*'. '*I f*ck YOU !!*'. '*I f*ck YOU !!*'... and finally, with his apoplectic gaze turned directly toward Christian at the head of the table, he delivered a final, most emphatic 'and, I f*ck YOU !!!'

With that, the door barely on its hinges, he was gone.

It was clear that my life was going to get very interesting, very quickly.

I now found myself in a very strange situation, being quasi-autonomous was fine, just like the old days in fact, but I was being paid by Toro Rosso, but working at Red Bull.

I was now a dog with two masters, and this can make for a

very perplexed dog. Largely left to my own devices, my blind obedience to Christian, combined with my sympathy for the way that Franz had been treated, left me in, what would turn out to be, a very exposed position.

Whilst I plugged on, trying to keep the masters happy, the organizers of F1 were doing their best to throw a complete set of spanners into the works.

The balancing act of trying to provide everything that Toro Rosso needed on time, without impacting the preparations of the Red Bull team was a diplomatic effort of epic proportions. Ultimately, I could never seem to satisfy one without upsetting the other.

Meanwhile, outside of my Toro Rosso Bubble, the team was growing exponentially around me, and with the arrival of Adrian Newey, it wasn't long until Red Bull would enter a period of total track dominance, winning 4 championships in succession from the 2010 season on.

As predicted, lots of money, aligned with the continuity of senior management and technical staff, seemed to do just the trick. Amazing.

This formula is not rocket science, and though a gross simplification, it's something that the mighty Scuderia Ferrari haven't managed to replicate, since their heyday with Michael Schumacher in the early 2000's.

The customer car arguments continued to rage on throughout 2007 and into 2008, with many teams unhappy with the way in which Toro Rosso was believed to be utilizing a thinly disguised version of the Red Bull race car, and as time went on, it became clear that moves were afoot to make this illegal within the sporting regulations and Toro Rosso would soon have to design and build their own car in Faenza.

This sounded the death knell for the UK office and my role within Toro Rosso.

I believe that I am loyal, often to a fault, and would often naively expect a reciprocal loyalty in return, most importantly from those that were above me.

My 12 years of loyalty counted for nothing at the end of the day and being offered redundancy was the ultimate insult, from a team that I had sweated blood for.

The ennui that I felt was profound, and I was unable to muster any enthusiasm for the box ticking HR offers of internal interviews, for jobs I had no interest in doing.

No signed rear wing end plate for me, no watch, no leaving drinks, just a fat cheque.

Feeling rejected and worthless, I checked the jobs section of the Autosport website.

***

Pete Ford, or Fordy as he is universally known in F1, is one of those unsung backbones of Motor sport.

At Stewart Grand Prix he had been, very briefly, installed as Production Manager in the very early days. His infectious laugh when he would launch his regular but affectionate piss taking banter at me, made it very hard not to like him.

He taught me a lot - his mantra was *'They can't kill you'*. He was right, they can't, only you can do that to yourself. I wish I had let this sink in a bit more.

He saw the writing on the wall very quickly, and witnessing the growing carnage caused by the technical boss Alan Jenkins, and he was not prepared to endure the inevitable political war.

I don't blame him, the job is hard enough as it is, without fighting internal battles on a daily basis. His prediction was spot on, considering how badly his successor, Ian prior, would go on to be treated.

If I knew what I know now, I probably would have done the same thing, but unlike me, he wasn't blinded by the excitement of entering F1 and he jumped ship, knowing he could find something better, and he surely did. He would ultimately join the fledgling BAR team, based in Brackley, in 1999. S

Some 9 years later, in his position of Head of Operations of the team, now known as Honda Racing F1, he would approve the placement of an advertisement in Autosport Magazine for a Purchasing Team Leader.

*　*　*

(nana korobi ya oki) English Translation: "Fall seven times, get up eight."
- Japanese Proverb

I left the stark brown and white reception area, accompanied by Sean Gutteridge, then the head of Purchasing at Honda Racing F1, and climbed the narrow spiral stairs to the waiting interview room on the next floor.

Half way up, a familiar voice boomed out *'Diet not working then!'*.

It was Fordy, same infectious laugh, same gags.

All nervousness gone, I instantly felt right at home.

Sean, was understandably far less comfortable, clearly unaware of our shared history, and initially dumbfounded at this highly unusual greeting.

We settled down to the least stressful interview I've ever had, and it was obvious that the job was mine and it was just a question of haggling over the wage demands.

12 years at Red Bull had led my wage to grow considerably and reflected both my Head of Department role and the period of tenure. I had learned to go high and stick to my guns.

The interview over, we shook hands and I left with assurances of an imminent job offer. In my first experience of corporate inertia, the 'imminent' job offer took over three months to arrive, three months that saw my Red Bull redundancy payment dwindle down to nothing.

But arrive it did, and in October 2008, I arrived, bright eyed, in Brackley to take up my new position as the Team Leader of the Honda Purchasing team.

* * *

Honda Racing F1 was less than 30 miles away from Red Bull , but it other ways, it was a world part. A giant operation, owned and operated by one of the largest multi national conglomerates in the world.

* * *

Honda has had a chequered history in F1 - but Motor Sport, and especially F1, was central to their brand from the very beginning.

First entering F1 in 1964 with their own chassis and engine, just 4 years after the launch of their first road car, Honda ultimately failed to overcome the dominance of Ferrari and, what Enzo Ferrari would sneeringly refer to as, the British 'Garagistes'.

The undisputable lowlight was the tragic death of Jo Schlesser in the Honda RA301, during the 1968 French GP.

This profoundly shocking event would lead Honda to leave F1 at the end of the season and they would not surface again until 25 years later, when they would finally find success, albeit as just an engine supplier, with Williams and, finally, McLaren - powering six consecutive constructors championships between them both, from 1986 to 1991.

In 1992, for once leaving on a high, Honda withdrew again, citing financial pressures from the asset bubble as their reasoning.

As I wandered the corridors in late 2008, observing the sea of Japanese engineers and technicians, I was, unknowingly, arriving at the very end of Honda's third period of involvement in F1.

Just 8 years after their previous withdrawal, they returned in 2000 to supply the new BAR team with engines and support, offered free to the team as a semi-works arrangement.

In late 2004, despite not winning a race, Honda were encouraged enough by BAR's 2nd place in the constructors championship to purchase 45% of the team, and the following year, purchased the remaining 55% to confirm their position in F1, once again, as a full manufacturer.

I had barely got my feet under the table, when Sean Gutteridge, my boss, called me out into the mezzanine floor above the race bays, and told me, in confidence, that Honda were withdrawing from the sport.

PUNISHMENT OF ANSWERED PRAYERS.

It had not yet been made public, and shockingly, Honda initially wanted to close and lock the factory and send everyone home that day. This seemed bizarre, even from Honda, with their swing door attitude to F1.

They had spent huge amounts in 2006 and 2007 securing the means to win again. The arrival of Ross Brawn in late 2007, one of the principle architects of Ferraris period of total dominance of the early 2000s, was stark evidence of this, yet they were throwing their cards in yet again.

Citing the economic downturn, seemed to be a convenient way to divest themselves of the team, but for a company that spends $5-6 billion on R&D each year, the argument that $300M for F1 is unaffordable, really doesn't stack up.

Yet another example of a large conglomerate failing to understand the very simple basics of F1 - you need money, ideas and continuity. Without all 3, sustained success will not come, no matter what you do.

As I braced myself for 'last in, first out', I kept my ear to the ground and waited to see what would develop. The more I learnt about the way that the Honda team operated, the more horrified I got.

I seemed that practically anybody could create a purchase order, seemingly with minimal, if any, oversight, and rumours of unnecessary and duplicated requests were rife, as were the inevitable insinuations of fraud surrounding the lackadaisical way in which some of the purchasing was carried out.

My first direct exposure to the fallout of Honda's withdrawal from the sport, was memorable to say the least. I was despatched to a local supplier of carbon fibre components, to give them the good news before it was officially announced. The supplier provided the overwhelming lions share of components that were not made directly in house by the teams own composite department. It seemed that we sent them the designs, they made everything that we needed, and then told us the price.

The purchase order seeming to a bit of an afterthought, clearly not the contract by which goods were to be supplied.

* * *

After a brief phone call with the owner of the company, I set off, alone, for a meeting that I will never forget.

Strangely, no one wanted to come along on this little jaunt.

Soon, I was walking into a large, spotlessly clean modern composite factory.

I broke the news to the owner, and he took it, putting it very mildly, quite badly. Clearly the shock of Honda's exit was about to be reverberating far wider than the factory in Brackley.

He was apoplectic, absolutely beside himself with rage.

"You have destroyed my f*cking business!", "YOU!", he kept repeating, over and over.

My efforts to pin the blame on Honda failed dismally - he was taking this very personally, and he clearly wasn't done yet.

He shouted and screamed at me repeatedly - *'How was he going to pay his fucking staff'* and other such expletive laden tirades.

Honda had committed to a generous commitment to all of their suppliers. Not only would they pay for all outstanding purchase orders, they would ALSO pay for all work commenced without one, and even more remarkably, they would cover the cost of any materials that suppliers had obtained, in the expectation of making further parts for Honda.

This staggering generosity fell on deaf eyes, and even as I reminded him that I could be out of a job very soon too , he was continuing to lay the blame for his self-produced mess, squarely at my door.

His failure to protect his business from shocks such as these was lazy and greedy.

I felt like shouting at him, *'Rather than expand your clientele, and maybe reduce your overall profits a little (one Porsche rather than 2 maybe?), you chose the highest risk strategy possible, head stuffed in the trough, and you are now suffering the inevitable consequences.'*

I resisted the urge, but I had little sympathy for him.

As the weeks went on, rumours were rife of draconian redundancies, factory closures and sales to the usual roll-call of scam artists, assets strippers, billionaires, and those that thought they were billionaires.

News also started to slowly trickle out about how close Honda actually came to canning the whole project overnight, and just laying off everybody.

Only through the diligent work of the team management, and the interjection of the British Government, did this scorched earth policy get avoided. Is there even a world in the Japanese language for Loyalty?

Honda's demise would, however, give rise to one of the oddest championships in the history of F1.

The team was for sale for £1 on the understanding that the new owners would be liable to underwrite the $40M+ needed to complete the 2009 season. Further seasons would require much higher budgets obviously, as, for this year only, they would be getting an almost complete car (*though designed around an unavailable Honda engine*).

※ ※ ※

Shortly after the Honda withdrawal announcement was made, I was confidentially told that I would be staying at the team, and furthermore, going forward, I would become the only person authorised to create and release a purchase orders, until a new buyer was found.

I assumed that this catastrophe was being used by the management as an opportunity to weed out some of the elements that had led to a dysfunctional purchasing function that allowed literally dozens of people all over the estate, to order whatever they wanted.

This was far from the 'last in, last out' that I suspected was coming.

I also suspected that this unique situation had been grasped by the Finance department, as a great opportunity to get this tiger by the collar, and stick it in its cage.

The days of open purchase orders, and no purchase orders were well and truly over.

Soon, rumours began of a buy out by the team's management. Seemingly, they had convinced Honda to hand the team over for the token £1 and instead of spending an estimated $100M on closing the business down, they would provide not only the assets of the team, but a similar sum as a running budget for the team.

For this to turn out to be true is utterly remarkable, considering Honda's originally avowed desire to throw the whole lot in a trash can and not look back.

With careful budgeting, and a huge headcount reduction, it was thought that the $50M (*the annual staff cost that would have been paid in redundancy*), along with other benefits and payments from F1 organizers, could maybe stretch enough to last two seasons, giving the team the breathing space to find some sponsors and, try to rebuild themselves back.

In March 2009, Brawn GP was officially born out of the ashes of Honda racing F1, and it was announced to the world that Mercedes would provide the engines to power the car for the season.

The name may have been Brawn, but the design of the car was Honda's and the raw materials and spares in the stores were also Honda's.

The profligacy of the previous regime meant we had enormous stocks of raw materials and consumables - by some estimates, enough to last 2 seasons without buying anything.

As the purchasing gate keeper, I remained tasked with creating every single order, ostensibly to protect our 'tiny' budget.

As it turned out , the team was in a massively better financial position than they ever let on, but that, as they say, is a whole other story.

* * *

Honda, in an epic piece of bad timing, had handed over a chassis that would turn out to be, far and away, the best that Honda would ever produce, providing that it was mated, ironically, to the far more impressive Mercedes power plant.

The car was immediately quick and, more importantely,

it suited the minimalist driving style of the lead driver Jenson Button. Jenson was a driver that needed to feel secure in the car, and was not one to drive around inherent deficiencies. He made the most of what he was given, and to the astonishment of the world, he delivered six race wins and was part of a seventh 1-2 finish with his team mate Rubens Barrichello.

On paper the championship win looked easy, but it was far from that.

In a further effort to conserve funds, and seeing that the car had a phenomenal performance advantage over the other cars at the beginning of the season, the team carried out next to no performance development from race 1 to the end of the season.

As expected, the bigger teams weren't standing still and watching this fairy tale unfold, and the second half of the season saw results much harder to come by as the opposition caught up, and narrowed the gap to such an extent that if the season had been extended by a handful of races, most observers felt that Button would have been soundly defeated.

Thankfully the season ended as planned, with Jenson in an emotional first place, but closely followed by Sebastian Vettel in his Ferrari, a scant 9 points behind in second place.

* * *

The Brawn year was a dreamy roller-coaster of emotions.

The elation of winning the first race with a dominant 1-2 was swiftly squashed flat by the 350 redundancies (*roughly half the workforce*) that were announced immediately after the cars left the factory for Australia.

For those that were forced to leave, I am sure that it felt like a huge betrayal after the immense efforts everyone made to get the cars to the first race. As the season went on, it was clear that this was something very special, but for those that were shown the door, it was no fairy tale.

As the season concluded, it also felt to some of us at least, that we were robbed in some way of our winning identity, and our right to celebrate. No sooner had the dust settled from the last race, it was announced that Brawn had been purchased by Mercedes.

The Brawn signs came down, the walls soon bare white again. Gaps where the pictures of the championship winning BGP-01 once hung. Brawn branded clothing was not to be worn.

We were eradicated, we were now Mercedes.

Like a fever dream almost, we all woke up and thought, did it really happen? According to the record books, I was part of the most successful Formula One team of all time (*statistically, that is*).

One championship, One win.

I'll take that.

* * *

As we woke from the Brawn dream, the Mercedes era began with a shock that no one was expecting.

The loss of our reigning champion driver, Jenson Button, was disappointing in the extreme, some feeling that this lack of faith in our future reflected quite poorly on him, but he had the chance to go to a proven super team, McLaren, so, personally, I found it hard to blame him.

Rumours were rife of new drivers, so as we all gathered

expectantly in the auditorium, hoping for some good news this time. Ross Brawn led us up the garden path with a speech of many words, but scant real news. It turned out, that he was playing for time, to allow our new lead driver to be secretly whisked in to the factory, up the back stairs, and outside the auditorium door, ready for the unveiling.

'Ladies, and gentlemen, I am incredibly proud to present our new Driver', and as Ross began to mouth the first syllable of the word Michael, the place erupted in incredulous cheering and whooping joy.

From the door in the far corner, a bronzed and athletic Michael Schumacher bounded on to the small stage, grinning ear to ear as he soaked up the deafening rear of 300 ecstatic people.

His brief, and very humble, speech betrayed just how overcome he was by the power of the reception. A Ferrari legend was coming out of retirement, and coming to an English based team. He was replacing an English world champion. He expected boos.

He must have had some trepidation, but he need not have worried. Though he was standing before a group of workers, firstly, we were just fans. He was a winner, and we needed a winner. We left the meeting with a giant spring in our step.

The singular focus of Mercedes was to exploit the wide ranging rule changes due to come into effect for the 2014 season, and in particular the introduction of a revolutionary new V6 Hybrid Power Unit.

The subsequent success of the Mercedes team is almost entirely down to this ultra long term vision. The boffins at the Mercedes engine division in Brixworth began beavering away as soon as the ink was dry on the rules.

This vision, as it turned out, was unique to Mercedes.

In stark contrast, their main rival, Ferrari, inexplicably continued to develop their soon to be out of date V8 engine right up until the very end of 2013 - a decision that inflicted pain within Ferrari that would still be felt some four years into the new era.

* * *

The subsequent weeks and months would see the team begin the very long road to growing back to its former glory, with some lucky souls enjoying the bonus of taking the Brawn redundancy payment and then returning to their old job. Nice work if you can get it.

Mercedes had serious ambitions to not just win in Formula One, but to dominate it for multiple years.

Old faces melded with new faces and we soon began to grow. Some faces sadly didn't fit this new staid corporate world, and over time the likes of my old friend Pete Ford, and the Machine Shop Manager Richard Smith would fall to the corporate sword, their faces not fitting the template of what a Mercedes manager was - a template that seemed to demand subservient, obsequious and unquestioning support of the senior management.

Yet another alarm bell that I failed to heed - something of a habit. Is is loyalty, or just plain old inertia?

The team was changing, and as one colleague who, as a veteran of the engine division, was steeped in the Mercedes ethos, would tell me something along the lines of...

'It's not necessarily WHAT you do, it's HOW you do

it. You need to promote yourself if you want to get on here.'

I fundamentally disagree with this way of management - principally because I am no good at it, but also philosophically - I believe that a great part of a managers job is to delegate work, mentor his staff, and recognize talent before rewarding it.

Recording artists need promotion, not me.

What you end up with is *'performing seals'* - people who talk themselves up, and others down, and do tricks for the management, rather than serve the cause.

Sadly Mercedes had a fair few of them, and as time went on, it became clear that some would do absolutely anything to promote themselves, at the detriment of myself and Sean.

Empire builders were rife in the team, running around unchecked by the one of the weakest senior management team that I have ever worked for.

One of my many failings, if you can call it a failing as such, is that I simply cannot get excited about working for someone that I do not fully respect - but for those that I do, I will move heaven and earth.

Such was the situation at Mercedes, and rather than have the courage to walk away from a toxic environment, again, I struck at it, getting more and more depressed as the weeks turned into months.

Daily life seemed to compose almost entirely of dissecting the minutiae of life in the tedious daily production meetings.

I got the distinct impression, that the management valued **talking** about stuff far higher than **doing** stuff - a classic justification for a top heavy organization.

PUNISHMENT OF ANSWERED PRAYERS.

Meetings, and their output, act as a perfect smokescreen to give justification for a lack of real action, development or improvement.

I was spending more and more time in meetings, endlessly talking about the same things over and over again, ad nauseam.

* * *

This is where the pigs come in.

Not those intensively farmed pigs that provide the nation with meat as pale as milk, and bacon that tastes of fresh air, but rare breeds - exotic names like Gloucester old spots, Tamworths, Saddlebacks, and my own personal favourite, Oxford and Sandy Blacks.

The first sign of my first mid life crisis, was an all consuming fascination with self sufficiency - we even went so far as trying to find land locally to raise some pigs.

This was text book deflection. We didn't have the money to do any of it.

I was profoundly unhappy at work, and for my sanity to remain intact, I needed desperately to focus my mind on something else - this time it happened to be pigs.

I bought books, I watched documentaries. I devoured everything that I could find about living 'The Good Life' but Tom & Barbara we were not, and sadly it wasn't to be.

But thankfully, fate had something some extreme in mind.

* * *

Another 'Groundhog Day' in Brackley.

My silenced company blackberry buzzed in my pocket. A welcome distraction, providing as it did, a brief respite from the endless *(and, for me, largely pointless)* fascinating discussions about, among other things, the tricky machining of the worlds most complicated wheel nuts.

I glanced down at my phone, and read the notification of a LinkedIn message notification that fleetingly appeared on the screen.

Opening the app, I was astonished to see that the message was from someone claiming to be from the Human Resources department of the Ferrari Formula One team. I read it more than several times.

Amazingly, each time it said the same thing.

They were inviting me to Maranello to discuss a job opportunity. I put the phone back in my pocket, convinced this was a joke or at very best, an unfortunate misunderstanding.

They don't have buyers in Italy?

Either way, there's no way I'm getting a job offer from Ferrari. Ridiculous.

* * *

Whenever I go through an airport or a train station, as some kind of minor ritual, I invariably buy a copy of Viz magazine and a copy of Private Eye.

On this occasion, I forgot. I had a lot on my mind.

As the plane gently touched down in Forli, Northern Italy, I was still trying to fathom just what had happened in the previous seven days, and my brain was still mush.

Nervously striding through the Airport, I almost walked past an olive skinned, raven haired, and impeccably dressed gentleman, in sunglasses, who was holding a simple sign - the unmistakable shape of the Prancing Horse. The symbol of the most famous racing team in the world.

He nodded, I nodded, and off we went.

Looking through the dark limousine passenger windows of our black Lancia Voyager, it was quite surreal. The sun lit countryside flashed past, as my unspeaking chauffeur sped along as only an Italian can.

Ferrari is Maranello, and Maranello is Ferrari.

As we took the slip road from the SP467 into the outskirts of Maranello, we passed the largest representation of the *Cavallino Rampante* that you are ever likely to see.

It's clear. You have left Italy, we are now in Ferrari country.

Before long we would arrive outside one of the most fabled places in Motor Sport. The racing factory was painted almost entirely in the blood red of Ferrari, save for a 30 foot long illuminated yellow sign, spelling out the word F E R R A R I .

Parking under the sign, I was greeted by my HR contact and ushered into the building, passing trophies, old race posters, and photographs of some of the most iconic moments in motor sport.

It was too much to take in, just a blur.

Deposited in a small waiting room. I nervously rearranged the bottles of water and admired the potted plants, and pictures of red cars. Lots of red cars.

'Nigel! How are you.' Swinging around, I greet the familiar smiling face of Michele Ciavola.

Michele, the ever dapper Head of Human Resources & Legal for Scuderia Ferrari, was known to me from my time at Red Bull. Prior to heading the HR activity at Ferrari, he carried out the same function at Toro Rosso, and we spoke regularly in my role as liaison between the two teams.

I like Michele, but I have to say, in hindsight, he was about to well and truly lead me up the garden path, and all the way to the river, that he would inadvertently sell me down, without a paddle.

When you know your interviewer, it's always an easier task to be interviewed, but despite this, I was about to experience an interview like no other.

Michele explained to me that, in his opinion, this was a perfect time for me to join Ferrari. The crippling interference of the Fiat parent company, that had blighted the team in the past, was coming to an end.

He likened the situation to a graph, which he proceeded to draw, with huge peaks and troughs and used a quite bizarre analogy to explain it.

Ferrari was likened to a woman suffering repeated abusive relationships - she would initially be attracted to a strong and exciting man (*top of the graph peak - signifying a period of high FIAT control/interference in the team*'), the man would eventually beat her, and she would inevitably leave him, seeking instead a nice boring man ('*bottom of the graph peak - signifying a period of low FIAT control/interference in the team*').

Drawing this frequency chart on an A4 sheet of paper, he triumphantly told me, with a flourish of his marker pen, that we were about to enter a long period of low interference.

Once I had recovered from the analogy, I asked a few questions, and Michele convinced me that Ferrari were interested in understanding how other teams worked, they wanted cooler heads, access to UK suppliers and wanted to learn how to replicate the most successful English team, Mercedes.

Seemed to me like a perfect opportunity.

The language was all *'when'* and not *'if'* so I left for the airport feeling much more relaxed than when I arrived.

My still silent driver whisked me rapidly back to the airport and a few hours later, I was having dinner with Linda in Greens Norton, quietly confident that things had gone pretty well.

If what Michele had told me turned out to be true, this could be the very best thing that had ever happened to me. I almost allowed myself to get excited. Almost.

***

4

Pain without purpose.

> *"Some are born mad, some achieve madness,
> and some have madness thrust upon 'em."*
> **— Emilie Autumn**

The 15 tonne truck was taking up way more than its fair share of Blakesley Hill, and soon caught the attention of the local constabulary.

They'd had complaints from the local 'curtain twitchers' apparently.

I politely asked the female officer if she knew of a less *'irritating'* method of transferring our worldly goods into a truck without parking it outside our house.

Despite my best efforts to mask the simmering sarcasm in me, it appeared that I had failed dismally.

She eyed me wearily, and we settled on an agreement that we'd get it done as soon as we could. She departed, hopefully, I thought, to deal with something a little more important than my Italian movers.

PAIN WITHOUT PURPOSE.

* * *

Just under 3 months earlier, after a brief tennis game of offer and counter offer, we had settled on a package, and I was about to become, as far as I could tell, the first ever UK born buyer to work for Ferrari.

People kept telling me that I was brave, for some reason, but I didn't exactly feel brave. I was running from one failure, in the hope of producing a better outcome.

Time would tell, just how intelligent the move would be.

As Einstein, and Ian Prior, would often say, *'Insanity is doing the same thing over and over and expecting different results.'*

Maybe I was insane, but as least I was going to be insane with a better climate and food.

When I nervously handed my notice in to my immediate boss at Mercedes, Sean Gutteridge, he was immediately pleased for me.

We both felt the same way about the way that Mercedes was going, and he was far from surprised that I wanted out. News flowed around the factory, but only Sean knew where I was going, and I was determined to keep it that way for as long as I could.

Knowledge is power, so they say.

A little after lunch, I was called to see the CEO for a chat.

Sean had warned me in advance had he had blocked out a couple of hours to speak with me, and he was likely to try to understand why I wanted to leave, and maybe even try to convince me to stay.

I arrived back in the office after 10 minutes.

'Meeting cancelled?', said Sean.

'Nah, finished mate', I said. He chuckled, he knew there was

no way I was staying, particularly after the way in which both of us had been treated in the previous 12 months.

The meeting consisted of the CEO asking me why I wanted to leave. I gave a simple and direct answer.

'Is there anything we can do to encourage you to stay?', he said.

'No.', I said. Well, that's that.

Sean then did me a huge favour, completely without my knowledge. His unorthodox leaving present was to convince the management to send me home on gardening leave for the 3 months of my notice period.

This helped me immensely, as the mountain of things to do before we left for Italy was big, and growing bigger all the time.

Never one for goodbyes, the insincerity can be nauseating, I let a few people know what was happening, and skipped out of the door.

Yet again, no signed Rear Wing end plate, no feigned good luck speeches. Seven years of my life, but the introvert in me tends to prefer it that way.

* * *

The timing of my departure would add further weight to the long belief that my presence in a team is a powerful 'jinx', preventing them from winning championships.

I left Red Bull, immediately prior to their 4-year back to back championship run, and as I departed Mercedes in December 2014, they had just won the first of an unprecedented 8 championships on the trot.

The bonus payments from 12 championships could have come in handy, but such is life. Timing, as they say, is everything.

To compound the complexity of what we were doing, we were taking a dog and a car to Italy. Ferrari would cover the flights for us, but not the dog express.

We agreed that I would drive over, and Linda would fly with Oliver. The plan was impeccable, as I would take 2 days to arrive in Maranello at our Ferrari provided accommodation, and the rest of the family would fly out to Bologna in the morning of day three.

The air traffic controllers of France, however, were having none of that. Typical French industrial carnage was planned for the day of their flight, and BA duly cancelled the flight at the 11th hour.

I was in Maranello, and Linda, in a state of near panic, was back in the UK. Once the French workers had been placated, flights went back to normal, and a few days later, I would collect Linda from the airport.

We could now begin our Italian adventure.

My first Italian lesson was a suitably chastening and embarrassing one.

A few days in, needing fuel, we dropped into a petrol station and I confidently inserted my credit card into the self-service payment machine. All fine, assuming the station wasn't closed. It was.

Card machine 1, me Nil.

Luckily, not long after our arrival, we had made the acquaintance of the unelected leader of the Ferrari WAGS, as they were known.

Louise Salters was a huge help to us when we arrived. Her husband David worked in the engine design department of the F1 team, and she ran an unofficial social club for the expat workers of Ferrari.

They were immediately likeable and approachable, and would become great friends in the short time we shared in Italy. Louise rolled up to the petrol station and chuckling, directed me to the huge sign at the entrance that read *'CHIUSO'* - which I now know to be Italian for *'CLOSED'*. I felt a complete fool.

Louise, it turned out, was also the font of all Ferrari related gossip.

'Have you heard about the new organization chart?' she enquired conspiratorially.

I hadn't. It was 16th December 2104, less than 3 short weeks away from my January 5th start date.

I knew precisely nothing about anything.

I was to be dumbfounded, as she recounted a set of changes to the structure that could profoundly affect my position.

Importantly, the new structure no longer included my old friend Michele Ciavola, the HR director who had brought me to Maranello. This was worrying in itself, but coupled with the most recent change at the very top of the tree, possibly terminal.

Marco Mattiacci, the very person that had signed off my contract, and who himself was only appointed as Managing Director and Team Principal eight months earlier, was also gone.

This was beginning to smell like a train wreck.

My nervousness was compounded further, when I received an email the next day from Ferrari, informing me that my start date had been shifted to the following week.

A painful first introduction to the unique ways of Ferrari, and a very clear sign that Michele's infamous 'domestic abuse' chart might well be complete and utter b*llshit.

The day finally came, and I went into Ferrari with my eyes fully open, and certainly didn't underestimate the magnitude of what I was attempting to do.

To travel to another country, work for a team notorious for its eccentric ways, and do it all in a foreign language that I could not speak. Surely I must be certifiably mad.

I had mentally prepared for most things, but what I really didn't expect, was the early revelation that my boss hadn't asked for me, didn't want me and certainly didn't know what to do with me.

They didn't even have a desk for me, let alone a computer or phone.

As I sit forlornly in the corner of an office within an office, it would take well over a week to get a computer and even longer to get a phone.

A went home wondering just quite what I had done. I had been told that I was there to share my knowledge of the UK teams, and their methods. To help Ferrari modernize there practices, in the image of Mercedes.

Despite repeatedly trying to engage with my Boss and share my knowledge, there was zero interest.

My colourful charts and PowerPoint presentations were accepted, but I doubt any of them were actually read.

The purchasing department at Ferrari was tiny in comparison to the UK teams, and the compliance was almost non-existent, particularly, as I would find out later, on the engine side.

It was like going back 20 years.

The only person that was genuinely interested in my experience was Mauro Falcone. We shared an office and was a great help to me in understanding who was who, and what was what.

Later, it would become apparent that he had drawn the short straw, as he was also the only person in the room with a reasonable grasp of the English language, but, to his credit, he never showed it.

Mauro was the deputy manager in all but name, and over time, I determined that he was the only one in the room that was remotely interested in change, the rest, pleasant and friendly though they were, they were stuck in their little silos, dealing with their stuff in isolation.

It was not a recognizable team as I would have expected.

We never met together, we could go all day without speaking to another member of the team. The half a dozen or so staff in the department were expected to manage the entire purchasing needs for both the chassis and the engine side - something that Mercedes employed, by my estimation, around 18 people - 3 times the quantity at Ferrari.

They were staggeringly under resourced yet saw no reason to change.

At the end of my first week, I was utterly depressed.

Could this really be Ferrari? The Ferrari of Fangio, Lauda and Schumacher?

This mob were never going to win anything, from what I could see.

What had I done?

**

The Ferrari factory was an aged rabbit warren of overcrowded offices and workshops, built over 50 years - organically evolving over the decades as the needs of the teams changed.

It was dark, it was pokey, and it was a very long way from what I expected and what I was used to.

Thankfully, Luca Montezemolo, the legendary former leader of Ferrari, had done at least one good thing. He signed off on a new state-of-the-art campus that would rival any other team in the world, a few years before he would be unceremoniously thrown under the bus of change, driven on this occasion by one Sergio Marchionne.

The first building was almost complete when I arrived, and soon we would be installed as the first 'guinea pig' residents. Built as an 'Eco building,' it was effectively a giant green house. The building incorporated a newfangled air conditioning system, that was swiftly shown to be unable to cope with what turned out to be the savagely hot summer of 2015.

The lights were controlled electronically, and had a mind of their own, coming on at their brightest for no apparent reason anytime after lunch. Technology at its finest. It didn't bode well.

Whilst this was going on, other personal changes were afoot.

We had moved from our temporary accommodation at the Maranello village hotel complex, and had found a Tardis like house in the low hills surrounding Maranello.

Yet again, with both feet first, I jumped in without haggling the rental, committing ourselves to a rental of 1600 euros per month. Looking back now, this was a ridiculous sum of money and way above our means, particularly when we had to consider the exorbitant fees of the International school to educate Oliver.

We were living, but it left precious little in the pot for

fully enjoying what Italy had to offer. Living on the edge, financially speaking, is something that I have done all my life, and it's one of my biggest regrets, that and selling an old classic BMW M3 around 20 years ago, to a toff from London for next to nothing. £75K car now. Oh well, some are born to save and some are born to spend.

Just as we became settled in our new environment, the Ferrari gods were not yet ready to let us grow comfortable in our chairs.

The last person who had any involvement in my original requirement, my direct Purchasing boss, was to be replaced. Only recently, had we finally reached some sort of understanding that I would work on establishing a UK supplier base for Ferrari, as my detailed analysis showed that they were paying disturbingly high prices for their simple, and medium complexity components.

Now, uncertainty arrives at a gallop again. Anxiety not far behind.

He unceremoniously left the office, moved to the road car function on the other side of Via Abetone Inferiore, and after a few months would take a role at one of the F1 teams biggest local suppliers.

This post-Ferrari career path would be repeated again some months later when the senior buyer for engine components was 're-allocated' to the road car division, in a very similar way.

This career trajectory left few doubts in my mind as to how purchasing was being managed in the past, these personnel changes coincided as they did at a time when Ferrari was due to be launched on the New York Stock Exchange (**NYSE**) in October 2015.

PAIN WITHOUT PURPOSE.

The consequences of a NYSE listing were profound - so, it was now as clear as crystal, that despite the assurances of my old friend Michele, we were about to get absolutely battered by a very aggressive new boyfriend.

The Sarbanes-Oxley Act (**SOX**) is a law enacted by the US congress in 2002, and is designed to protect shareholders and the general public from both accounting errors and fraudulent practices by listed companies.

Ferrari would need to comply with every last bit of it.

There is a very good reason that large automotive manufacturers house their racing teams outside of the realm of their primary manufacturing activities - and this is it.

Compliance with SOX would pour down an avalanche of process and procedure on our heads - everything that goes against the effective creation of a dynamic racing environment.

This is another trigger point - I should have taken this as a very clear sign, and left at the end of my first year, but no I soldered on into the oblivion.

> *"It's not always the most popular person who gets the job done." -*
> **MICHAEL DOUGLAS as Gordon Gekko in the movie 'Wall Street'**

Our new boss was the epitome of a young, thrusting, FIAT executive.

Tall, slender and impeccably groomed at all times. Teeth like a primetime game show host. Very soon his slightly awkward and almost apologetic arrival would give way to reveal the real character of the man, a character that exuded both the confidence of a wall street master of the universe, and the paranoia of someone way out of their depth.

He had clearly been tasked with an agenda to clean out the dead wood, implement a set of new processes and do whatever is necessary to pass a SOX inspection.

I was completely back to square one.

A new boss, and new doubt as to what my role actually was. I updated my charts, tinkered with my presentations, and proposed yet another new structure for the department. My proposal would require a significant head count.

His face said it all, he was not here to increase headcount, he was here to beast us into shape, and draw blood if necessary.

The department was always flat out busy, summer and winter, and this, remember, without any consideration of the impact that the SOX regulations would have on our purchasing activities.

In a UK team, it's expected that staff work the hours that are necessary during the car build period from October through to March, and then as much as possible, they are encouraged to work at their standard working hours.

To expect staff to work 6 days a week, and 12 hours (*or more*) a day, is very last century and from a practical standpoint, ineffective. In an environment that encourages and rewards long hours, the law of diminishing returns comes into effect. People pace themselves to suit the hours that they are expected to work.

Bosses who haunt the corridors at night, seeing who is still there, are not leaders.

If I left before 7.30pm I would be sarcastically accused of working a half day. I had done my 15 hour days 20 year before at SGP, a team without the money and resources to work in any different way.

Ferrari did not have these excuses, only a tired, undermanned function, working in an outdated macho culture that favoured those who paced their work all day and worked late in to the evening.

It was more and more apparent that the toxicity of the management would get a lot worse before it got better.

Despite my best efforts to learn Italian, the hours I was expected to work, and drain on my emotions that it caused, left me little time to improve from beyond basic conversational Italian.

Instead of being offered more lessons, I was regularly criticized about my poor Italian, and unfavourably compared to other expats in Ferrari, most of whom had been in the team for upwards of 15 or 20 years. Having been there for less than 18 months, this attitude was thoroughly demoralizing. It was just a part of the toxic management style that were were subjected to.

My new Boss was entirely inexperienced in F1 or Motor Sport in general, for that matter. He had come from a high volume road car division of FIAT, but gave the distinct impression that he had little to learn from us.

As the weeks turned into months, old staff were pushed out, young (*cheap*) graduates were bought in, and we all plodded along, mostly keeping our heads down, not knowing what to expect next.

***

What came next, was the reward of more work.

In 2015, HAAS F1, a new team from the USA, would well and truly set the cat amongst the pigeons, arriving as the did, at a time when the F1 regulations allowed for a wide ranging catalogue of chassis components to be supplied by another team.

HAAS had settled on a partnership with Ferrari to source the engine, power train and anything else they could lay their hands on. You can surely guess who was going to responsible for managing this additional manufacturing activity.

Rumours of an extra headcount in the department to make up for the increase in workload did little to improve our feelings of depression. As if we didn't have enough to do already.

Importantly, as a new team they were unrestricted in their testing (*including wind tunnel time in the facility they shared with Ferrari*) until they officially entered F1 at pre-season testing for the 2016 season.

This 'black hole' sized loop hole led to lots of allegations about collusion with Ferrari and unfair advantages. FIA investigated thoroughly and found nothing to see, so there.

The HAAS team was managed by my old Jaguar/Red Bull friend, Guenther Steiner.

The last time that we had met, was just before I left Mercedes. A brief but sweary chat in the corridors of Mercedes GP, at the end of his visit to discuss a possible Mercedes deal for HAAS.

In the following days we spoke briefly about a possible job at HAAS, but nothing came of it.

Now, as a Ferrari customer team, regular meetings were planned in Maranello, and despite never officially being told, I started to get emails suggesting I was somehow the liaison between the two purchasing functions.

My opposite number at HAAS was another old Red Bull F1 mate, Andrew Cumbers, who, like Maradona, is known only by his second name, but there, despite being a keen fan of the beautiful game, the resemblance abruptly ends.

We had worked together briefly at Red Bull and I liked him a great deal - hugely enthusiastic and hard working. We would speak regularly on the phone and occasionally met in Maranello.

The first HAAS meeting at FERRARI headquarters was a classic Guenther encounter, with his inimitable German accented, expletive peppered reaction to seeing me for the first time, going something along the lines of *'F**k me Betsy, what the f**k are you f**king doing here? I thought they would put someone in charge that knows what he is doing. F*ck me, we have no chance...'*

My boss, standing beside me, was stunned, but I was not.

I mumbled, *'usual story'* and greeted a chuckling Guenther with a handshake.

I don't think my boss ever got used to Guenther, his mixture of German directness and British sarcasm being very hard to translate into Italian. I believe that it also added to his growing paranoia that I knew everyone in F1. I did not, but you don't work for 3 of the biggest teams in the paddock without getting to know a few people.

I got invited by Jock Clear[20] to a BBQ at his house not long after I arrived.

The *'who the f*ck are you'* looks from the Italians among the guests, left me in no doubt that I was flying way above the clouds.

We weren't invited back, and I don't blame him at all.

* * *

Ferrari is all about the cult of hierarchy.

For me, it is the absolute antithesis of what an F1 team should be, and how it should operate. My Boss would aggressively discourage communication that didn't directly involve him.

I once made the egregious error of speaking to the Head of Purchasing in the road car division, on behalf of a supplier.

They simply wanted to know if they could contact a buyer to present their products for a road car application. Not worthy of involving my boss for something so low level, you would of thought.

When he found out, embarrassingly, whilst we were dining together in the staff canteen, he almost swallowed his silk tie. My explanation that I knew him socially within the ex-pat community, only added unnecessary oil to the fire - he was beside himself at the sheer treachery of it.

I was genuinely baffled.

In Mercedes or Red Bull, I could talk freely to anybody about anything and was trusted to either involve my boss or not.

Trust, a world that was alien to my boss. No one was to be trusted, everyone and everything was dangerous. The atmosphere that this attitude created was a war like *'batten down the hatches'* attitude that stifled communication, and his explosive reactions to situations like this, led to us involving him less and less with what was going on.

We would discuss problems within the team first, and only share it with him if we already had a solution.

He would often panic and turn small problems into big

nightmares - badgering people continually, to micro manage problems until there was a resolution. Trust is a vital element to leadership, and he trusted very few, to do very little.

My mental health was starting to suffer, and this was only the start.

* * *

The weight of the SOX procedures, the failure to expand our overworked department, and the ever more erratic Boss led me to seriously consider leaving the team.

I was on a call to Cumbers at HAAS F1 one day, and he mentioned that they were looking for a Purchasing Manager, and would I be interested.

When you considered that I was coming up to the last 3 months of my first 3 year contract and soon would be expected to re-sign a new contract or push off, it seemed worth talking about, at least.

What's to lose? I knew Guenther, I knew what to expect. Most of the senior people there, I had worked with before. I said OK, and naively told him to get Guenther to give me a ring, and we could have a chat about how serious he was.

Oh boy, what a mess.

A week or so later, I mentioned to Cumbers that I hadn't heard from Guenther, and he told me *'Oh, I think he was taking to Mattia about it yesterday at the circuit.'*

What? You're kidding right? He spoke to Mattia before speaking to me? I never heard from Guenther again.

It turned out to be as bad as it sounded. Monday morning I was summoned to HR, and an hastily prepared contract was shoved under my nose.

'*You must sign this today.*' In a rare display, I put my foot down, I needed time to consider the contract, it was entirely in Italian for a start. I could be signing anything.

I got a friend to translate it, and compared with the old contract, it was substantively the same.

I can't regret signing, as the wage they were offering far exceeded what I could reasonably expect to earn in the UK, and I was starting to have plans for that money, big plans. I do regret how it made me feel, and the severe effects on my mental health, that still reverberate with me now.

* * *

Mattia Binotto was someone I respected very highly in the early days. Before he became the big boss at Ferrari, we would occasionally bump into each other in the corridors and lifts, always cordial, always chatty.

After his ascent to the throne as Team Principle, less often, for obvious reasons, but when I did see him, always the same cordial and chatty Mattia.

I liked him, he had genuine enthusiasm for what he was doing.

From the day that I signed my new contract, I din=t recall ever speaking again.

He appeared to studiously and self-consciously peer at his phone when we passed in the corridor or shared a lift.

I can only assume that my fleeting thought of abandonment affected him quite badly.

* * *

PAIN WITHOUT PURPOSE.

Daniele 'Dan' Casanova spent most of his career in the UK, he was quite non-Italian in his Italianness.

Born in Italy, he spoke perfect English with just a trace of an accent.

We had briefly worked concurrently at Red Bull, but at Ferrari I would get to know him well, both at work, and socially.

During the early part of 2018, we worked closely together on a 'secret squirrel' suspension project.

I liked him.

His sudden death was a profound shock to me.

The morning after his death, my Boss informed me that he had passed away in the night, presumably of a heart attack. I was stunned. We had a meeting planned for that morning - it seemed so surreal.

It put my life into stark perspective, and just how fragile existence was.

Dan was very well liked and appreciated in the team, and on the 20th October 2018, we drove to the Church of San Germano in Rivanazzano with heavy hearts, to honour his life and bid him a fond farewell.

Despite the funeral coinciding with the USA GP in Austin Texas, the church was packed to bursting with Ferrari employees. Unexpectedly but touchingly, Binotto had returned early from Austin and attended the funeral, giving a warm speech of appreciation for Dan.

As we mingled outside on the large expanse of the church steps, awaiting the sad departure of the hearse, Binotto left the church and appeared to slowly and methodically shake the hands of every Ferrari employee who stood there, every single one, including the one standing to the left of me, and the one standing to the right of me.

But not me.

An oversight maybe, but I couldn't help taking it personally.

From that day, my mission was to leave, and live my life in a better way.

* * *

By 2018, Sergio Marchionne, the sword wielding cost-cutting titan of the automotive world had turned his attention to the F1 team in earnest.

With Montezemolo finally gone, the train set was his, and his alone.

Rumours were rife that he was clearing the path for Ferrari, and particularly the F1 team, to be his singular semi-retirement focus. A day rarely went by without a new rumour about the team management.

The team under Arrivabene was failing on the track, and his rumoured blame culture was destroying morale. Coupled with his notorious reluctance to speak to the press, observers were beginning to accuse him of harming the reputation of the team.

It wouldn't be long before it was chief number four in the space of five years for the men in red.

Marchionne was rumoured to want to bring the Italian culture back to Ferrari - everyone was instructed to create an identically formatted CV of their career and outline their repeatabilities within Ferrari.

Critically, it had it be in English.

This made me popular for a while, and I would edit 30 CV's from Italian speaking members across the team.

PAIN WITHOUT PURPOSE.

There was no explanation for this request, so this information void was naturally filled with lurid and panic driven speculation. The most popular theory being, that Marchionne wanted to kick out all the (*highly paid*) non Italians.

He had been vocal about not hiring foreign *'white knights'* in the future, to *'save'* the team - he believed that Ferrari was quintessentially Italian, and should be managed by Italians. This noble and crowd pleasing philosophy conveniently ignored the glaring fact that Ferraris last period of domination was managed almost entirely by foreigners.

You couldn't help thinking that it was much more about reducing the wage bill, than a patriotic urge to promote Italian prowess.

As it turned out, the rumours were half true. Save for the major, and inexplicable, loss of James Allison, the Chassis technical Director, a man that Marchionne never saw eye to eye with, there was no wholesale cull of non-Italians.

The numerous career *'mercenaries'*, going from 3 year contract to 3 year contract, could expel a sigh of relief, and get back to keeping their collective heads down.

We did see an increase in the internal promotion of native born managers, and ultimately in late 2018, it would see the elevation of Mattia Binotto to the leadership of the team, following the overthrow of the incumbent Arrivabene.

This made for a interesting situation for my boss, as in the fight for the throne, he had clearly aligned himself with Arrivabene, and was convinced that should the day arrive of a King Binotto, he was straight for the Tower and the chopping block.

Days passed into weeks, and the guillotine remained unused. It must be said that no one was more surprised than my boss.

The elevation of Binotto to the top spot came in the wake of the shocking death of Sergio Marchionne.

His micro-managing control of Ferrari would cease abruptly on July 25th 2018. When the dust had settled, many within in the team would consider this to be, despite the tragic nature of his passing, a good thing for Ferrari, in the long term.

Marchionne had propagated the culture of fear and blame that Binotto was so obviously opposed to. The loss of Marchionne would ultimately herald the beginning of a period of stability for the managerial and technical structure. Something sadly lacking at Ferrari for so many years.

Like Honda, and Toyota, FIAT (*former owner of Ferrari*) is an incredibly large organization, and their instinct is often to use their racing departments as either, short term rewards for the rising manager class, or a kindergarten for their most promising engineers, or indeed a combination of the both.

Neither brought about success.

* * *

Meanwhile, as things were finally settling down for Ferrari, I was rapidly descending into a deep dark black hole.

With a clear eye, looking back, I can actually trace my problems back to the early days of Red Bull, but I had successfully managed to keep a lid on my anxiety over the years, mostly by distracting myself, and by moving roles and ultimately teams.

The triggers were always the same. Specifically, working for people that I did not respect and carrying out work that I felt was unnecessary to the end goal or being done *'for the sake of it'*.

***

Everything came to a crashing head in the winter of 2018/2019.

It was not pretty.

The understaffed purchasing department were now being subjected to their portion of a company wide financial audit of forensic proportions - they would delve into our practices and procedures - pulling activities at random to check their compliance with the endless policies and procedures if a SOX compliant business.

The policies, whilst important to prevent large scale fraud, were so rigid, they completed removed any freedom of action for the buyer, and required massive amounts of justification for many of the buying decisions made.

This was hugely time consuming, and largely pointless in my opinion. I have always achieved the best result for my employer - I spend the least that I have to, to achieve the target.

With over 22 years experience, I expect to be trusted to do this as I have never made a single transaction that betrayed that noble aim. What began as stifling oversight in Mercedes GP, led to my melt down in Ferrari.

Buying in Ferrari required you to negotiate the negotiable, and the non-negotiable and also to predict the future with 20/20.

Two decades in Formula One had taught me a few things, one of which was there are some suppliers you can push and some that you cannot. Formula One is a niche business and some components are only supplied by one supplier - normally for performance reasons.

Components are often bespoke, i.e. designed especially for the team, in what is, in effect, a collaborative process. The opportunities to negotiate price reductions is hugely limited, yet my boss, not coming from an F1 background, believed that they could be, and I spent hundreds of wasted hours having fruitless negotiations with big ticket suppliers that I knew would not budge, rather that working on things where I could get a result.

The demeaning way in which all of us buyers were treated when we failed to find a reduction was mentally wearing. You begin to doubt your own worth.

Much like a oft beaten dog, you become depressed and shy of your master.

Overwork nearly always leads to corners being cut, as it did for me. Due to the complexity of the parts that i managed, the suppliers were often not willing or able to give me a price until the pieces were in manufacture, and sometimes almost complete.

To be compliant, an order must be in place before any work begins. This leads you to create an estimated order, and once the real price is made clear, to remain compliant, the order must be updated with the new value before the first parts are delivered.

For high value orders, they would need to be electronically signed by my Boss.

The gap between the correct price being known, and the parts arriving could be as little as a few days. In this time I was expected to carry out a detailed financial analysis of the prices and provide a justification to my boss for the final price.

A failure to provide a %age reduction in the previous year was an abject failure, even if the design from one year to the next was radically different.

This lack of trust in my ability and demeaning way I was treated, led me to delay some large value orders and not seek the re-approval, leading them to be outside the procedures and a failure of the audit. The dog was made to cower in the corner.

I couldn't bring myself to highlight the mess I had created and, ashamed to tell anyone, the sand seemed very inviting and in popped my head.

My boss was unapproachable, often rude and very sarcastic. He would routinely sit in his glass sided office, and shout our names out like a Drill Sergeant if he wanted you to come to him.

It felt like we were dogs in kennels, except we very seldom got a pat on the head. I've never felt so disrespected or undervalued in my life.

Occasionally given to explosive rage, I could imagine how he might react to me informing him of the small list of orders that were not complaint.

Regretfully, I sat on it, and sat on it, until it became like a cancer.

My anxiety was sky high, facial ticks, bowel churning stomach upsets, the full gamut arrived over time.

I am in no way likening what I was experiencing to PTSD, but I definitely suffered a number of similar symptoms, though in their milder forms.

The insomnia, anxiety and loss of focus was one thing, but the weirdest one was the sound of his shoes.

Sometimes a sound can automatically trigger the *'fight or flight'* response and fear, anger and anxiety.

In my case, it was the sound of my bosses leather soled brogue shoes as he marched purposefully across the tiled floor of our offices. A day without my boss was like a working holiday - the whole office relaxed, so much more would be accomplished, with remarkably less stress.

In the darker times, the sound of him coming was enough to make me tense, anxious and my blood pressure spike.

The interminable audit, was finally completed, but after my Boss had been promoted and replaced by a human being.

The sharp suited youngsters had found me out, and crisis meetings were held.

In my defence, I wrote a long memo to my bosses explaining my mental state, and the reasons why it got the way it got. To be fair, they were hugely supportive, but it's my greatest regret about this affair, that the new guy had to deal with the fall out. God knows, the job was hard enough.

The stress of work and overeating/drinking meant that my general health was in about as bad a place as it had ever been.

Two hours of driving an automatic car each day to Ferrari, and then sitting behind a desk for up to 10 hours was slowly killing me.

My body was crying out - both ankles seized up and it became painful to walk.

The only answer was exercise, severely allergic though I am.

My mind was effectively saved by Adam Buxton[21].

Specifically, the parlous state of my body led me to spend an hour lunch break fast walking, rather than fast eating, and the unexpected by-product of this fitness push, was an equivalent

PAIN WITHOUT PURPOSE.

improvement in my mental health, directly attributable to listening to Adam Buxton podcasts, principally, but also those of the deliciously named Scroobius Pip[22] - listening to other people talking about their own mental struggles was a huge help and just that one hour a day of fresh air, exercise and mental stimulation, brought me away from the cliff edge, and lifted the fog from my bar, just enough to keep pushing on to the end of my second 3 year contract.

The other thing that kept me from falling over that imaginary cliff, was a dream, a dream that would lead to the single biggest decision of my life.

The decision to walk away from the best paying job I'd ever had, and risk it all on a *'shit or bust'* plan to drive along the Pan American Highway in an old land Rover Defender.

The carefully prepared plan was set and was beginning to be executed - however, in the background, a *'little bout of the sniffles in China'* was about to spectacularly blow everything into a thousand pieces.

II

Part Two

"If you really want to escape the things that harass you, what you're needing is not to be in a different place, but to be a different person."
*— **Lucius Annaeus Seneca***

5

Plans and pandemics.

"But it affects virtually nobody. It's an amazing thing."
- President Trump speaking about Covid in 2020

Undoubtedly, by any reasonable measure, I have lived a privileged life. I know this, and to suggest otherwise would be entirely disingenuous.

As a child, I sat cross-legged in front of the TV, watching those blood red cars racing around racetracks in exotic parts of the planet, but never once dreamed that I would spend 6 years of my life in Maranello, in the very heart of that same red machine.

In this *'insta'* world though, appearances can be hugely deceptive, and from the outside, I was surely living the dream, but inside?

Something was very broken inside me and I had determined that Overlanding would be the answer to a question that I couldn't readily define.

I was hungry for something that would fire my soul,

something that would drag me from the stupor of over work and stress, and like many addicts, I sought the company of other addicts to feed my hunger.

The dream of overland travel was always in the back of my mind and I devoured all the TV shows and magazine articles I could get hold of. I wanted to know the who, the what, the where and the why of adventure travel.

Then one day in 2016, I stumbled upon an article on the BBC Travel website entitled *'The neverending road trip'*.[23]

* * *

Looking back at it now, that day in 2016 was surely the official start of our dream – the moment of conception, if you will.

The idea that someone was doing what we dreamed of doing, right now, at this very moment, was intoxicating.

But the crippling doubts lingered… How could **WE** do it, how could we even afford it?

It seemed utterly impossible as they were surely eccentric millionaires, or trust fund kids living off Daddy's money.

The Bell family from South Africa, or A2A Expedition as they are collectively known in the Overlanding world, may be eccentric, but they are no millionaires and not held aloft by Daddies bulging trust fund.

They are a normal family doing very unusual and inspiring things. For me, they define the authentic essence of Vehicle Dependant Overlanding – they travel for the joy of travelling.

It's clear that, for them, the destination is most definitely **NOT** the goal.

* * *

I found them quickly on social media, and after some very brief interactions through Facebook, I thanked them for their kind encouragement for our aspirations, and made the customary offer of hospitality, if they should ever find themselves in our neck of the Italian woods.

I certainly didn't expect the swift reply from Luisa, that they could be with us by the end of the week.

What followed was, what I now understand to be, a typical overlanding experience. Come for a day and stay for three. Use the Wi-Fi, showers and eat everything available.

We didn't mind at all, we loved the experience. In true South African style, on the final evening, Graeme cooked the famous beer can chicken (*variously known as chicken on a throne, beer butt chicken, coq au can, or even dancing chicken*), braving the pouring rain to produce this Louisiana speciality on our garden BBQ.

It was absolutely delicious.

This topped off a visit very nicely indeed. A visit that begin with a stark illustration as to why you don't underestimate the alcoholic capacity of a South Africa. A first night demolition of a litre bottle of Glenmorangie, amongst other things.

Most overlanders we have met, seem to arrive with a fearsome thirst, and a lot of washing.

Meeting the Bells got me thinking, a lot. They had kindly and enthusiastically answered a million questions, and left us curious but still dubious.

Could it be possible for us?

The first issue was money, with the exorbitant rent, the costs of Olivers International School fees, and the general costs of living, we were existing from one pay check to another, and really not enjoying it as much as we should have.

We needed to make radical change to turn this around and give us the funds we needed, both to build the vehicle and to travel for at least the first couple of years.

The biggest consideration was that I would have to do another 3 year contract at Ferrari despite my complete disgruntlement with my working environment.

In retrospect, this was easily the biggest sacrifice, but without it, none of this would have been possible.

In 2016, I bit down hard on the bullet, and mentally committed to another 5 years in a job that was slowly killing me.

Over the next two years, we would move house, Oliver would move School, twice, and we would reduce our monthly outgoings by well over 50%.

This staggering turnaround made the dream seem more like a possibility.

Linda still refused to believe that it was real, until such time as we had bought the vehicle. She wanted action, physical stuff, not just my fancy plans.

By the end of 2018, we had a kitty of around 10,000 Euros to buy the vehicle, and the dreaming became a serious search for a vehicle.

* * *

"Look no further than the holy trinity of off-roaders, Jeep the Father. Land Rover the Son. Toyota the Holy Ghost." - **Tom Collins**

In the first months of 2019, I avoided work misery by

spending an occasional few minutes scouring the internet for a Defender 130.

Why a Defender, you ask?

Wouldn't a Toyota be more reliable, and wouldn't a Jeep be cheaper? Well, yes to both, probably.

Obviously, I just love the smell of warm engine oil on my shoes and the regular company of a varied selection of auto mechanics who specialize in these wonderful but temperamental vehicles.

There was only even one possibility for the vehicle that we would choose, and it was bound to have been born in Solihull, UK.

The Land Rover v Toyota v Jeep debate is as about as old as Land Rover itself. It's rather like my preference for Canon photographic equipment over Nikon, in that there is no point delving too deeply into the reasoning, as you will find precious little to study.

I know what I like and that's what I like – nothing more scientific than that, I'm afraid.

In all seriousness, we wanted the practicality of 4 wheel drive, and with Oliver needing separate roof top accommodation (*apparently Linda snores*), there wasn't very much in our price range that would have the roof space to fit 2 tents.

The 130 was perfect. Cheap standard parts, and the huge range of after market overland kit available, was a distinct bonus.

* * *

In May 2019, after a six-month search across most of Europe for a reasonably priced LHD Defender 130, we found our perfect one limping forlornly around Frankfurt, Germany.

Despite her dodgy steering and her alarming lack of brakes, we completely fell in love with her. She was definitely the one. She came with heavy-duty everything and, like a derelict old farmhouse in the Cotswolds, we could see the stunning potential, but we were going to need a lot of stone, and a lot of slate.

Romantically speaking, it felt like we were about to save an old warhorse, and give her a second chance of life.

After tracking down Hamid the relentlessly positive, but worryingly elusive, salesman, the deal was eventually done. Deposit was made, and plans were hatched to come back in a few weeks and drive her back to the UK.

To our huge relief, Mandy, as she would be named, was born at last – now the real fun could begin. When looking at the recent prices of 130's, its clear we got her for an absolute song at around €9K, albeit after some cringe worthy haggling. Our dreams were slowly beginning to turn into reality. Linda was starting to believe at last.

Unlike most German girls, our Mandy was neither tidy nor reliable, so we knew very well that, before she was ready to be our Overland house on wheels, she was going to need a lot of love, affection and money.

Now, the only thing remaining was the seemingly simple task of returning her to the UK for her much needed makeover.

In the words of Jeremy Clarkson[24], *'What could possibly go wrong?'*.

* * *

On Thursday 16th May 2019, I flew in to Frankfurt from Italy and Jon Norman arrived separately by plane from the UK.

An old friend and former motor racing colleague, Jon had kindly agreed to take on the mammoth task of rebuilding and upgrading the Defender. Before that could begin, he had the unenviable task of being *'track side support'* for this mad overnight caper from Germany to Essex.

Top of the agenda on day one, was for him to change the Brake Vacuum and PAS pumps, or we weren't going to get very far at all.

Under the knife - the surgery had begun.

Friday 17th May 2019 dawned – D Day was an overcast and chilly day in Frankfurt, we were ready to go at 9am as agreed, but the normally uber organized German state apparatus decided to go all Italian on us, and did its absolute best to foil our plans.

Providing export number plates with the wrong year on them, was definitely not helpful – even less helpful was the fact that you could not simply swap the number plates for correct ones at the office, the whole export process would have to be begun again, and to compound the pressure even more, the offices were due to close at lunchtime on a Friday.

If poor Hamid the salesman failed, we would be stuck in Frankfurt until Monday.

Just before Midday, our saviour appeared in a dense and acrid cloud of 2 stroke scooter smoke, grinning like a Cheshire cat and clutching a set of correct export plates under his arm.

With the new plates fitted, and notwithstanding some initial wrong side of the road shenanigans, we were finally on our way.

Now, just the small matter of the 605 km to Calais, where the 21.55 P&O Ferry to Dover would be patiently waiting to carry us to Blighty. We had almost exactly 9 hours, to drive, what should take us no more than 6 hours, at the most.

It should have been plenty of time… you would have thought.

* * *

Jon is, thankfully, highly experienced in the skilled art of keeping an ageing Defender on the road, and, as it turned out, proved to be worth his weight in gold.

Armed with slightly more than my usual tool kit of a large hammer and a can of WD40, we were ready for anything.

Unfortunately, we didn't have long to wait to be reminded of the old adage that 'Land Rovers have been turning drivers into mechanics since 1947'.

Speed is all about perspective, and travelling at 120 km/h in a Defender on the Autobahn feels quite quick enough, thanks very much.

Until, that is, you are parked on the hard shoulder of said Autobahn, in the pouring rain, holding a very weighty bonnet up with one weedy, quivering arm. I nervously scanned back up the packed lanes of speeding Audi's, BMW's and Porsches, as they whizzed past my right shoulder at race pace. Jon, head buried deep in the engine bay, wouldn't stand a chance if we were hit, so I was ready to scream **JUMP** if someone strayed into our lane on a collision course.

The fuel cut-off solenoid had failed in the closed position (*a common fault apparently*), so with no diesel flowing, we were going precisely nowhere. Thankfully, Jon is a veteran of many a 300tdi powered adventure, and knew exactly how to get us going again, and coincidently, it would involve the direct application of our trusty large hammer.

As the engine had cut out, Jon had the presence of mind to coast to a halt underneath a wide motorway bridge.

The only water we had to contend with, was now limited to the 'pressure washer' wheel spray from passing HGV's as they skimmed past us in the inside lane. With every passing truck, I rocked on my ankles, and the heavy old Defender drunkenly rocked on her knackered springs in sympathy.

With light now fading, and famously poor headlights, the last place we wanted to be was a lame duck on the hard shoulder of the Autobahn.

After some precision hammering, Jon removed the errant

solenoid housing, but only after considerable swearing and knuckle damage. An auxiliary wire was run from the fuel pump to a permanent live feed under the bonnet to bypass the closed cut-off valve, and restore the vital diesel flow. The 9pm check-in for the ferry from Calais was starting to look fairly unlikely.

At this rate, it was going to be a very long and nerve wracking 605 km to Calais. Thankfully, an hour or so later, we were back on the road and heading towards Brussels.

Time to get fuel.

* * *

There are few more sickening feelings in the world than when that ignition key gets turned and the engine stubbornly refuses to fire.

You guessed it. Time to get the hammer out again.

It seems that the previous *'Heath Robinson'* bush repair type wiring solution, was only rated for around 200 km, not the full 605. We were eating fuses fast and running out of permanent live wiring feeds under the bonnet. After some sterling roadside innovation, Jon rigged up a much more robust wiring set up, that, crucially, was much more acceptable to the hard to please fuse box and, after a swift injection of coffee, crisps and chocolate, off we went again.

Having used up most of our wiggle time already, previous thoughts of a cheeky stop off at the museums of Dunkirk were, rather like the light, fast receding.

The flag had dropped, the worlds slowest race was officially on.

Considering the delays due to the fuel pump solenoid issue, coupled with the increasing volumes of early evening traffic, it became clear that our optimistic attempt to reach the ferry at 9pm was a thoroughly doomed one.

Defenders are not sports cars, and options to push on and make up the time were non-existent, even without considering the decidedly dodgy brakes, seriously suspect steering and their infamous 'candle like' headlights… we were going to get there, when we get there, and not before.

As darkness began to fall, we plugged on to Calais without suffering further mechanical issues, but the closer we got, it became clear that we had made much better time than we had any reason to predict.

We were going to be achingly close to the cut-off for our

ferry.

Despite arriving just before the departure time, the computer said no, and we would not be able to board the ship. Frustrating close as we could see the ship right in front of us with the bow doors open.

With the next ferry not due to leave until 11.35pm, we had some time to kill.

Jon busied himself trying to understand the whacky wiring system on the Defender and hopefully head off any more potential electrical gremlins, as we still had a long way to go.

Jon's workshop was based in Essex, so we had the unappetizing prospect of a further 3-hour drive in the early morning after a midnight arrival in Dover.

This was swiftly becoming a 24-hour marathon journey.

PLANS AND PANDEMICS.

Neither of us fancied reliving those golden days.

Just after midnight, UK time, Mandy finally returned us to the land of her birth. After a relatively uneventful drive from Dover, passing through the Dartford tunnel and the M25, we wearily arrived in rural Essex, around 3am and very worse for wear.

The Solihull girl, with a German accent, had ultimately done the job.

As we dropped her off at the workshop, I bedded down in the office and fell into a deep sleep, a sleep full of adventurous dreams no doubt.

I never dreamed, however, that it would be another 1 year, 10 months and 25 days until she would be fully ready to hit the road again, as our new permanent house on wheels.

By then, the world would be a very different place entirely.

* * *

Not unlike the knowing where you were when Kennedy died (*my father was in the bath apparently, by the way*), do you remember where you were when you heard the word 'Coronavirus' for the first time?

Working in Italy, we had a front row seat to witness what quickly evolved from a severe 'flu' outbreak, to the beginning of the end of the world.

Soon we would see reports of military trucks carting bodies away from Italian hospitals for mass burial. It was mind blowing.

We'd seen the reports from China leading up to Christmas 2019, but like the vast majority of the world, plodded on regardless. As I earned some money, I would send it to Jon, and he would do a little more on Mandy. Each month a little more stripping down and old parts replaced with new.

Life was good, we still had 12 months to get her ready for the journey of a lifetime. The plan was fixed and very simple, I would finish my contract in December 2020, fly to England, drive her back to Italy, say our goodbyes to our Italian friends, and off we would go to Nordkapp to test her out.

Simple as that.

* * *

What followed would prove to be as simple as threading a needle in a gale, while wearing boxing gloves, and just about as frustrating. Even before the all pervading Covid had struck, the first blow to our plans was much more mundane.

Jon had gone from being a self employed race mechanic, to having a full time position. Obviously, this would reduce the time he would have to rebuild the Defender and the endless stop/start would severely impact on his productivity.

I was gutted, but tried not to let it show.

I was anxious to get her done, testing and ready for our adventure, and progress was frustratingly slow.

I had not budgeted to use a professional restoration business, and needed all of my diplomacy skills to keep Jon motivated on a job that now, he really didn't want to complete.

Jon's employer somehow managed to work throughout the Covid period, so even the virus wasn't going to help me out, and anyway, he was somewhat reluctant to work on her during the lock down periods. Understandably, I guess.

The stress induced by this situation was immense.

I was paying an awful lot of money and progress was so

slow, I had very serious doubts that he would ever get her completed, even enough that I could at least drive it away from his workshop. Depression was never far away.

The old doubts resurfaced.

What right did I have for this dream to become real?

Once the severity of the COVID virus was clear, I would spend the vast majority of 2020 either on holiday (*mandated by the F1 authorities*) or working from home due to the COVID restrictions employed by Ferrari.

I have never been more frustrated in my life. I could not travel to the UK to try to help with the rebuild of Mandy. I was stuck in Italy, trying to gently motivate Jon, as much as possible, to complete her.

It's a horrible situation when you are beholden on a friend to complete something that they clearly don't want to do. He never said it out loud, but that is the price that you pay for trying to cut corners I guess, and I didn't want to lose him as a friend, but the frustration was hard and real.

Commitments mean something to me, and rightly or wrongly, If I am honest, I felt abandoned by someone I had trusted.

* * *

In parallel with the ongoing battle to get Mandy rebuilt, I was channelling my under-developed marketing side. Despite my instincts, it seems that I have one, and it works quite well, in writing at least.

They say that you should never go racing with your own money. So, taking a leaf out of the F1 marketing handbook, I set about trying to encourage as many Brands as I could to support our project. But first, we needed a name.

We named the project 'Itchy Feet Overland', and soon, along came a logo, website and the dreaded social channels.

I am hugely ambivalent about social media. I like that Facebook can keep you in touch with friends, but the dark side of Facebook is very dark indeed. I came off it completely during the first COVID lockdowns as my mental health was being continually assaulted by the pseudo-scientific idiocy from both ends of the spectrum. I had to walk away.

Instagram is, in my experience, a friendlier space and as I love photography, I would end up spending most of my time there.

The problem is that social media is now inextricably woven throughout most of our lives, and I knew that the companies we were seeking sponsorship from, would require payment in social media posts and likes. I needed to learn fast.

This is the real conundrum of living the life we lead.

I don't have a skill that can earn me money while we travel. Neither am I natural exhibitionist, far from it.

As a card carrying introvert, the last thing I really wanted to do was to post endless selfies and videos of me opening boxes and waxing lyrical about the the latest fire pit or whatever. But that is what I had committed to.

So, not for the first time, and maybe not the last, it's time for *'Fake it, until you make it'* time.

* * *

The first business to yield to my advances were Safety Devices International, designers and manufacturers of some of best Roll Over Protection kits in the world.

The one thing that everyone can agree, about the old Defender, is that you don't ever want to roll it on to its roof.

The roof will easily collapse to the tops of the doors, and unless you are 2 feet 6 inches tall, you will struggle to come out of it without, at the very least, life changing injuries. They offered me a free of charge internal/external roll cage. I must admit to be being slightly gobsmacked at this initial success, but this was just the beginning.

Buoyed by my early success, I widened the search to include some of the other major equipment and services that we would need.

Over the next 8 months I would identify, chase down and get positive commitments from around 80% of the brands that I targeted.

The hardest part was often finding the person within their organization that could give the commitment - the real decision maker. A LinkedIn Premium Business Account is a must, and was a huge help in identifying the right person in large organisations, despite the *'b*llshit bingo'* used by HR 'Business parters' to obfuscate what people actually do.

My biggest target was to find a supplier of the roof top tens and awning - these were one of our biggest potential expenses, and after long but ultimately fruitless discussions with a number of potential supplier, my final target, Darche of Australia came on board with a tremendous offer.

They were willing to supply two roof tents, a batwing awning and a pile of other stuff. This was absolutely incredible, and totally exceeded my expectation.

Over the months that followed, we would gather together a great selection of high quality brands that shared our adventurous vision, all on the promise of our life changing project to travel the Pan American Highway from top to bottom.

Now, we just had to deliver, and deliver big.

*　*　*

As the fallout from COVID 19 ground grimly on, the delays to Mandy were mounting on all sides.

Parts were piling up all over the place and the the truck wasn't even painted yet. Trying to keep the ball rolling, the paint shop placated, and the parts coming in, was right up there with one of the most stressful things that I have ever been involved with.

All the while, stuck in Italy, trying to keep Ferrari happy, and my sanity intact.

Days turned into week, which turned into months. Little further progress was evident on the truck, and my old mental frailties returned.

I slumped into a deep negative trough, and couldn't see a way out.

Everyting was being compressed into the tail end of 2020 - the registration of the vehicle, the fitting of the roll cage, the repairs to the doors, the final painting, the bumpers, the electrics, the transmission, the interior - everything.

Then just as the Defender was finally painted, Covid struck again, hard.

October 31st 2020 saw the next UK lockdown, and restrictions would continue until March 2021.

The impact of this was massive, as nothing meaningful was happening to the truck, but after a great deal of cajoling, Jon agreed that he would make the Defender available for RST in the new year, with the majority of the big stuff fitted and the engine running.

It was crucial that the engine was running so we could move the vehicle from his workshop to RST for the new gearbox, and trans axle to be fitted.

The slot that I had booked at RST Land Rovers to fit the new gearbox and Transfer casing was being shunted further and further forward in the diary.

Christmas 2020 is one that I definitely want to forget.

Clearly, our original plan to collect the truck in January 2021 and head for Nordkapp was in absolute tatters, and even with the most optimistic outlook, a June departure to Canada for the Pan American Highway seemed highly unlikely, and anything later would risk us arriving in Alaska in the dead of winter.

That prospect was unthinkable (*and would result in my divorce*) - a years delay to the project seemed the only possibility. I was gutted.

All of the planning, the effort, the sacrifice.

3 years of pain and it had come down to this.

A half built car 1500 kms away, parts stuck all over Europe and the world reeling from an invidious virus.

I was ready to just walk away.

* * *

As I finally left Ferrari in December of 2020, the imagined joyful feelings of relief and released tension were conspicuously missing. Replaced as they were, by the almost unbearable weight of seeing my meticulous plan shattered before me, like a cherished crystal vase.

I managed the bereavement in the only way that I knew how, by blocking it out and dealing with one day, and one problem, at a time.

It was obvious that with travel restrictions and lock downs in place, we wouldn't be leaving Italy anytime soon.

Linda was becoming more anxious by the day to get moving, but I wanted to wait until the Defender was on the road, but as things dragged ever further on, I finally accepted that we had to make forward progress.

We would leave Italy in our battered Land Rover Freelander on the 4th February 2021, during the COVID lockdown.

PLANS AND PANDEMICS.

***

6

Nothing behind, everything ahead.

"A journey of a thousand miles must begin with a single step."
– Lao Tzu

It is the early hours of 4th February 2021. Outside our beautiful stone built farm house, in the Apennine hills of Zocca, It's pitch black and forbiddingly cold.

The Freelander is packed to the very gunnels, with barely enough space to fit the three of us. Poor Oliver is wedged in his seat, legs clamped tightly, and partially cocooned by bags, boxes and rolled up duvets.

After weeks spent holding garage sales, and minus the few items we decided to store in Italy with our friends, we were left with the remnants of our worldly goods.

Every conceivable hole in the Freelander had been stuffed with what remained.

This was it.

Anxiety levels were at an all-time high.

NOTHING BEHIND, EVERYTHING AHEAD.

The migraine inducing mathematical juggling of receiving our COVID results before arriving at Mont Blanc, and for them still to be valid when we reached Calais the next day was a mind-numbing calculation, and relied on, in no small degree, a dose of pure luck.

Thankfully, at least our negative test certificate emails had arrived earlier that day, and more importantly, they were in English, as necessary to arrive in the UK.

The game was on - we had just 72 hours to reach the UK coast or our test certificates would be invalid. Normally, an easy target, but courtesy of the French government, we now had the additional challenge of a nightly curfew in France from 18.00.

I felt like I was about to embark on a very low rent version of a Top Gear challenge.

* * *

We set off north, directly for the Mont Blanc Tunnel, and made good progress as a beautiful dawn broke over the approaching alps.

As we got closer to the Tunnel, the large electronic signs above the dual carriageway were flashing their urgent message - I managed to glance at it, as we sped along.

Did it really say that the tunnel was closed?

A frantic search online and nothing suggested that the tunnel was closed - despite that familiar sinking feeling in my stomach, I tried hard to convince myself, and everyone else in the car, that I **MUST** have misread it.

Simplest answer, not to worry, just plough on.

Just a few minutes later, more electronic signs, and this time, there was no way of convincing myself that I was mistaken this time. The indisputable message, writ large in orange flashing lights - *'**TUNNEL FERMÉ**',* and alternating with its Italian translation. They were screaming at me... **Closed!!**

I felt the cold sweat and hot hives of anxiety.

To arrive in Northern France by 18.00, we **HAD** to take the tunnel, to have to turn around and make the much slower crossing via the Brenner Pass, in February of all times, would mean that we would have to drive during the French curfew.

Disconsolately, I thought 'Why me?'. Always me.

Six years in Italy had taught me at least one good thing, however. Never, ever, believe a *'Road Closed'* sign.

I gamely ploughed on, in the back of my mind expecting to reach an impassable concrete barrier very soon.

Adding to the general feeling of Apocalypse, the motorway was almost deserted. We had passed a handful of cars and the occasional truck in the last 30 minutes, and next to nothing was coming the other way. I had never seen it so quiet.

As we made the last twists and turns past Courmayer and towards the entrance of the tunnel, we saw no concrete barrier, no blocked road.

Slightly dumbfounded, we slowly drove up to the deserted border and pulled up next to a pair of French border police.

Initially they seemed confused as to why I had stopped the car, and even more confused when I thrust a handful of COVID documents at them - the very documents that the French government, their employer, demanded that we provide to get into their country.

They didn't seem to have a clue what to do with them, with one of them even trying to hand them back to me at one point.

It's worth mentioning that our Freelander had Italian number plates - but even so, with France in complete lockdown with a curfew, this greeting was very bizarre.

It got a little stranger still, when I tried to show them our UK passports - they looked at them, looked at me, and one of them burst out laughing *'Ha, Ha, Brexit, Brexit!!'*, he roared, much to his friend's amusement, both shaking their heads in pity, as they handed the passports back.

In the door mirror, he was still chuckling to himself as he waved us goodbye, and off into the Tunnel.

Ciao Italia, and Bonjour France.

* * *

The rest of the journey was relatively uneventful. We arrived at our Hotel in Northern France just before the 18.00 curfew, and enjoyed a great socially distanced meal, before having our first longed for sleep for over 30 hours.

The next morning, bright and early we headed to Calais for the Channel Tunnel and were met with the British variety of Border Force comedian.

My answer *'Wellingborough'* to the question *'Where are you a heading'* made him suck his teeth and wince, *'Really?, Why would you want to go there?'*.

A little harsh, I said, as I half-heartedly defended the town of my birth. As it turned out, he was somewhat of a psychic, in a depressingly predictable way.

He waved us on our way, and after the short journey under the sea, we alighted the train, and headed North, amongst the busiest pandemic lockdown I had ever seen, in my life.

Unlike Italy, and France for that matter, in the Oxford English Dictionary, the word *'LOCKDOWN'* was now defined as *'Do pretty much as you please'*.

Having lived through COVID, and suffered its many privations in Italy, it was shocking to see how little things had changed in the UK. The roads were busy, shops were open and life seemed pretty normal.

* * *

A couple of weeks prior to leaving Italy, I had checked with my sister, Jenny, to see if she was still OK to accommodate us for the mandatory 10-day quarantine period when we arrived in the UK.

Despite our negative status it appears that, for whatever reason, she was not.

Staying with her would have broken no rules that I was aware of, and the rules at the time did not require her to isolate in the house with us.

I was crestfallen.

Later I would learn from more than one friend, that they would have stepped in and offered us accommodation if we had asked. We didn't ask.

The company she worked for had a one-bedroom flat in the centre of Wellingborough, and Jenny arranged for us to use it for the mandatory 10-day isolation period. Beggars can't be choosers, and despite everything, we were grateful for the offer.

No mention was made of rent, but I was clear that I was more than happy to pay for all the utilities etc. The flat had been empty for some time and was impossible to rent during the COVID lockdown anyway, so maybe, in some small way, I was doing them a favour too.

The flat was in the wrong part of town, which presupposes that there is a right side of town, but we were at the top floor of an old building that had been converted into offices.

It seems that we weren't doing the owners a favour at all. At no time after the 10 days were up, did my sister offer to accommodate us, so as the Defender was delayed, and the time in the flat increased, our funds were heavily dented with paying rent that was never budgeted for.

A lesson really should have been learned, but I managed to blindly walk into an identical situation immediately afterwards, much to my shame and embarrassment.

* * *

Formula One is essentially one giant cottage industry.

If you are in it long enough, you will bump into the same faces over and over again, though they may be wearing different colour shirts each time you see them anew.

It is the same with the suppliers that the teams use. The same ones will crop up with most of the teams, if they are any good that is, and over the years you can build a rapport with some of them.

Stable Fabrication was one such business.

They were steeped in the history of Formula One - spawned, as it were, from the wreckage of the notorious Hesketh Formula One team of the 1970s. Originally based in the old Stable block at Easton Neston House - the home of Lord Hesketh, eccentric leader of the team that bore his name, Stable would grow into a major supplier to motor sport teams throughout the UK and Europe.

In the days before the widespread use of carbon fibre, their metal fabrication skills would become renowned throughout the racing industry.

For most of my working life, I have known Mark Halleybone. His shock of blond hair, and explosive laugh, would feature regularly in my life from the early 1990s. We first met working for Ray Mallock Engineering, at the time, a ramshackle racing team operating out of a rat infested farmyard in Castlethorpe.

He was a fabricator and I, a newly appointed and very green production assistant to Ray Mallocks, one legged wife, Sue.

We both had the dubious honour of being 'made redundant' on the same day - though, when considering the half dozen of us who went, the criteria for redundancy may have much more to do with the quality of the relationship that we each had with 'she who must be obeyed', otherwise, less charitably known as 'Peg leg'.

Neither of us were on her Christmas card list, that we could be sure.

Whilst Mark would soon resurface at Stable, I would end up rattling around a few more touring car teams, until I would really need him in, what would become, close to my darkest hour.

In 1996, Stewart Grand Prix proudly told the world that their embryonic SF1 racing car would be entirely designed using the wonders of Computer Aided Design (**CAD**).

They were nearly right, but they had neglected to consider the small matter of the tangled web of aluminium pipes, snaking like Medusa's hair around the gearbox and engine assembly.

Always amongst the very last things to be designed, the pipes would carry the lifeblood of oil and water, vital for her successful operation as a racing car.

In the final days of the construction of the first car, it became obvious that, clever though it was, CAD was not going to give us design drawings of pipes anytime soon.

The next day, and to the astonishment of the young designers and engineers, two men in overalls arrived - armed with a load of welding wire, a ball of string, some sticky tape and a box of old old bits of bent aluminium tube.

Mark, along with one of the original Hesketh F1 fabricators, the legendary 'Pop', swarmed all over, around and under the car. A few hours passed, and after a quick trip back to Towcester, they returned very late in the evening with a set of *'mock-up pipes'* to test.

Anything was possible if you knew who to ask. This, more than anything, briefly cemented my favourable position with the SGP Technical boss, Alan Jenkins. It didn't last long (*as you may recall in chapter 3*).

Pipes have long formed a significant part of our professional relationship.

Mark loves nothing more than to remind me of a now notorious exchange that happened in the late 1990s. I managed to lose my legendary composure in a most spectacular fashion, when the continued absence of some vital new welded pipes, caused me to scream down the telephone at Mark - *'Where's my F*CKING pipes!!'*

I've been paying for my outburst ever since, as there is literally no conversation over the last 20 plus years, that Mark has failed to weave this anecdote within.

Fast forward to 2019, and its time to ask for Marks help again. By now he's a co-owner of Stable Fabrication - a much larger and more capable organization. As it was looking certain that when we return to the UK, we were going to need some fabrication work done on the Defender, and somewhere under cover to complete the build of the car.

Mark came up trumps as always.

They had just been joined in the business by a third partner, and he had arrived with a small factory unit on a farm just outside Towcester, that was pretty much unused - we could use it, and they would also do whatever work we needed on the Defender.

This was a huge weight off my mind. I assured Mark that we were happy to cover the utilities on the building, which seemed fair, as they were not using it and were already paying the rent regardless of our occupation of around half of it.

I was about to get another hard lesson.

When we arrived in the UK, I spoke with Mark.

Things had changed at Stable. He seemed unsure, vague and even a little embarrassed when we discussed moving the Defender into the factory unit.

Marks position in the business had seemingly changed and he was no longer able, through no fault of his own, to make good on the informal agreement we had.

Just another drama to add to the list.

* * *

A few weeks earlier, the transfer of the Defender from Jon to RST had gone spectacularly wrong.

Despite assurances that the vehicle could be loaded onto a trailer under its own steam, this didn't happen. Flat battery I was told. Two Odyssey Extreme batteries?

RST tell me they didn't have a winch trailer, so refused to

collect it, and no one is telling me any of this, this until it was all too late.

Stuck on the end of a phone in Italy, I was fast losing the will to live.

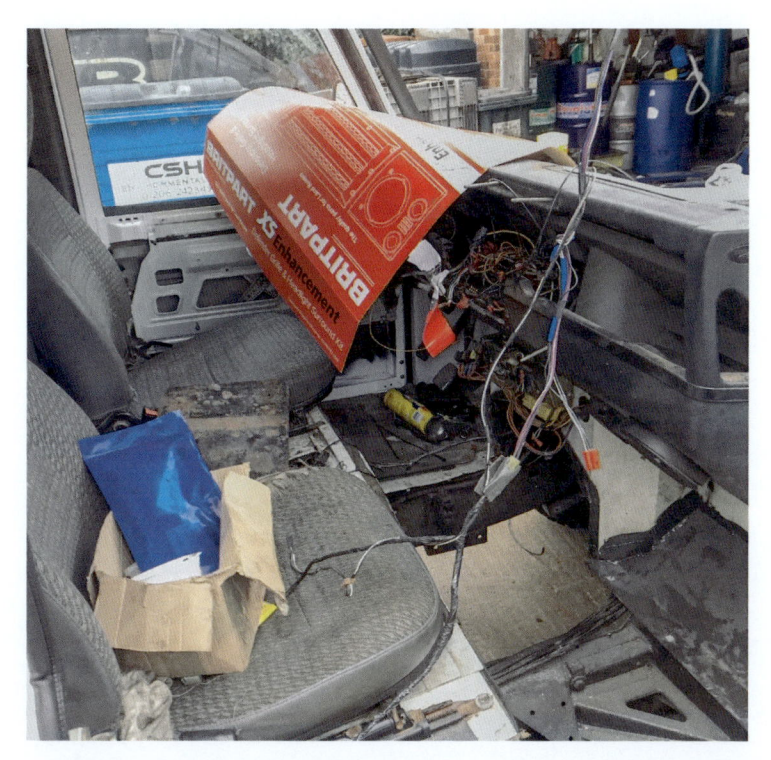

I would now have to hire a local recovery truck to move the Defender to the workshops if RST. More time lost and more money spent. Tick tock.

The Defender was still missing it's front bumper, rear bumper, roof rack, interior seating, headlining, auxiliary lights, winch, underbody protection - the list was endless. It arrived at RST with piles of parts stuffed inside the defender.

Linda cried when she saw it.

Once delivered to RST, the list of problems was long, with fuel leaks, loose dampers and brakes, and the engine timing was catastrophically out. I had to call upon my diplomatic skills, yet again, to get RST to try and finish the work that had not been done.

I was partially successful and they bolted the front and rear bumper on, fitted a windscreen and got it running (*though, audibly, it resembled a hugely underpowered Panzer tank, complete with plumes of oily smoke*).

The gathering frustrations were eating my soul.

Every day, another imploring plea for someone to do something that was either already agreed, or easily within their control to do. It's never been so hard to give people money. The difference between building F1 cars and defenders was stark.

Once RST was finally finished with her, I needed to get her engine running straight. In the best silver lining fashion, I was about to be introduced to one of the few positive aspects of this whole saga.

Mick Loughran, of the Towcester Loughran Brothers, is a local legend. With a wit far drier than the Sahara Desert, he spends his life repairing Land Rovers of all shapes and sizes, but only the ones he wants to.

We felt privileged that he agreed to take on our half built pile of scrap.

Operating since 1976, he has never needed to advertise, as his order book is always full, as it has been from day one.

If you are bold enough to tell him what the problem is before his expert boys have looked at it, he is, as likely as not, liable to tell you to *'P*ss off and repair it yourself'*.

Like I say, a true legend, and the most reliable garage I have ever used.

Another old SGP colleague, Leigh Pettifer, from Circuit to Circuit, agreed to collect Mandy from RST and bring her to Micks comforting care.

As Mick was tending to the Defender, we took on the factory unit, in preparation of its pending arrival, and the much anticipated final assembly stage.

The unit was a complete mess, piles of old equipment and general tat everywhere. We offered to help clear it, clean it and tidy what remained.

We set to work enthusiastically - we had literally had nothing else to do and weeks were ticking by relentlessly.

* * *

On the 29th March 2021, exactly 6 weeks after leaving COVID isolation, we excitedly took delivery of Mandy at the unit near Towcester.

But still, with no other place to live, we were still in the one bedroom flat in Wellingborough.

A flat that was seemingly a magnet for *'fly tipping'*, each morning I would nervously draw the curtain back to view the overnight *'delivery'*, the best of which by far, was a complete builders house clearance of debris, including toilet bowl and cistern.

Welcome to Wellingborough.

COVID caused numerous problems for us, not least the logistical delays for our roof top tents. Darche were kindly providing 2 tents. An RT1600 for myself and Linda, and a smaller RT1400 for my son Oliver. We could do nothing without these tents.

Due to Covid, their Chinese suppliers were in disarray. Whilst they managed to find a large tent in Australia, the shipping times were horrendous, and the smaller tent would have to be made in China and then shipped.

We filled our days in the unit, fiddling around with the Defender - Linda helping to fit the Exmoor Trim cubby box, seats and generally tidying her up.

I am not a mechanic and only know what a spanner is, by looking in the mirror.

To try and keep the momentum going, I called in every favour that I possibly could.

Two heroes that answered the call, were Scott Antoniou and Alan Strachan - two more disparate characters you could not meet.

Scott, a mild mannered, bespectacled encyclopedia of Defender parts, and Alan, a tall, wrinkled chain smoking Scot who used swearing as punctuation.

Both give up multiple weekends to help Mandy come alive.

The weeks in between were the most frustrating of times, but slowly as the weeks progressed, the winch was fitted, then the auxiliary lights, the under body protection, the door and roof linings - it was slowing taking shape.

I doubt that I ever thanked them enough.

* * *

The UK's lamentable decision to leave the EU, *'Brexit'* as it has become known, was just another unwanted impediment to our project in an already substantial list of them.

By April 2021 we counted ourselves pretty lucky that we hadn't really been affected too much. In 2019, we jumped too soon and swapped our UK driving licences for Italian ones, but other than that, nothing had changed.

I had managed to import the vast majority of the the big pieces of the jigsaw, into the UK, before Brexit customs problems began - the final thing left to come was a bespoke storage pod that would be mounted in the back of the truck, designed to house our huge 90L Fridge/Freezer combo, and a set of integrated storage drawers.

Tembo, the manufacturer, was based in the Netherlands, and had already supplied the rear bumper assembly and full length roof rack prior to the Brexit transition deadline of 31 December 2020.

It came as a shock when the storage box was turned back at the Hook of Holland and the export was denied - apparently, I would have to run around finding someone with an EORI number, required for the importation of all goods from the EU.

Luckily our vehicle transport friend, Leigh Pettifer, had the required status within his Business and kindly arranged the import for us.

More delays.

The whole world seemed to be against us.

**

We really needed some good news, and we needed it soon.

Shoulders were sagging heavily, and the driving from Wellingborough to Towcester and back, each day, was draining us all.

The much needed boost to morale came in the form of a short phone call from Clare at Trek Overland in Yorkshire.

The first post-COVID sea container of Darche products was about to arrive in the UK. It should contain our large tent, our 270 degree awning and our storage bags. Christmas was finally coming.

Like war, we were experiencing long periods of boredom and delay, interspersed with short sharp bursts of action. The only thing we lacked for, was being shot at.

Now we had a battle on our hands, we had to have her ready for her first significant journey since returning her from Frankfurt 2 years earlier.

The first weeks of April were spent at Stable Fabrication, frantically completing the necessary work - the priority was the mounting of the full length Tembo roof rack (*essential to allow the tent to be fitted*), the rear storage box and finally, the modified second row seating. Kev did a superb job.

On 20th April, we braced ourselves and set off up the M1 motorway, and headed north to Yorkshire.

Mandy was nowhere near complete - missing door panels, roof lining, and internal matting. The noise was utterly deafening - wind whistling through the holes behind the dash and bulkhead, like a wildly out of tune Peruvian Pan Pipe orchestra.

Thus, we began our first real journey in Mandy.

Deafened, frozen and hunched up like the famous Parisian resident, Quasimodo. If you had asked me right then, why I had bought a Defender, I would have struggled to give you any sort of reasonably coherent answer.

As we dodged the HGV's on the inclines, I began to seriously doubt what was left of my sanity.

The feeling was amplified when we arrived at the base of Sutton Bank, a very long climb with a 1 in 4 (*or 25% if you prefer*) incline, and a few hairpin bends thrown in for entertainment.

Bearing in mind, the vehicle was totally unproven, particularly the engine, which had been largely untouched since we drove her back from Germany.

The roar of the engine was even more deafening than usual, and we laid down an effective smoke screen as we chugged up the hill. Sweat forming on my brow, and cheeks clenched tighter than a giant nut cracker, we crested the brow of the hill and the engine note dropped with a palpable sense of relief that was shared by both of us.

We had made it, the engine seemed to be in one piece, new new rattles detected, so far.

My mouth was as a dry as the Sisters of Mercy's drinks cabinet.

* * *

Trek Overland looked after us handsomely.

Within a few hours, and after the welcome imbibement of some reviving Yorkshire tea, we were now, at last, the proud owners of a Darche RT1600 Roof Top Tent. With still no sign of the second tent, we bid our farewells to Clare and the gang, and headed back south.

The arrival of the first tent meant, at last, we could move out of the weekly '*World Fly Tipping Championships*'.

The final cost, at £17 a day (*around £500 per month*), was a little hard to swallow, If I'm honest, but maybe I was naive thinking someone would cut us a break. They hadn't so far.

More money that we didn't plan to spend.

The unit that awaited us was freezing cold but dry. We had a tent to sleep in and a flushing toilet. The lap of luxury.

In the absence of the second tent for Oliver, we agreed to all sleep in the large tent, on top of the Defender and, inside the unit. Three little piggies, wrapped up tight, looking forward to a peaceful night..

All was fine until one of the piggies kept oinked far too loud for the young piglet to sleep, and soon, everyone would start throwing their trotters about.

* * *

In a selfless act of peacemaking I withdrew from the tent in the early hours of the morning, wrapped myself in a duvet, stuck a woolly hat on my head, and settled down in a chair to try and get some sleep.

I was woken around 6 am, cold, stiff and utterly dejected.

This wasn't going to work.

Luckily we had a set of inflatable mattresses that would become a makeshift bed on the floor of the unit, and used by Oliver until the second tent arrived a few weeks later.

Unsurprisingly, our second tent found itself stuck in the multi billion dollar traffic jam behind the jack-knifed container ship in the Suez canal.

I didn't know whether to laugh or cry.

* * *

16th May 2021 turned out to be a very big day for us.

Exactly 106 days after arriving back in the UK in our battered Freelander, we would be camping as a complete family in the Defender, for the very first time.

The day before we had finally got the second Darche tent, and we had been invited to represent Darche in a Land Rover magazine feature for Roof Top Tents.

We nervously drove to Quarry Events in Kettering, not knowing quite what to expect. This was a far more public camping initiation, that I would have liked, as would be among a group of a dozen or so other Land Rovers, representing the many other Tent options on sale in the UK.

The fact that the business had 'Quarry' in its title, really should have had the alarm bells ringing, but I blissfully followed Andrew, the owner, through the farm gate.

In his very light, but very battered Defender 90, he effortlessly glided around the tree line and ascended a 45% incline on the narrow tree lined track.

I looked at Linda, and she looked at me.

My off-road experience amounted to little more than parking on the grass at Towcester rugby club.

I had that sickening feeling of impending doom. I was going to park it squarely in the trees, the very first time I ever went off road. My face was heating up at in anticipation of the inevitable embarrassment.

I snapped out if it. I'd spent my life blagging, so one more go couldn't hurt - bravado dial turned to 11, and off we go.

I launched Mandy from a standing start, but up the hill she would not go. Not a chance - she spluttered to a breathless halt, less than half way up.

'*Jesus*', I whispered to myself. What now? The deep mud ruts in the track meant I should be able to roll back down comfortably to have another go - but Linda didn't know this. Understandably, she was beside herself.

I care way too much about what other people think of me, and would probably still be there now, wheels spinning, if Andrew hadn't trotted back down the hill, and asked a very simple question.

'*Are you in low range?*' - he said, balancing himself in the claggy mud by hanging on to my wing mirror.

I could have died. Low range! What an absolute idiot. How could I forget the most basic rule of off road driving. I mumbled, and sheepishly engaged the low range shifter.

As he walked away, he inadvertently saved my brand new gearbox, by yelling 'Use second gear, first is too harsh'. I popped it from first into second.

A couple of goes more, including a big run up, and *voila*,

we had managed to crest the hill with all 3.5 tonnes of our Defender intact. You could smell the relief in the vehicle.

I silently gave praise for the foresight to pack a crate of beer. I was ready for some, very soon.

* * *

Now, replete with two tents, we needed to get out of the factory unit.

The free use of a unit had turned into a money pit, so despite clearing the place up, we were expected to pay their rental payments and the utilities.

As a buyer in Formula One, as I was for over a quarter of a century, many assume you to be corrupt, taking bribes and favours in exchange for offering work.

I know some that may well have, and probably made a lot of money doing it, but I am not one of them.

What I did do, and I am not ashamed to admit it, was to, in the lean times, favour some companies over others to reward them for the extraordinary support that had given to me over the years. Quid pro quo, nothing more then that.

Suppliers do not need to drop everything, and react instantly to your urgent requests, but some do, and the best ones, don't charge you extra for it. That's called a relationship.

There were few, but one such relationship was with Mark Halleybone of Stable Fabrication.

I trusted him, and he trusted me.

He got me out of incalculable dramas over the 25 years, often working late into the night, and at weekends to do the jobs that no-one else wanted to do.

He got us to races, no doubt about that.

When the economy tanked, he would call me, and if I could, I would ALWAYS send him some work, just enough to keep his machines working. That's called a relationship.

When I was finally charged for the work done on Mandy, and expected to cover the full rent of an unused building along with utilities that we had used, I didn't say anything.

What could I say? It was the time of Covid, everyone was struggling I guess, but I was disappointed more than anything.

Regime change was happening at Stable, and I knew that Mark had no say in it.

It's clear that it's easy to invest in a business, but not so easy to run it. It's even harder to have the vision and character to build the types of relationships that keep businesses afloat in the good times, and the bad.

Yet more expense that I wasn't expecting.

The kitty was getting smaller by the day, with every £50 spent, being roughly one day less on the road.

A hard lesson learned. Everything changes, all the time.

* * *

As we left the factory unit without looking back, we finally caught some luck.

An old acquaintance of Linda had a farm not too far from the factory unit and Tony, the very generous owner, kindly offered to let us stay in an unused paddock for free.

We had no facilities but we absolutely didn't care. It was perfect.

Finally, we could stand still and not spend any money - the relief was palpable.

We set about sorting, what we hoped would be, the very

last bits and pieces on the Defender.

* * *

For a while, I had been growing increasing concerned about the steering in Mandy. It felt really loose and indistinct, in fact, it felt as precise as a bucket of blancmange. It had become increasingly difficult, and stressful, to drive.

This difficultly was superbly illustrated by Linda who, inadvertently I must stress, almost killed us on the A5 near Weedon.

The Defender had started to gently fishtail at 50 mph, as we descended a series of sweeping bends. The weight transfer was causing the unstable Defender to act as a pendulum.

The necessary correction is supremely counter intuitive though - keeping the steering wheel rock steady will get the wallowing, top heavy Defender back under some sort of control, but your brain is screaming at you to steer against the swerve, but this is 100% wrong.

Trying to correct the it in that way , will just accelerate the fish tail. 100%.

It's easily the scariest moment of my life, and I have crashed a few cars in my time.

As we drove through a final gentle down hill corkscrew bend, I could see a 18 wheel HGV heading directly at us, if our course wasn't corrected immediately.

It's the first, and so far only, time that I have ever been compelled to grab the steering wheel of a moving vehicle. I gripped it solidly in my left hand until the lurching stopped and Linda braked to a slower speed.

Anything over 40 mph, on anything other than a smooth

and dead straight road, had the potential for instant and unexpected catastrophe. It had steadily got worse as the Defender had gained the weight, in particular once the roof tents were fitted.

I ordered a new steering column from RST and booked her in to Loughran's again. More expense.

* * *

The quarry hill debacle was a clear (*as mud?*) reminder that we desperately needed some off road driver training, and we needed it fast.

As part of my marketing campaign for the Pan Am trip, I managed to convince the legendary Vince Cobley to provide a two day off road driving course. As it turned out, he had volunteered his son Edd, to do the hard work.

Edd is the renowned chief Instructor at the Land Rover Experience at Rockingham Castle, and in his spare time, races madly powerful Defenders in Hill Rallies. We were going to get on just fine. Oliver loved him, especially when he let him loose in his own personal 110.

Day one was spent at Rockingham with the basics. He looked over the truck and was very worried about the suspension because of the weight we were carrying and, in particular, the high centre of gravity.

Despite a new steering rack and a general tightening up of all things steering related, she still felt very skittish through bends and under heavy breaking. My buttocks were perpetually clenched as I drove her, a sigh of relief when we arrived without incident.

A phone call to Glyn Lewis in Wales ended with an agreement to order a set of monster rear springs and a set of old man emu heavy duty dampers.

This, I was reliably informed, was as much rear suspension as we ever going to get, short of designing our own mega springs... I took his word, and ordered a kit.

The rest of the day was spent on approach angles, departure angles, and how far we could lean her over before we made like a drunken turtle.

Worryingly, Scooby Doo scary arrived at just 15% from horizontal.

Our sky high centre of gravity and the blancmange like suspension was giving Edd recurring palpitations - more discussions followed at the end of day, would lead us to speak to one of our partners, Terrafirma, and order a full set of monster, heavy duty front and rear Anti Roll Bar assemblies.

Day two began early with a change of location. This time we were at the HQ of Protrax, the driver training business owned by Edd's father, Vince Cobley.

Despite this being our first visit to their Tixover Quarry facility, the vague familiarity of the location was explained by it's use as the off-road course featured many times in the BBC's Top Gear TV show. Most memorably, who can forget Richard Hammond's, now legendary ,'I *am a driving God*' Bowler Wildcat feature in 2010.

Linda had barely driven the Defender, and after her recent terrifying episode on the road, her confidence was shot to pieces.

This was kids-stuff for Edd. His easy going but direct teaching style was just what she needed. He dismissed her worries out of hand, and got her to drive Mandy in a way that none of us dreamed she ever would.

Driving through deep water, cresting see-saw ridges and testing that 15% angle to the limit. She was on fire.

I left Tixover feeling a mixture of genuine happiness, after successfully testing ourselves in a hostile and very foreign driving environment, and a persistent niggling worry regarding the rear suspension on the Defender.

If the upgrades we had ordered didn't work, what on earth were we going to do?

* * *

Over the next weeks, Edd helped us in so many other practical ways. On day one of our driving course, he had quickly identified some problems with the prop shaft UJ's.

Despite all the things going on in his life, he kindly offered to show me how to replace them myself.

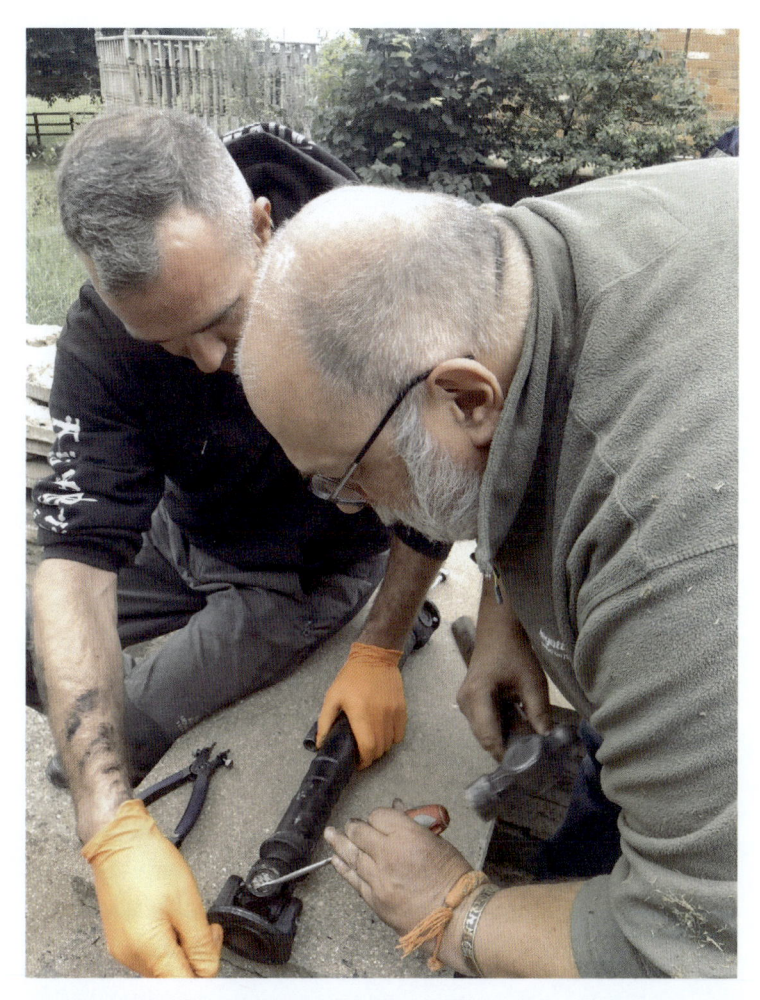

He clearly had no idea just how mechanically inept a man can be. After watching me flailing around with shiny things that he referred to as *'tools'*, the purpose for most of which will forever remain mysterious to me, he took great pity on me, or more likely, he was eyeing the impending darkness, and felt duty bound to step in and rescue me.

Either way, together we replaced the loose propshaft UJ's and I learnt some useful stuff for once.

Over the next couple of weeks, Mick at Loughran would also fit the new heavy duty OME dampers and worlds stiffest Defender springs.

I had the presence of mind to ask Loughran's to measure the height of the rear tub with the old suspension fitted, so we could compare the difference with the new kit.

Incredibly , the rear ride height had risen by 2 whole inches - with standard length dampers and standard length springs. Staggering difference.

* * *

The final piece of the handling equation was the mystery that is tyre pressures. The endless jawing about tyre pressures amongst the experts of the online '4x4 community' is legendary. I went my own way.

The standard pressure recommended by Land Rover for the 238/85/16 tyre is 38psi, so using the well-worn maxim that more is better, I took the decisions to take the pressures up way higher.

The Falken tyres were rated for a massive 80psi - much to Edd's incredulity. Edd helpfully informed me that the tyres increase in pressure around 10% at highway speeds due to the build up of heat.

I settled on 65psi for the rear tyres, well below the maximum, even allowing for the heat build up when driving at motorway speeds.

The transformation of all 3 changes was nothing short of

spectacular.

I could finally drive the car with unclenched buttocks.

* * *

By June 2021, we were desperate to get going, but with Europe still requiring full vaccinations and onerous quarantine requirements, it was impossible.

Oliver would not be eligible for his first Jab until later in the year.

Any thoughts of the an American Highway, or even Nordkapp, were a cruel joke.

The negative feelings engendered by, what I perceived to be, my failure to achieve the central goal of the whole project, was starting to weigh heavy on my mind.

Anxious thoughts of having to return to work began bubbling up in my mind.

How long could this Covid mess continue?

All of my childhood inferiority complex came slowly creeping back. *'Maybe this is no more than I deserve'*, the voice said. *'It was never going to work, you idiot'*, it taunted. *'You've just wasted your life savings.'*, it mocked.

Blah, Blah, Blah. Yakety yakety yak..

My mid June Birthday was cerebrated not in Halifax, Nova Scotia, but Greens Norton, Northamptonshire. This only served to emphasise just how little I had achieved.

A night spent with the friends in the local pub, eating stone baked pizzas was a welcome distraction, but, enjoyable though it was, it was never going to shift the *'Charlie Brown'* dark cloud over my head.

The itch, that was the need to travel, was becoming unbearable again.

* * *

In the following days, trying to keep busy, I contacted Presson UK, the company that had kindly offered to apply our stickers on the truck. Based just south east of London, in the historic naval town of Chatham, in Kent, we arranged a mutually agreeable date to have the livery applied.

Stickers are a divisive issue, I know, but we had a lot of partnerships, and we had agreed to carry each of their branding in exchange for the products and services they provided.

It would mean that we would stand out even more than a huge white Defender 130 ordinarily would, which is a fairly high bar to begin with.

Their facility was about a three hour drive to Portland, long time home to Linda's younger brother Michael, so we arranged a rare family get together as part of our trip around the South of the UK.

We had booked a small quiet campsite neat Chatham and arrived the day before the appointment, to avoid a very early start.

* * *

Up early the following day, we packed down, and set off to find a car wash service to give Mandy a good scrubbing.

We found a hand car wash a few miles from the campsite. It looked slightly grim and deserted as we drove past, but it was supposed to be open, and with not much time for shopping around, I turned around, went back and pulled onto the forecourt.

What following was like something out of a low rent *'made for TV'* film.

As I pulled to a stop by the pressure washers, a dirty and dishevelled young man appeared from a shed in the corner, smoking something that was once a cigarette.

In his dirty, screwed up tracksuit, he looked like an extra from *Lock Stock, and Two Smoking Barrels*.

But rather than a cheeky cockney accent, he spoke in short staccato sentences with a heavy East European accent, further testing my understanding by leaving out every other word.

What remained was barely intelligible.

'Want full wash?, he mumbled, blankly, staring through me with his dead eyes.

'Er, yes' I said, *'but don't use the pressure washer on the windows and side doors please, there are lots of gaps.'* I had visions of swimming to our next appointment.

'Huh', he grunted flatly.

I took that as OK. Maybe. Maybe not.

By this time, he had been joined by his mate. Similarly attired, but this one was seemingly mute. He had the inappropriate smile of a highly contented mass murderer, and the brooding eyes to go with it.

As he picked up and tested the Pressure Washer, I repeated my request not to blast the windows and doors. Too late, he was off like a maniac. I tried again, he stopped washing this time, smiled at me like Charles Manson, and then carried on regardless.

I gave up. I had mentally resolved to having to deal with an inch of water in each of the footwells, and an auxiliary electrical system that would take at least day to dry out, if it ever decided to work again.

We handed our money to the 'Manson Twins' and beat a hasty retreat, considering ourselves lucky that the car wash was on a main road and in full sight as passers-by, and not tucked away in the back corner of a deserted trading estate.

Making a mental note to never darken their door again, we sped off the forecourt in a cloud of diesel smoke.

* * *

Arriving at the factory unit, we were met by a much nicer, and far less homicidal looking,Paul , the Managing Director of Presson UK. He loved our vehicle, and shared our enthusiasm for the project.

We commiserated together about the effects that COVID had had on our ambitious plans, and his team got down to work.

With lightening speed, his expert livery crew had all the stickers applied by early in the afternoon. Expecting the work to take all day, or maybe even more, we had booked a local campsite for the night, but looking at the weather, a biblical storm heading our way apparently, we elected to head straight to Portland.

Thanking Paul and his team for a sterling job, we shook hands and headed off to Portland, where the weather looked to be much more favourable.

* * *

Early in the evening we wearily arrived in Portland, setting up camp hastily in a field not far from the famous lighthouse, Portland Bill.

Passing the many deep cars to the landscape, a reminder of the past quarrying for the much sought after Portland Stone.

The Portland Limestone went to build much of the monumental buildings in London, including Saint Pauls Cathedral and Buckingham Palace. This highly prized stone was also used to produce all of the gravestones to commemorate the Commonwealth soldiers who fell in battle, during both the First and the Second World Wars.

As the beer began flowing, the sun was beginning to slowly sink into the sea over the dramatic Jurassic coastline, marking a beautiful and inspiring end to a very long day.

* * *

Portland is a small island, tied to the rest of the county of Dorset by the impressively long Chesil beach.

It is home to not only the famous Lighthouse, but to some of the most dramatic coastline in the UK. We have visited many times, and never tire of the challenging walking across and through the cliffs of the UNESCO protected coastline.

The next evening, Michael and his wife Andrea brought a feast of local Fish and Chips over to the campsite - it's a maxim that they always taste better when you can see the sea.

Another great end to the day, sitting in the dying sun, chatting away about nothing.

The following morning, we left Oliver in the field guarding our camping kit, and headed over to another one of our partners, GTC, in Poole to collect the Garmin InReach personal locator, and a Satellite Phone, that they had kindly agreed to rent to us free of charge.

Remote communications were really important to us, as we would be travelling solo for the vast majority of the time.

Considering the uncharacteristic Italian weather that was expected over the following days, we decided to hang around for a few days and take advantage of it.

Compared to the wet and windswept days in Tonys field, it was absolute bliss.

Life was great, and soon we would be heading back to Italy at last.

* * *

Back in Tony's field, I lit the stove and started to cook dinner.

My whole body went haywire. I began to shake uncontrollably, my teeth were literally chattering, clattering together like a live version of a *'Tom and Jerry'* cartoon.

I mumbled to Linda *'I don't feel so well'* and left her to finish the half cooked meal that I had felt I had to abandon.

Climbing gingerly up the ladder to the tent, I crawled in and wrapped myself like an Egyptian mummy in the duvet, still fully clothed, and with a heavy winter coat on. The fever was so intense, I was struggling to focus my eyes.

Being a man, I instinctively knew this just had to be toughed out with nothing stronger than paracetamol. No medical intervention would be required, and a good nights sleep would see me right as rain again.

It is easily the most wrong that I have ever been.

Linda, not so stupid as I, immediately saw the potential seriousness of the situation, stripped me off, got me to drink plenty of water, and thinking it might be COVID, arranged to pick up a self test kit from a local friend, Janine.

It was negative. See, told you, more paracetamol.

The next morning, I felt a tad better and coincidently, I had an appointment at Northampton General Hospital to carry out an MRI scan on what, my doctor expected to confirm, was my frozen shoulder (*the terrible pain from which, is something that I cannot adequately describe*).

MRI done, paracetamol still being taken, I was still manfully resisting the chorus of demands to go to the hospital and find out what was really going on. Linda, having none of it, had booked a full PCR Covid test for the following morning.

That night, I went down hill fast, unable to keep my eyes open for long, a heavy fog had descended upon my brain and, privately, even I was worried.

However, I still didn't go to the Hospital. Man, remember?

The following morning, I awoke late.

Still very drowsy, I looked at my left leg and was stunned to see that from knee to ankle it was the brightest red possible - not sunburn red, think fire engine red.

I sheepishly showed Linda, and we were going to the hospital. **Now.**

No arguments this time, I know when I am defeated.

* * *

With the pre-booked PCR test completed in Towcester, we drove the twenty minutes to Northampton, and pulled up at the Accident and Emergency department (*A&E*) - I was still not sure it was either of these, but it was definitely something.

Covid restrictions meant that I was assessed (*if you call it that*) from behind glass, by a triage nurse that was at least 6 feet away from me.

In her wisdom, it wasn't urgent and she directed me to a clinic, attached to the hospital, where a doctor would assess my leg.

After a brief wait, I was ushered in to the Doctor. With the briefest of looks and touch to gauge the searing heat coming from my leg, she said, *'Wow, you need to go back to A&E and have blood tests'*.

So, escorted by a nurse, back past the triage nurse I went, and onward toward the next stage of what would become a very long day.

* * *

Despite having a PCR test that very morning, to be allowed into A&E, I would need yet another one. It was negative.

Time for a blood letting - not exactly an armful, but plenty for them to play with. I was sat in a chair just outside the Resuscitation area.

'The results should be back in an hour or two.', said the Doctor.

Great. I shut my eyes for a couple of seconds.

'Mr Betts, Mr Betts. Wake up Mister Betts.', the nurse was shaking my frozen shoulder.

Where was I, what was going on?

Who are these people?

Stop shaking my bloody shoulder!

'Your blood test results are back Mr Betts.', the calm voice of the Doctor bringing me back to earth. 'Sorry, you'll be staying with us tonight'.

My heart sank, knowing that I would be leaving Linda and Oliver alone, in a field, on top of an old Land Rover. The coming weather was some of the worst that we would ever see.

I phoned Linda and told her the bad news.

It was an unknown infection and could be the early stages of Sepsis (*Blood Poisoning to you and me*). I neglected to tell her that the Doctor had told me that it was 24 hours away from something potentially life threatening. There is such a thing as too much information in one day.

What followed was 4 days in a medical ward. Daily blood tests, intravenous antibiotics administered every 12 hours, and woken every 6 hours to have my vital signs recorded.

I found myself in a male only ward, almost entirely made up of elderly dementia patients. Including a number of patients who were docile in the day, yet raging maniacs at night, as their dementia turned to fear and loathing of those doing there utmost to help them. What nightmares are made of.

From the second day, despite my confusion with the COVID visiting rules, I managed to get Linda in to see me on the ward. Poor Linda burst into tears the first time, betraying the pent up stress that she had been holding in since I was kept in.

I could only imagine what she was going through.

Stuck in a tent, in the freezing cold, feeling very alone.

Each day my blood test results revealed an improvement in the infection markers, but it was very slow going. There was a lot of discussion about whether I could leave on the 4th day, but I was more than ready to go.

An untended consequence of taking on such a huge amount of liquid antibiotics, and being seated for nearly 4 days, is that all the fluid has to go somewhere, and as the inflection was in my leg, I ended up with one leg that was twice the size of the other.

The argument over the management of the 18 inch long fluid filled blister on the back of my left leg, was decided in my favour.

Thankfully, I could leave the ward, and return instead to the outpatients department to receive clean dressings every 2 days until the blister was fully under control. My leg looked disgusting, rotten even.

It would transpire that I would need 2 weeks of outpatient care, and another 6 weeks of care at my Doctor.

**

> *"It's the friends you can call up at 4 a.m. that matter"*
> **- Marlene Dietrich**

With a left leg that had now ballooned to twice the size of the right hand version, there was no way that I was climbing a ladder before bed each night. I could barely walk.

Both my left knee and ankle were locked solid with litres of fluid, and left me with a walk like a drunken penguin. My size 13 fake Croc barely containing my baby elephant-like, swollen foot.

They say that in times of adversity, you get to know who your real friends are.

It seems we are truly blessed with ours, as over the next few weeks, my recuperation would not have been possible without firstly, Janine Mold, and old and dear friend of over 20 years. A truly selfless individual who, despite having no spare bedrooms, immediately welcomed us into her home, turning her front room into a sickbay in the process.

Her generosity was equally matched by Steve and Viv Middleton, who subsequently invited us down to their beautiful farm in Essex, to finish off my recouperation. These final days, until I was well enough to travel again, were spent in the lap of luxury.

Without these people, we would have been utterly sunk.

In the end, it took almost 9 weeks of industrial strength antibiotics, before the infection was completely under control. All this from, what is believed to be, an insect bite, but contrary to some humorous suggestions, I had had recently visited the Jurassic Coast of Dorset, **NOT** Jurassic Park…

* * *

We still desperately needed to get back to Italy.

Lots of important equipment, and much of our clothes, remained there, and we would need to collect it all before we headed anywhere serious, but whilst the leg related delay was a frustrating delay, the world was still steadfastly against us travelling anyway.

The COVID related logistical costs of getting back to Italy remained very high, so, regrettably, we determined to wait a little and hope the quarantine and testing regimes would be relaxed soon.

This decision put an end to any hope of being able to arrive in Nordkapp in reasonable weather.

In any event, my doctor wasn't happy for me to make that type of journey, with my leg still in recovery. He informed me, ominously, that, for ever more, I would be highly susceptible to sepsis as I had suffered from it previously. Just what I needed.

BLOOD, SWEAT AND GEARS.

* * *

By early August, we were running out of letters for new plans.

We had received our second Covid jabs in mid June, but Oliver was officially not eligible to get his first one until he was 18 in November.

We were going nowhere, anytime soon.

The obstacles to EU travel were changing all the time, and we couldn't afford to be in France or Italy if they suddenly locked down and quarantined us for a period of time.

I was also becoming hugely disheartened at the general lack of travelling. I didn't leave my job to sit in a field and endlessly discuss vaccinations and quarantines.

So far, after almost 8 months back in the UK, the farthest we had managed to get, had been the southern coast of England. Depression was never far away.

I was losing heart. How could I repay our partners, and supporters, and importantly, how could I keep money flowing in? Trying to find interesting things to post on Instagram was becoming more and more difficult. I was losing heart in everything.

We desperately needed some excitement, some adventure to rekindle the fire in our travelling souls. Souls that were feeling completely battered after the last 24 months of preparations.

I had an idea. Sadly, it turned out to be one of the bottom three worst ideas of my life. Not quite as bad as accepting my Sisters dare to swallow a whole boiled egg, when I was 6 years old, but pretty close.

Little did I know it, but I was about to test our commitment to overland travel to the absolute limit.

NOTHING BEHIND, EVERYTHING AHEAD.

* * *

We have long loved the rugged West Highlands of Scotland, and I have often secretly entertained the romantic notion of retiring to a slightly run down croft in the West Highlands, and writing a devastating successful, and highly lucrative, series of malt whisky fuelled Sunday Times bestsellers. Dreamers will dream.

With rumours that quarantine rules may soon be relaxed in Europe, and jabs possibly available to under 18 year olds, I suggested we head North to the Highlands of Scotland, and kill a few weeks, camping on the beautiful and dramatic west coast.

We set off with a vague plan. Friends in Newton Stewart, friends near Oban and we'll run the gauntlet of the anti NC500 crowd, and try some *'wild camping'*.

The leg was still not 100%, so we gratefully accepted a very welcome invite from Simon and Pen Graham, old friends from Red Bull Racing days, that had recently moved to the Scottish Borders. A lovely few days spent drinking and reminiscing soon came to an end, and the northern trajectory resumed.

The common thread of all our travels so far, regardless of the ups and a few spectacular downs, the golden thread, remains the people that we meet along the way, and the overwhelmingly positive experiences that we have enjoyed through those people.

Two such people were was Andrew Morrison and his wonderful mother Gillian, a more welcoming pair of human beings you could not possibly meet.

I had worked with Andrew at Red Bull, many years before,

and though we had socialised a few times back in those days, we could not truly consider ourselves friends. Despite all that, and learning of our trip to the Highlands, he immediately invited us to his mothers house near Oban as a possible stop over.

Happily, he also happened to be on holiday there with his family at the same time. We were welcomed like long lost member of the tribe. Unforgettable times, that make this life so much more than the sum of its parts.

After a beautiful evening, cooking, eating and drinking together, we bade our farewells and made our way yet further north into the heart of the Highlands, and our final destination, the majestic Loch Torridon.

* * *

Many years earlier, we had spent some very memorable holidays in the Torridon area, always renting a large property on the Ben Damph estate.

We visited with friends, with family, and on our own with a very young Oliver.

We experienced the very best and the worst of what the Scottish climate could offer, over those multiple trips. Often travelling *'out of season'* we experienced some of the worst weather that I have had the misfortune to endure.

Our most memorable 2 week trip, would turn out to be our last one. Unfortunately, we were compelled to leave early, at the beginning of the second week.

Oliver was a very adventurous toddler at the time, and the weather was so atrocious that we could neither leave the house in the day, nor sleep through the night.

It was like a prison sentence, just with added malt whisky.

The wind and driving rain, tearing unhindered across the bottom of the vast valley, within which our unprotected house stood, was epic.

Finally reaching the end of our collective tethers, in the early hours, we piled everything into the back of our brand new Land Rover Discovery 3, strapped Oliver into his child seat, and we headed off along the unlit and windswept single track roads towards Inverness.

No more than 5 miles into our homeward journey, my complacency led me to make a terrifying and potentially fatal error.

Gliding supremely along the single track road at 40-50 mph, the Discovery was easily soaking up the bumps along the narrow and undulating roads. I settling into a comfortable driving rhythm.

Though already tired, we had a very long way to go, and I wanted to get home.

I pushed on.

The product of the weeks deluge of rain was filling the lower portions of the many dips in the road. In the early morning dark, the wet tarmac looked almost identical in colour to the water sitting in the bottom of the dip, silently waiting fir the unwary.

KABOOM!

The steering wheel was viscously ripped from my hands. Briefly airborne, we crashed back down on to the tarmac with a sickening thud. Stunned, the Land Rover coasted to a halt with a stalled engine.

We had hit a solid 3 foot wall of standing water of at something approaching 50 mph.

Linda swore, Oliver cried, but I was just stunned.

I looked at the dashboard of the Discovery and, somewhat worryingly, it was lit up like a control panel in the Space Shuttle. Every light was on or flashing, including ones that I had never seen before.

Hands still shaking from the shock of the impact, I turned the ignition off, and back on again. The big diesel engine roared into life.

To my relief and incredulity, it had fired up immediately, and all warning lights were extinguished.

If I was a religious man, this would have been an excellent time to thank the supreme being.

Linda called me an idiot, and on we went, slowly, arriving home in Northamptonshire some 6 hours later.

One of the nine was definitely lost that day.

* * *

Driving from Oban, and further into the highlands, we were determined to finally live our life in the way that we had always intended.

This was our first real test of living as a family, day to day, camping informally as we travelled. I intentionally don't use the phrase 'Wild Camping', and I'll explain why.

The term 'Wild camping' is highly contentious. There is much confusion in the public discourse, particularly in Scotland, between the legal right to roam and illegal vehicle based camping. The rules are simple, camping on or in a vehicle is pretty much *'verboten'* in most of Europe. In Scotland it is specifically excluded from the right to roam legislation.

We hit this contention head on in the Highlands. We know what we do is illegal, but this is not an annual holiday for us, but a permanent life choice.

With some trepidation, we drove northward looking for somewhere that would fulfil our own set of values - a secluded spot (*unseen from the road*), not posted as private land, and as far away from the locals as possible. We would not make fires, and we would leave no trace.

It proved much harder than I thought.

* * *

After a day long drive from Oban, the first stop that fitted the bill was Loch Garry.

We backed ourselves into one of the many grassy spots at the side of the A87 highway and got ready to set up our camp for the night. We were tucked away from the road with no restriction signs, so felt pretty secure to stop for the night.

BLOOD, SWEAT AND GEARS.

A few minutes after stopping, Linda let out a long moan of disgust.

It was an understandable reaction to the fetid smell of human excrement all around the rear of the Defender. Along with clumps of toilet paper, human waste littered the whole area. It was disgusting.

The West Coast of Scotland is one of nature's most beautiful gifts, but some people clearly didn't know how to take a gift with any grace.

My mistake was to add a post to the Facebook Page 'NC500 - the ugly truth'. My post was an attempt to commiserate with the locals, who doubtless were sick and tired of this ugly and disrespectful activity on the door step, and to suggest some improvements that may well help the situation.

I admit I was naive about the issue, but boy oh boy, I got

absolutely hammered.

I was told in no uncertain terms that I was not welcome, and should not use the term 'Wild Camping' in this context, and I was ignorant to do so. Ouch.

The NC500 is a designated driving route around the Scottish Highlands.

Whilst commercially driven in the beginning of its life, it is now increasingly used by government tourist organizations to promote the wider area of the Scottish Highlands.

Sadly this promotion had led to a considerable increase in traffic in the highlands, and there is mounting opposition to it, from locals and others, who feel that their bucolic surroundings are being totally overrun by legions of inexperienced first time motorhome users, and inconsiderate supercar drivers.

The amount of motor homes that we saw on the roads was mind bending, and whilst it's clear that COVID brought about an explosion of touring in the UK, the problem is much wider than that.

Whilst I am sure that many visitors share our values of concern and consideration for the environment, so many that we saw clearly have absolutely no care for anything other than themselves.

The lack the consideration or self awareness when parking was astonishing and must be infuriating for the locals.

We are not on holiday, this is the life we have chosen and we are anxious not to be lumped in with the inconsiderate moronic masses - we believe in leave no trace, we even tidy up others rubbish when we leave an informal camp, but is this enough?

Being called a *'freeloader'* by the Facebook keyboard warriors sticks in my gullet.

We buy food, we buy fuel, we buy everything that we need in small retailers, when we travel in remote areas like the highlands - we pay our way, and we leave no trace.

So what's the real answer?

Education, education, more education and some amenities - not just from Government but those myriad companies enjoying the Covid windfall of Motorhome hire, many of whom publicly extol the joys of 'Wild Camping' to their clients.

Spend some of your profit on educating your clientele - if not, dark days are ahead, and you don't have to look far to see what some locals are willing to do, when their environments are threatened.

If the Scottish Government backed tourism strategy is to invite as many people as possible to their beautiful land, that same government must provide sufficient infrastructure to cater for them, and avoid this brewing animosity between locals and holiday makers.

In France, you will find a huge network of cheap or even free municipal camp grounds, chemical waste dumps, public toilets and refuse bins. They understand that people spend their money in the villages near to these amenities.

Finally, screaming into the echo chamber void of Facebook is pointless.

The locals need to organize and petition their government to make the changes that want to see.

Once the amenities are in place, fine the transgressors to death for all I care, but use that revenue to maintain and grow the amenities for all visitors.

This is **NOT** a zero sum game - everyone can win.

NOTHING BEHIND, EVERYTHING AHEAD.

* * *

The following morning, despite the fact they we forgot to buy any wine, we awoke in good spirits, having enjoyed a peaceful and undisturbed night under the canvas.

We spent 30 minutes picking up two black bin bags worth of rubbish that was scattered around the area, including (*with the aid of gloves*) some of the human waste.

I was anxious to get further off of the beaten track, and itching to get to the familiar territory of Loch Torridon, but first I wanted to tick a box.

Weeks ago, when researching our trip to Scotland, I came across the Glenelg to Kylerhea Ferry, which crosses the shortest gap between the Isle of Skye and the mainland, across the Kyle Rhea.

Our ferry boat, the Glenachulish, is believed to be the last manually operated turntable ferry in the world. Certainly in Scotland, anyway.

There has been a car ferry service crossing the Kylerhea straits since 1934. However, this closest point to the Isle of Skye has been a regular crossing point for hundreds of years.

I love Skye, but we had been there many times. I was just intrigued to arrive in Skye in a way that is travelled by so few.

Ferries are like a drug to us. We absolutely can't get enough of them. Maybe being the children of an island has something to do with - channelling the child like joy of travelling to another country.

Either way, it really doesn't feel like we've been anyway until we've been on a ferry.

It was a long and hair raising single track drive to get to the ferry, but thankfully, it turned out to be well worth it.

As we waiting alone on the shoreline for the ferry to come, and as it hove into view, the excitement levels were off the scale.

We gingerly pulled onto the tiny Ferry and were met by the happiest ferry workers I have ever met.

The introvert in me was mortified when Linda decided to hop up on to the bonnet, so she could video the whole crossing… thankfully she had decided to sit down (*but still on the bonnet*) when we disembarked.

* * *

The next day, with the sun shining in a very uncharacteristic way, and nary a cloud in the sky, we finally pulled into the familiar surroundings of Torridon village.

Just maybe, our weather jinx was over, and we might enjoy a few days without rain.

It was great to be back on well known territory, but the Loch Torridon area is largely grazing land, and what little forestry there is, is clearly private land, complete with deer fencing.

The small free municipal campsite was closed and chained up. Well done Scotland.

We were going to find it hard to hide away.

A mile or so out of the village we found a patch of grass just off the single track road, but it was well used, as evidenced by the usual detritus, including the seemingly universal signs of human excrement.

We did the usual, and cleared it up as best we could and set up camp.

. We asked in the village and it seemed that lots of people

stay there and, apparently, no one seems to mind. It was uncomfortable being so close to the road but we stayed for one night.

Being close to the coast in Scotland is a twin edged sword. It's beautiful, and dramatic but also, with no warning at all, you can be consumed by a billion dreaded midges, and so it came to pass.

We had taken a late afternoon walk to the village to check out the tiny shop, which was now closed, leaving Oliver as captain of the good ship Mandy.

After a consolation walk along the shoreline, pausing to admire the majestic Deer in the sanctuary, Linda decided that she was going to swim in the sea.

Regardless of the time of year, the waters of the West Coast of Scotland have never struck me as enticing, but in she went, completely naked, save for her beach shoes.

I stood guard on the beach as she walked, Reggie Perrin-like, from a neat pile of clothes, out into the approaching high tide. That's an extrovert right there - no question.

Despite promising no photographic evidence, I managed to shoot off a couple of blurry shots to commemorate the event, before she came storming back up the beach, screeching and shivering like a leaf.

As we stumbled back to Mandy across the stony beach of Upper Loch Torridon , giggling like naughty little school children, it felt that finally, we had really begun our journey.

Those brief euphoric feelings soon subsided as we approached Mandy. Oliver was nowhere to be seen, and the rear of the Defender was a teeming mass of Highland midges (*think acid fuelled mosquitoes*).

As thick as smoke, they covered every surface and were

spreading all around the vehicle. Oliver was found taking refuge in his tent on the roof, reacting as though he had been attacked by a fleet of Daleks.

Irritating though they were, this was just the start of our problems.

***

We awoke the next day to heavy rain and dense dark clouds.

Not wanting to break the camp down in the wet, we looked for a break in the weather and it looked like we would get a chance late in the morning. Thankful, the wind had picked up and have ruined the flying conditions for the midges, so at least we were free of those little blighters.

I didn't like staying like this, so near to the village, so we decided to carry on further up the coast of the Loch and head towards one of our favourite places - Diabeg, the dead end of a 20 mile single track road from Torridon. It was beautiful and remote, flanked as it was by the Outer Loch on one side and the imposing peak of Beinn Alligin on the other.

The weather finally broke, and taking the opportunity to quickly pack up, we soon set off to find somewhere more remote.

It may be only 20 miles to Diabeg, but the road is steep, twisting and very narrow. We took our time but grew increasingly frustrated as anything approaching suitable for us to camp was either directly on the road or was blocked with wardrobe sized boulders to prevent any access for vehicles.

I was beginning to take it personally.

As we got to Diabeg, tempers were fraying, the temperature was dropping, and the rain was falling. As the light receded, I made a management decision to get a little way back down and stay in one of the road side cuttings that would just about accommodate our tents.

The rain began falling heavier. It was starting to enjoy itself.

We set up camp, and celebrated by having a massive row, about nothing in particular.

Linda went for a walk.

We all hated the grim weather, but Linda suffered from the cold very badly. Her happiness quotient dropped as the temperate dropped, and rain made it just that much worse.

Not being able to sit in a warm motorhome became a big issue. I tried to put a brave face on it and push through, and that, understandably, pissed her off even more.

We agreed that we would head north the following day and find a campsite in a place called Laird, apparently now owned by an old Red Bull Racing colleague.

If it was reasonably priced, we could wait out the diabolical weather.

For me, hot showers were always the answer, but for Linda it was something else that she needed.

That something was, is as yet, unidentified.

* * *

We set off, the drizzle and low cloud mingling with sea fog from the Loch, as was passed back down the track to Torridon.

Setting the Sat Nav for Laide, around an hour and a half, or so, up the coast, we headed off to check out the campsite.

Around an hour into the drive, Clickety, clack, **BANG!**

Startled, I watched as the first, and then the second windscreen wiper came loose from their mounts, spastically flayed around a little, and then clattered across the bonnet, and finally, disappearing over the edge into oblivion under the Defender.

I pulled over as quickly as a 3.5 tonne Defender will allow, and Linda, may god bless her, ran back down the road, in the pouring rain, to try and retrieve the errant wipers, impressively managing a 50% success rate. The other one had been driven over and comprehensively destroyed.

After 30 minutes in the rain trying to refit the remaining wiper, I admitted defeat. Both elements of the splined mounting mechanism were almost smooth, and for its intended purpose, entirely knackered.

I briefly thought about reminding Linda that she had trod on the RH wiper when she was clambering on the truck for the video she shot on the Glenelg ferry, earlier in the week, but valuing my teeth more highly, I decided to hold my own counsel. I like my teeth.

It was starting to rain heavily.

Ever tried driving without wipers? This was my second go, and it was no more fun this time.

Looking online, I found a garage in Aultbea, a few miles back from where we were.

We headed straight there, dodging the raindrops as we went. He looked at Mandy, said he could have the parts in a couple of days, and we left happy.

Simple you would have thought.

* * *

Without wipers, we weren't getting very far in Scotland, a place not noted for it's extended heat waves, even in summer.

At least we had finally received one bit of good news though, as Olivers first COVID jab was now booked for a weeks time, much sooner than we feared it would be.

Once the wipers were fixed we could head home and, more importantly, this meant that as soon as the French quarantine regulations were removed, we could finally return to Italy and collect the rest of our belongings.

We couldn't wait.

* * *

We headed to the Guinard Bay Caravan park to park up and wait for the wipers to arrive.

A lovely looking little campsite, located in a rugged little cove with access to a small beach, but at £30 a night, it was way more than we wanted to pay, but choices were slim to none.

Hopefully it would only be a couple of days.

As it turned out, my ex-colleague had no recollection of me, despite working in the same team as him for the better part of 5 years. Oh well, any chance of a mates discount went straight out of the window.

They were great hosts though, and the facilities were very good.

We set up, showered and settled down for a restful evening. The wind had been simmering all day, but now the kettle was truly boiling.

All night we were battered with gale force winds. The Darche tents stood up heroically to the onslaught but the deafening noise meant sleep was not an option.

Linda was becoming more and more disenchanted with life

in Scotland, and with overlanding in general.

I had pinned my hopes on getting the wipers fixed after the weekend, and then a slow trundle heading back down south, in time for Olivers COVID jab.

As so often, in times of adversity, the clouds will present a silver lining of some sort. In this case, it was in the shape of James Locke.

When the wipers let loose, I had put out a request to the Scottish Land Rover owners Facebook page, asking for any recommendations for garages or people with spare LHD wipers.

James had got in touch, and whilst he didn't have any wiper arms in his garage, what he did have was some epic Caribbean street cuisine. Even better.

After visiting us at the campsite in his fantastic old Series 1, complete with vintage 1960s Roof Top tent, he told us about his B&B business a couple of miles up the road, that also included a street food stall called, the Black Pearl Creole Kitchen.

James, it turned out, had not always been a creole cooking Land Rover lover. In a previous life, he had one been one third of 'The Chimes', a 1980/1990s pop trio who had some notable success with their version of U2's 'I Still Haven't Found What I'm Looking For', which peaked at no.6 in the UK charts in 1990. You meet all sorts.

We chatted away like old friends in the drizzling rain, discussing 1980s pop, Land Rovers, the wonders of Creole food, and, strange as it may seem, Calor gas bottles.

* * *

If you live in the UK, and have ever had a need for a 3.9kg Propane Calor gas bottle, you will know well, the extreme difficulty in obtaining one.

Frustratingly, it's easier to find a pregnant, 3 legged, unicorn.

The myths surrounding the reasons for the nationwide shortage of these simple, yet highly useful, gas containers, are many and varied.

My favourite one is the notion that the IRA used so many of them in Northern Ireland, during 'The Troubles', that their love of road side bombs led to Calor restricting the manufacturing of the bottle. Got to be nonsense, but great story.

Less intriguing, but eminently more likely, is that Calor, hit by a massive COVID surge in UK demand, reacted very slowly to this change in demand and when they finally ordered a load of new bottles from a low cost country (*think Crispy Duck*), the logistical challenges have thoroughly defeated them.

Either way, it's a nightmare.

* * *

As we stood in the entrance to the campsite, leaning up against his Series 1, I noticed a large bright red Calor gas bottle in the back of his pickup..

This promoted me to tell James the bitter story of our search for our first gas bottle. A two week scouring of numerous Calor gas dealers earlier in the year, that finally involved '*lifting*' a bottle from a local Recycling centre, as a staff member studiously looked the other way.

Ridiculous chicanery, just to get some propane to allow us

to cook our dinner, but it does illustrate, yet one more, of the many reasons why I married an extrovert.

James chuckled at my gas related tale of woe, and then casually asked if we needed another bottle.

I was speechless.

He thought he had one of the right size in his shed, and if he did, he would drop it off that evening when he delivered our Creole feast.

The evening came, and we were treated to some of the very best street food I have ever tasted. For that brief period, all our troubles were gone. To cap off a beautiful evening, we were now the proud owners of a bouncing baby Calor gas bottle.

Life felt good, for once.

* * *

We spent the remainder of the weekend trying our best to amuse ourself at the campsite.

The wipers were due to arrive on Monday from Inverness. I called the garage, Monday was now Tuesday.

More frustration, but hey, we're in the Highlands, deep breaths.

* * *

Tuesday comes, we break camp and head over to the Garage in Aultbea to have the new wipers fitted.

Thankfully it wasn't raining - but that, as it turned out, was as far as my luck was going to stretch that day.

We needed to get on our way South to get Olivers Jab -

delays were not an option.

Highlanders, in my experience, are wonderful people, but they are different.

Quiet, somewhat reserved and sometimes very direct. I've met enough people in my life to know the difference between direct people, and rude people.

We drove the handful of miles back to the Garage, and walked into the office. All good so far. The wipers were here, it would take an hour or so. Perfect.

It's my habit to try and watch when work is done on the Defender, as I need to learn as much maintenance as I can.

I wandered back into the workshop and stood in the corner, quietly watching as the boss replaced the splined spigots to which the new wipers would be mounted. He seemed fine with me being there, as we chatted away amicably.

As he left the workshop to go get the new wipers, one of his mechanics came over from the other side of the workshop, with a frown on his face, and barked *Customers shouldn't be in the workshop, you need to wait in the office*.

Hmm, he was angry and rude, not direct at all.

Thankfully, he was clearly English, and consequently didn't upset my positive bias at the lovely people of the Highlands, but served to reinforce my negative bias at most of my fellow Englishmen.

Instead of firing a biting retort to my angry friend, I gave my best *'F*ck you, mate.'* stare, and retreated back to the waiting room.

Thirty minutes went by, and then the confession came.

Despite spending 15 minutes checking out the vehicle the previous week, he had managed to order wipers for a right hand drive defender. Face palm.

Staying calm, I told him that I needed to get a set by the following day. The Formula One never dies in you. He looked blankly at me and mumbled, *'I'll try'*.

* * *

Tony Blair, former Prime minister of the UK, famously once said, that the biggest change that he had to get used to, once he had left office, was having to stop at red traffic lights. No more police escorts for Tony.

The equivalent for me is customer service.

Formula One has instilled in me an expectation of the highest levels of customer service that you can imagine.

Team suppliers would be mentored to a position that their service levels would be exemplary. If they failed to live up to that standard, they would be dropped and we would find another supplier.

My red traffic light moment was outside that garage in Aultbea.

In my head, I was screaming *'Get in your f**king car, and go to Inverness and get a set of fucking LHD wipers. Why are you still standing here?'*

I had no leverage, no ammunition to fight this war.

He had messed up, and we were massively inconvenienced, but *'He was going to see what he could do'*.

He wrapped some paper around the spline and jammed on one old wiper, so at least we could drive in the rain, sort of.

We left them *'seeing what they could do'*.

* * *

We returned, dejected, to the campsite and booked back in for another night. It was Tuesday and Olivers jab was booked for the following Saturday.

We had explained to the garage that if the wipers did not arrive on Wednesday, we would have to leave to go South, to be sure to arrive in time for Olivers jab.

As you will doubtlessly have guessed by now, the wipers did not arrive on Wednesday, and they could not guarantee that they would arrive on Thursday either.

I was fuming at this chronic customer service.

Was I expecting too much?

Was I projecting F1 standards of service on a tiny back street garage?

If we had waited, it would have been a full week to get a correct set of wipers the 77 miles from Inverness and fitted to my Defender.

A full week no less. 77 miles.

I messaged the garage that we couldn't wait, as they already new, and that they could keep the wipers as far as I was concerned.

A week later, incredibly, and despite their appalling efforts, that invoiced me for the fitting of the new spline shafts.

Slightly stunned, I made them wait 30 days and then paid them, against my better judgement, I might add.

**

We packed up again, and set off south at last.

The whole experience had left Linda very weary of the weather and, more worryingly, openly questioning the very basis of our lifestyle. I couldn't entirely blame her.

Though I asked Linda, many times, in the early stages of the project, if she was absolutely sure she wanted to do it, and painting the blackest version possible, her extrovert character is a feet first attitude to most things, and that's understandable.

It's who she is, but clearly, the realities of travelling around the UK was not what she had envisaged her new life to be.

Hopefully, things would improve.

On the drive back down south, we once again accepted the graceful hospitality of Gillian Morrison and this time, a very kind offer of a soft bed and a warm shower. After the privations of our Highland adventure, we were more than happy to accept.

We cooked dinner for us all, thanking her for her hospitality. A fine tradition that we maintain, introduced to us by the Bell clan back in 2016.

The trip back to Northamptonshire was broken up next by a welcome, and much overdue, meet up with my Cousin David.

Despite having the worlds smallest family, and being as busy as we all are, we are as bad as each other at keeping in touch. Another soft bed, In Boston Spa awaited us, and the years rolled away as we chatted happily over a wonderful meal, and a few local beers.

It's only when you slow down, that you realise just how fast you were actually going.

***

Oliver is no lover of needles, even pine ones make him sweat.

Thankfully, he overcame his trypanophobia and, on 21st

August, he finally received his first COVID jab.

The last piece of the jigsaw was almost in place, as 14 days after his jab, we were free to travel to France and Italy without an expensive quarantine.

The target was set, we would leave the UK to return to Italy on the 4th September - almost exactly 6 months since we stuffed our Freelander with the sum of our wordly possessions and headed into the uncertainty of a COVID world.

7

Back to the past.

With just over two weeks to kill before we could leave for Italy, we set about tying up the last bits and pieces with Mandy.

BACK TO THE PAST.

Our wonderful friend Edd Cobley, had kindly agreed to supervise my ham-fisted attempt to finally fit the upgraded Terrafirma anti roll bars. We passionately hoped that these bars would represent the very last piece of the suspension jigsaw.

The transformation brought about by the combination of the ARB's and the stiffer springs/dampers was remarkable, finally coming somewhere close to dampening the last of the high seas pitching motion, that we had suffered from for so long.

The cheeks of my back side unclenched that short measure further.

We were almost ready to go, with just that fiery hoop of COVID tests to jump through.

* * *

So it was, that we found ourselves in the vast car park of the Northampton Saints Rugby Football club, having cotton buds jabbed up our noses, and in the back of our throats. The price that must be paid for international travel.

The following day, as if travel in the time of COVID wasn't stressful enough, it soon emerged that I had made a fundamental error in the registration process for the email receipt of Linda's results.

Spending the morning of our departure, sitting at Tonys kitchen table, making ever more frantic calls to the 0800 number of the testing company, was very far from what I had planned.

As the hours ticked by, Linda saw her pot distinctly half empty, and grew more dispirited by the minute, but finally, with minutes to spare before we needed to leave for the Channel Tunnel, the test arrived. It was negative.

We all breathed again.

Heading South at last.

One of the things that we have learnt, is that the longest lasting memories of travel are so often about the little coincidences and synchronicities of life on the road.

* * *

We made surprising good progress on the usually congested UK motorway network, and with a little time in hand, we pulled into the services on the M20 in Dover for a short break, and an essential cup of tea..

As we drive into the parking area, Linda began bouncing in her passenger seat.

'Ooh, park next to Landy, **GO ON**, park next to the Landy', she exclaimed, insistently, jabbing her finger in the direction of a clean looking, newish, Defender 110 commercial in the distance.

Groaning under my breath, I cut across the car park and heading in its direction. I hate this sort of overt exhibitionism (*says he in a giant white Land Rover, covered in stickers, but you know what I mean*), and cringe slightly when she makes me do this kind of thing.

In a further illustration of the many benefits of marrying an extravert, Linda would force a meeting with Sebastian Hadfield-Hyde, the owner of the 110, and we would discover that he is a Whisky distiller, that has no Whisky yet, so he was making fine Gin instead, until the good stuff was ready.

Incredibly, he was touring the country, delivering his wares, all the way from his Orkney based distillery, Kimbland. The most northerly distillery in the UK, no less. A very long way from Dover.

After the shared pleasantries, and in the bargain of the century, Sebastian got himself a rare and highly collectable Itchy Feet Overland sticker, and we came away with a very nice bottle of Sanday No.1 Gin.

The lesson?

Parking rules should **ALWAYS** be applied, you never know who you'll meet.

We bade each other farewell, and headed off in polar opposite directions.

* * *

The time restrictions brought about by the COVID tests were extremely tight.

Oliver, with only one jab, had to enter France within 24 hours, and then we all had to be at the Italian border in 48 hours, which, once you consider that the first 24 hours was spent waiting for the results in the UK, it was going to be decidedly touch and go.

24 hours to get from Calais to Mont Blanc. Easy you might say, assuming you have no problems. A big assumption when you drive a Defender.

For this reason, we elected to drive through the night to transit France as fast as possible, just in case we had any problems and gave ourselves issues at the Italian border.

* * *

When you own a Defender, you soon become an expert in the fine distinction between the many and varied noises that they make.

Some noises come and go, some noises are there all the time, and some others make your testicles retract.

Our reliability fairy had got wind of this tight schedule, and almost exactly in the dead centre of France, and the very dead of night, I detected a very slight whine from the rear of Mandy, but only when we were at motorway speed.

Keep an ear on that. Not yet enough to automatically retract the testis, but a concern nonetheless.

We ploughed on, until an hour later, we pulled over into one of the many 'Aire de service' that litter the French motorways, to have a quick brew up and a bite to eat.

* * *

As I reached the back of the truck to open her up, there was the unusual smell of very hot oil.

Apparently, since the last time that we had stopped, no more than 2 hours before, Mandy had privately decided to spew up all of the oil in the rear differential, and silently deposit it in an even coating over the underside of the truck, along both spare wheels, all the up the rear canopy, and even on to the back of the roof top tent above.

It's the early hours of Sunday morning, we're all tired, the clock is ticking away, and we need to get to the Italian border.

There go the testis.

I felt like a helpless child again.

As this wasn't spotted for a while, I took the view that the damage, whatever it might be, had already been done, but we were going to need differential oil, and lots of it.

Our sponsor Pakelo Oil had been more than generous, giving us plenty of oil of all types. The only problem being, it's location.

I had only 1 litre of diff oil in my spares, and the rest was either in Italy, or in Mark Halleybone's garage.

It was clear that my meagre amount of spare oil would not last very long at all.

We parked up until daylight, and after a quick call to Christoph, an old French colleague from the Stewart Grand Prix days, we soon found ourselves clearing out the local French equivalent of Halfords of their entire stock of equivalent diff oil.

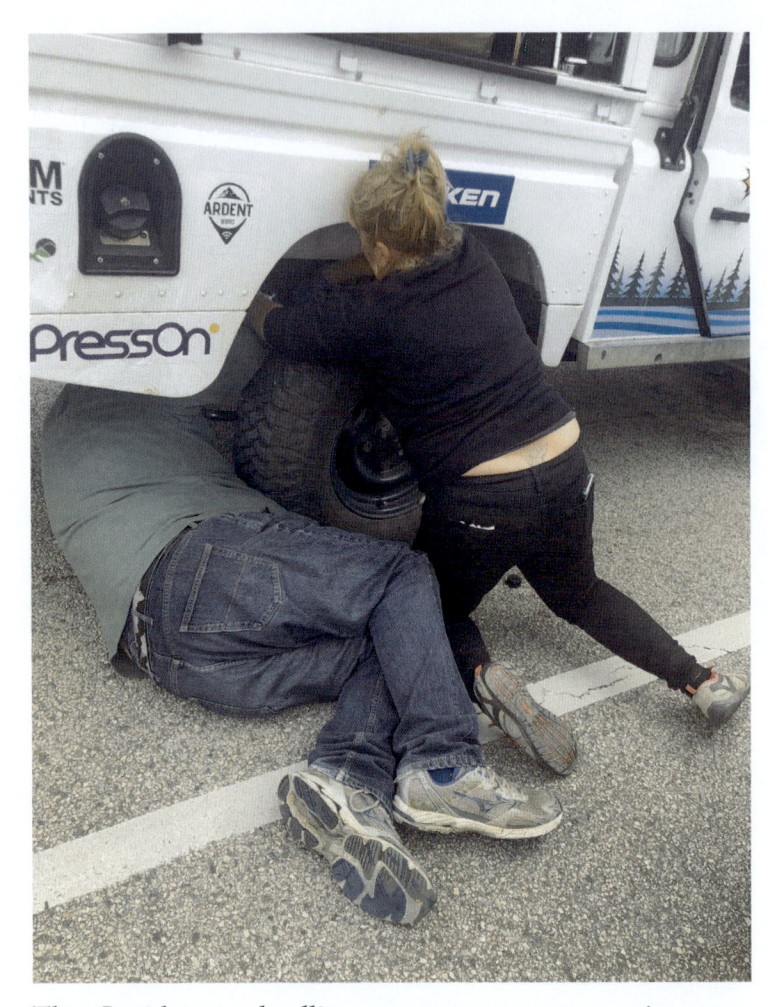

The Covid tests deadline was even more pressing now. Reducing motorway speeds to 70 km/h to protect the diff, and topping up every couple of hours, turned our journey into a nerve shredding 30-hour non-stop drive, dodging irritated trucks, and anxiously listening to every new whine, squeak and rattle - waiting for the almost inevitable and sickening **BANG** from the rear.

* * *

As dawn broke, we finally arrived at the French side of the Mont Blanc tunnel. The thought of breaking down in the tunnel only amplified our growing anxiety.

If only we could get on Italian soil, we could relax, but we still had to pass the COVID controls on the Italian side.

We entered the tunnel, cheeks fully clenched. The desperate whine from the differential bearings now amplified to an ear-splitting siren like modulating scream.

I couldn't look at Linda, my eyes were fixed 1000 yards ahead. The minutes passed as slowly as I have ever experienced.

After what felt like an hour, light began to appear on the roof of the tunnel. We were almost there. Another peak in anxiety, would they accept our documents? Were our test results still in time to be acceptable?

We slowly and noisily cruised into the strong Italian sunlight.

I began to slow down, ready to be met by the austere figures of the heavily armed Carabiniere, the Italian police that you don't argue with.

We approached the border control……..nothing.

I kept my eyes straight ahead and drove slowly toward the exit. Then, out of the corner of my eye, I saw two officers, with machine guns dangling from their backs, standing by a pair of freight lorries that had been pulled to the side. There was an animated discussion going on with the drivers.

Should I stop, or should I just keep going?

There was no physical barrier as such , not even any signs.

One of the officers briefly glanced at me over his shoulder, and then turned back to the truck driver as their *'discussion'* continued.

We looked at each other and quietly laughed. A laugh that ejected all the pent-up anxiety of the last 24 hours.

We were in Italy. We had made it. Oh, and did I not tell you, this was all on our wedding anniversary.

For Better or Worse baby. Definitely one to remember.

* * *

We crawled back to our old stomping ground of Maranello.

We desperately needed a rest after the stressful last few days, and as luck would have it, our wonderful friend Gilly, has invited us to stay in her house, and care for the cat Hippy, whilst she was back in England.

After a couple of days of relaxation, I needed to crack on and get my differential repaired. I had a friend in the town where we were staying that had his own garage.

Marco Mattana is a former race team mechanic for the Ferrari team in the Schumacher era. The walls of his workshops in Castelnouvo Rangone are peppered with reminders of those glory days. A young bright-eyed Marco, resplendent in vibrant red, looking back into the lens, joyously celebrating whichever past victory it happened to be.

I took Mandy over to Marco, and, as I suspected, the diff was a specialist job that he was loath to take on.

I could understand his thinking. So, in the time-honoured fashion with Land Rovers, I put my myself in the hands of

BACK TO THE PAST.

that modern day oracle, Facebook.

* * *

The response to my request on the Italian Defender Owner's Club page, was swift and fruitful. The consensus was, Musi was the man. He would sort me out, if he was not too busy, that is.

We exchanged messages and I explained what I needed, and we agreed to meet at this Bologna workshop in a week's time. He was close to finishing a big job, but he would squeeze me in.

His dimly lit workshop, in the outskirts of Bologna, was an Aladdin's cave of off-roading. A poorly looking 6x6 Man Kat1 Dakar style truck was wedged into the corner of the jam packed, double height, workshop. The walls were lined with heavy-duty racking, containing a cornucopia of parts and equipment for desert raid vehicles. Practically every piece of floor was covered with something. I loved it.

Who was this man?

It turned out that I was in the presence of a bit of a legend in the Italian Defender community. A fellow owner of a 130, we instantly hit it off.

Roberto Musi is a desert man. He looks it. Tall, broad, and

pony tailed with bright friendly eyes in his olive skinned face.

He has spent most of his adult life in the desert. At 22, he travelled with a friend to Morocco on their Cagiva Elefant motorcycles, and in some respects, at 56 years old, he has still not come back.

He hit the jackpot and made a career from his passion, and until the fall out of the Arab Spring in 2011, and the final COVID nail in the coffin, he was running a successful business conducting guiding desert tours across northern Africa.

Currently he splits his time between building off road vehicles for others, and running his own ex-Dakar Rally Range Rover, with the odd differential rebuild thrown in.

Due to the bursting workshop, he had arranged to take the diff off at a friends garage, which adjoined his own workshop. I got to witness the whole fascinating process, but was highly unconvinced by his continual assurances that *'it is quite easy'* and *'next time you do on your own'*.

He clearly subscribed to the old surgeons saying, *'Watch one. Do one. Teach one.'* I was no surgeon, sadly.

Spread over three days, to fit with his other commitments, the diff was rebuilt, refitted and off I went.

At last, no stomach churning whine from the differential bearings.

* * *

By the time the differential was repaired, and we have sorted out the belongings that we have in storage with my favourite beard sculptor, Elisa, it was the end of September.

Still smarting from the Scottish experience, Linda made it absolutely clear that we were **NOT** going anywhere that was remotely cold.

That comprehensively ruled out my plan to go to Nordkapp.

We decided to wait until Gilly, whose house we had occupied since we arrived back in Italy, returned from the UK.

We were like ships in he night, never in the same county at the same time. She would return in the second week of October.

**

Using the time to good use, we visited our old neighbours in Monteombraro.

This mountain village near Zocca, on the border with Bologna, was the last place we called home in Italy, and by the end, it was easily the most comfortable place that I have ever lived.

A large stone built house with open fires, down a long dead end road into the forest, and blessed with crazy, eccentric and inspirational neighbours.

Whether it was Gianni, mowing the lawn on his tractor, wearing only *'Budgie smuggling'* Speedos and flip flops, or when either Barbara or Lorenzo, the husband and wife herbalists, would cheerily run me off the road on their way to market, completely oblivious to my presence. Paolo, the 90 year old retired Carabiniere who kept peacocks and refused to let me pass his house without taking a glass of Grappa with him, regardless of both his wife's protestations, and indeed, the time of day.

It was never a dull moment in Via Roncadella.

If I settle anywhere, it will be with those crazy people. No

BACK TO THE PAST.

question.

Like many mountain communities, the locals can be very wary of outsiders. Sometimes that wariness can slide into rudeness.

When we arrived, we were clearly outsiders.

Overlooked for service at the bar by Mirko, stared at in the street by, just about everyone. It took over 2 years for us to be accepted into the community, but it's fair to say that many were equally as sad to see us go, as we were to leave.

We spent time and money in village - we bought our meat from the Butcher, our bread from the baker, and we ate often in the restaurant, and then there was the Doctor.

* * *

The wonderful Dottore Amore (*amusingly, literally 'Doctor Love' in English*), our general practitioner, had a character that would have fitted perfectly within any episode of Inspector Montalbano, the famed Sicilian TV detective.

With his tanned bald head, and his glasses perched in the tip of his nose, each visit would begin with an expansive ten minute lamentation on the parlous state of the Ferrari Racing team. We would then discuss wine, before eventually discussions matters medical.

Some of his prognosis's were, to put it mildly, a little eccentric, leading to the occasional raised eyebrow in the local pharmacy when proffering one of his easily obtained prescriptions, but we needed him to get Oliver fully jabbed, or we were going nowhere.

Amazingly, against all the Italian bureaucratic odds, he managed to get Olivers second Covid vaccination done in the village, and after much effort and correspondence, he would also secure EU COVID Green passes for us all. These passes would prove invaluable, as it turned out, as we travelled throughout Italy in the following months.

* * *

But the question remained, where would we go next? I was truly bored of driving around the same bit of Italy.

Borders were still shaky because of COVID, and it would be a risk to head into Eastern Europe, but like a modern day genie of the lamp, Facebook came to the rescue yet again.

The help this time, came in the form of a very timely invitation to visit a chap called Mark Attard in Sicily.

South means hot, Linda approved immediately.

The decision was made, we're going to take a slow drive down to Sicily, but first, we set about arranging a fitting goodbye to all of our friends, something that the COVID restrictions had cruelly prevented us from doing when we departed Italy, under cover of darkness, back in February.

* * *

In the rolling hills outside Maranello, the mid-October sun slowly set behind the endless acres of Lambrusco vines, stretching out across the valley towards the historic Levizzano Rangone Castle.

We warmly welcomed our many friends, as we gathered at our favourite restaurant, the incomparable, Lambruscheria Cà Berti.

BACK TO THE PAST.

Cà Berti represents a distilled version of everything that we grew to love about Italy. From the feeling of entering a pocket sized Tuscany, as you approach the restaurant through a narrow Cyprus tree lined single track road, to the breathtakingly wonderful, yet amazingly simple, local food.

Gian Matteo Vandelli, the owners son and the winemaker of the family, would always welcome us like old friends, occasionality chided us, gently, for our poor Italian, but always treating us to the very finest food and wine that Emilia-Romagna could offer.

He was a local radio DJ, and a musical encyclopedia, often despairing of me if I hadn't heard of some obscure 1970s English band or other.

The sublime pasta and meat dishes were all cooked under the ever watchful eye of his *'Mama'* in a giant farmhouse kitchen. A kitchen famed for having satisfied the hunger of, among others, the legendary Luciano Pavarotti, and even the great Enzo Ferrari himself.

My reward was always the food, her reward was a hug from me, to thank her.

In the beginning, she would chuckle and playfully shoo me away with her apron, but towards the end of our time in Italy, she came looking for me.

She spoke no English, but we understood each other through food.

Our first rented property in Italy was to be found a few kilometres along the same road, and back in 2015, Cà Berti. became a virtual second home, playing host to visitor after visitor.

Every meal was utterly exceptional. So many unforgettable nights of food, wine and music.

Memories that truly make the mouth water.

* * *

As our friends began to arrive in the large outdoor area surrounding the restaurant, I did my best to mingle among the crowd, a task that I hate almost as much as I am ill-equipped to carry it out.

Courtesy of the excellent work by my great friend Sara Garbugli, there was a great turnout from the Ferrari factory.

We drank, ate and talked about the future of Ferrari - there was a general feeling of despair as usual - I tried to be upbeat about our troubles, laughing as I span the Sicily trip as a good thing, even though, inside at least, the smoke of failure still clung to my clothes.

We were camping in the vineyard for the night, which gave everyone the opportunity to see Mandy up close and see the fruits of our long labour.

Everyone wished us luck, and a few even told the truth, and questioned our sanity, though in a friendly way. In the back if my mind, I struggled to disagree with them. This was not just me, I was dragging my whole family towards the cliff edge. More doubts.

* * *

In the morning, we had the immense privilege to watch *'Mama'* and four elderly ladies from the village, produce exquisite and identical hand made Tortelloni, a stuffed Pasta native to the region.

It forms the backbone of most meals at the restaurant and

served simply with sage and butter, was like eating history on the plate.

We kissed everyone, said our goodbyes and headed back to Gilly's house, to pack the last things and go. More kisses, more tears.

It had been a very long and gruelling 8 months since we left Italy, and those 8 months had been some of the most difficult, stressful and energy sapping months of my life.

I couldn't wait to get on the road.

The warm sun of Sicily could not come fast enough.

8

Always look a gift horse in the mouth.

"When someone shows you who they are, believe them the first time."
- Maya Angelou

The plan, such that it was, involved informally camping as much as possible on the way to Sicily - a reason born of economics more than anything.

We would begin by heading to Florence, our favourite city, and then roughly make our way down the west coast of Italy, taking in the long dreamed of Amalfi Coast, along the way, before taking the car ferry from the mainland to Messina in Sicily.

* * *

Travelling in slow mode in Italy can lead to some unusual experiences.

Off the beaten track, Sat Nav becomes less and less reliable, but that is part of the fun of Italian travel. You never know where you are going to end up.

Our trip to Florence would not be the last time that we cursed Google Maps though.

Our first challenge came early in the day, as in the process of negotiating the myriad of back roads to Florence, we were confronted with a first test of our vehicles overall height.

We carry 2 roof tents, and in between, two large Darche sailing bags, packed with clothes etc. As the bags can pack differently every time, we don't have a fixed height, though we hover around the 2.6m mark.

The height of the square concrete tunnel under the motorway looked uncannily similar to our own height. When you turn off Motorways on your Sat Nav, you get what you deserve, I guess.

With no sign for guidance, and a vague understanding of our actual height, Linda jumped out and had a look. Lots of 'chin rubbing' but in all honestly, I was never going to reverse back up the steep, twisting, single track road that we had just come down. If it came to it, I'd let the air out of the tyres first, before I attempted that!

Finally, I got the tentative 'thumbs up' from the co-pilot and I gingerly drove into the tunnel, braced for the scraping sounds of Darche bags against rough concrete, but none came.

We sloshed through the standing water and appeared out the other end.

That was a bit more like it.

After a stressful drive through the middle of Florence, we headed to the hills overlooking the city, to find our first stop for the night.

We camped among the trees just outside the small village of Castel di Poggio. I was a little nervous as this was the first time that we have camped without permission in Italy.

The small rural road was nearby but fairly quiet, with just the occasional car slowing to check us out, and a couple even giving us a shout of *'Bella macchina'* and a cheery thumbs up.

You can't underestimate the good will that a Defender engenders in so many different people.

A quiet and restful night thankfully, with no interruptions, save the usually barked dog chorus.

* * *

To find our informal camping, I mostly use a couple of Apps on my iPhone.

Park4Night and iOverlander have proved to be the best.

For our second night, we used neither and just happening to drive past a perfect spot, high up in the hills, and set back from the road. It was reasonably flat and with a space big enough for us that was shielded from the road by trees.

The 'Holy Grail' of informal camping.

Disappointingly though, it did suffer the same issues that we had first experienced in the Highlands of Scotland - it seems outdoor pooing is a worldwide issue.

Linda, however, didn't quite share my contented happiness. She was struggling to get a good night's sleep, waking routinely at 1.30 in the morning having only had 4 or so hours sleep.

The cumulative effect of a few days of this, the cold weather in the mountains, plus what she suspected could be the start of a cold, resulted in a demeanour that become known as *'Grumpy Mare'* syndrome.

Setting up and setting down the camp is highly physical, and Linda, being our *'Mountain Goat'*, or *'monkey on the roof'* as she self-describes, shoulders much more than her fair share of the burden.

She needed a break badly. A lesson I learnt very early on, is watch people closely, as you learn to calibrate your senses to tell how much more people can take.

The answer to most problems is always the same. Slow down.

Being static for a while lets everyone revive a little. If we are camping informally, I rarely feel comfortable stopping in any one place for more than one night, unless we have permission.

ALWAYS LOOK A GIFT HORSE IN THE MOUTH.

It's one of my phobias.

We had planned to head to the coast of Tuscany anyway, but now the priority was to find a couple of days cheap camping there, and for once, the weather forecast was predicting to be excellent.

* * *

Campiglia Marittima, 90Kms south-west of Florence, is one of my favourite places on earth. A dream like medieval walled village, and backdrop to an annual breathtaking festival of street theatre, music and the arts.

Long before we ever dreamed of living in Italy, back in 2008, it was the final destination of a road trip holiday that took us through France, Switzerland, Northern Italy and finally a week spent inside the village walls, enjoying the amazing artistic events in the narrow alleys and squares.

Our hopes of staying near to Campiglia were dashed, when it became clear, one after another, that all of the campsites were closed during the out of season period.

Whilst a lot of the bigger beachside campsites were similarly closed, we eventually found a great one near the Golfo di Baratti. The gulf is known by some as the Italian Caribbean.

A couple of days of sand, sea and sun - usually the very best medicine to combat *'Grumpy Mare'* syndrome.

* * *

Fully refreshed by those three wonderful relaxing days of sun and sea, we set off for the nearby tiny Tuscan island of Elba.

Disembarking from the short ferry transfer from the mainland, our excitement was soon extinguished, when it became clear that the entire coastline of the 86 square mile island was owned by someone or another, and they were absolutely determined to keep the entirety of the beaches to themselves.

Frustratingly, we could barely see the sea from the road, obscured as it was by the many hotels and beach clubs which were packed cheek to jowl, mile after mile.

We drove on and on with increasing frustration, concluding that there was simply nothing to do, other than head up into the hills.

Arriving in late afternoon had left us precious little time to find somewhere to camp for the night, so we headed into the centre of the island, up and away from the tightly packed villages on the coast.

We lost a few degrees in temperature, but it was worth it for a relatively quiet night.

The **'Absolutely NO Camping'** signs were huge, and everywhere on this small island, so naturally, in our paranoia, when we heard the sound of an engine and the flash of headlights around 1 am, we feared the worst.

Thankfully, it turned out to be the late arrival of some Austrian cyclists, and not the local police, looking to give us a hefty fine and our marching orders from our mountain top hideaway.

Still a little paranoid, as dawn broke, we broke the tents down, so as not to appear to have stayed all night.

* * *

This uncertainty and fear of being either fined and/or moved on, is one of the principle disadvantages we have with using

ALWAYS LOOK A GIFT HORSE IN THE MOUTH.

rooftop tents.

We are about as 'un-stealthy' as it is possible to be.

Unlike our fellow travels in commercial vans, we can't pass under the radar, and similarly, we can't just up sticks and move in a couple of minutes like the motorhome crowd.

We have a few advantages too, separated sleeping space being the main one, but it's very hard not to feel more than a little envious of the Sprinter gang, who roll up at 10pm, crack a beer, and then roll straight into bed. Particularly when it's raining.

* * *

The following morning, we headed off further into the interior of the island. It was great to find out that Elba has a reasonable amount of publicly accessible off-road tracks.

Occasionally we get shouted at in our Defender 130, but on this occasion, as we drove the dusty tracks, it was not related to my 'dominant' driving style, but rather an excited and very enthusiastic Italian Land Rover lover.

The weather was glorious, and as we made our way down a narrow dusty track, we paused by a beautiful rustic farmhouse to admire a red Defender 90, precariously parked on what passed for a verge. A disembodied voice shouted from the garden *'Land Rover Forever!'*

After a brief chat with the proud owner of the 90, who was overjoyed to see our 130, we rewarded him with a free sticker, and drove off in a dusty haze.

The passion of Land Rover owners always inspires us.

As we continued to follow our nose along the endless sandy tracks, we managed to get caught up in some sort of unofficial off-road motorbike event - there were no signs and the officials seemed unbothered by us driving straight through the middle of it.

I slowed to a crawl, as first one bike, then another, and another would come hurtling past us, waving and giving us the 'thumbs up' as they narrowly avoided ending up on our bonnet.

Only in Italy.

* * *

Rising up to 950 metres above sea level, the 18-minute standing gondola ride to the top of Monte Capanne takes you almost to the top of the highest peak on the Isle of Elba.

Before we left the island, Linda and I took up the suggestion of Becky, an old friend in Maranello, and squeezed together in a tiny tubular gondola, and clunked and screeched our way to the top.

Linda, for reasons unknown, felt the urge to re-enact the iconic 'Titanic' pose halfway up, but I'm sure she had good reason.

Once out of the tight metal cage, we continued climbing the mountain as far as you could go. Linda, the *'mountain goat'* obviously kept going until she arrived at the helicopter pad at the very summit.

30 metres down, I sat enjoying a well-earned rest, when I head the unmistakable whistle of a turbine engine winding up. The noise became deafening, as over my head a helicopter, nose down, powered away from the pad and dove all the way down the mountain to the town below.

Italians clearly fly their helicopters just like they drive their cars.

Once over the shock of it, my mind turned to Linda. I began to walk up to the pad.

She met me halfway, '*Oh my **GOD!***', she exclaimed., white in the face.

Apparently, she, along with a few other climbers had clung on to the rocks for dear life as the pilot powered away from the helipad.

We made our way back down to the car park. Oliver, the vertigo sufferer of the family, had staying at the bottom and held the fort. A fireman, he will not make.

This final memory gift from Elba made up for the lack of beach time.

Heading back to the mainland, we took another night at the Agricampeggio Sant'Ignazio in Golfo di Baratti, to wash the dust of Elba from our bodies.

* * *

> There are no strangers here; Only friends you haven't yet met.
> **- William Butler Yeats**

One of the enduring pleasures of our travels, is the many interesting and inspirational characters that we bump into on the road. With one or two notable exceptions, our experience is overwhelmingly positive.

Felix is one such character.

The Park4Night app had directed us to a lovely, secluded clearing, slap bang in the middle of a mountainous peninsular of Monte Argentario. A place famous, it would seem, for little other than being the place where artist Michelangelo Merisi, better known as Caravaggio[25], died of a fever in 1610.

The spot was high up in the forest, very secluded (*no barking dogs for a pleasant change*), and was empty when we arrived.

It's a sure sign that you're high up, when the only things higher than you, are the military weather facilities, and other giant antennae. We were a couple of kilometres down from the antennae.

It was going to be a cold and windy night.

* * *

A few hours after we had arrived and set-up, the deafening silence was broken by a large man on a very small old motorcycle.

When I say small, I don't mean the engine. He was at least 6 feet tall and the bike appeared to be the size suitable a 10 year old child.

He burst, full pelt, through the surrounding undergrowth into our clearing, knees by his chin, little engine screaming for its life. One sideways look of us, and he shot across the clearing, and up the steep rutted hill adjacent to our camping spot.

Swerving from side to side, mud and rocks spewing from the rear wheel, he bouncing and slid and swerved until he almost got to the top. Almost, but not quite.

Having lost critical momentum, he decided to roll backward down the hill, uncontrollably ricocheting from each bump, ridge and rut, until he arrived, still upright amazingly, in a cloud of dust at the bottom of the slope.

Undeterred, he glanced back at us, and without a word, set about attempt number two in what was fast resembling a fine attempt to gain his own notoriety in the world of YouTube Fail videos.

Cannily taking a slightly different line this time, victory was soon his, as he successfully screamed his way to the top of the slope. We cheered his persistence if nothing else.

He stopped briefly at the crest, stood astride his miniature motorcycle and looked back down, as if to take in the enormity of the achievement. Then off he screamed, never to be seen by us again.

* * *

On the second day in our clearing campsite, we encounter Felix, a fellow traveller. A young man, living in his van and following his nose - a greater life, it could be said, a man cannot have.

Over a coffee, we learned that he had damaged his foot climbing, so we got to use our Survival First Aid kit medical kit for the very first time. He seemed a little puzzled at our giggly excitement at getting the opportunity to bandage his foot.

Little things and little minds, so the saying goes.

Felix decided to stay the night in his stealthy unmarked white surfer dude van, and we shared a few beers and travel stories together, the temperature dropping, until the wind starting to make an unwelcome presence.

Many say that they want solitude, but actually, in my experience, what we actually need is solitude, interspersed with meeting interesting people for short periods. That's the best life there is.

We said our good-nights, and agreed to carry out the usual Instagram ritual of cheesy photos by the vehicles in the morning, before we went our separate ways.

Felix was going North back to Germany, and we, ever onward south to Sicily.

I was mindful that we needed to pick up the pace somewhat, as Tuscany was keeping a hold on us.

Beautiful though Tuscany is, we would never get to Sicily at this rate.

***

With rain expected anytime soon, Linda was up early as usual, and anxious to get packed up and ready for travel.

The night before, Felix had warned us of his hatred of sunrises, and that he was most definitely not a morning man.

So, to the sound of the local sparrow taking his first morning fart, Linda, undaunted by this information, decided to chance her arm and knock on Felix's sliding door.

Results were as expected.

A groaning German finally emerged, blinking mole like into the light. We agreed to send the photos later, and he gratefully crawled back under his duvet.

As we finished the pack up, and just as we were securing the bright orange Maxtrax recovery boards on to the rear wheel, a dishevelled Felix appeared, mobile phone in hand. We would do our photographs together. Top man, that Felix.

I backed Mandy up to a spot beside his van, and the ritual was complete.

ALWAYS LOOK A GIFT HORSE IN THE MOUTH.

* * *

The weather was now appalling, so we decided to have breakfast on the road and made our way down he winding roads of the mountain.

On the way up, we had passed a beautiful old monastery. It came equipped with a very rare commodity in this mountain, a Car Park.

Usually, I check the engine fluid levels every day when we are travelling, but that morning, I had forgotten, so we pulled into the monastery car park.

A group of American tourists on a cycling holiday started to gather in the car park. They were were curious as usual about our Defender, and our strange, to them at least, lifestyle.

I popped the bonnet, and was met with a wide scattering of what looked like Demerara sugar, that golden-brown large grained sugar used in cooking, so I'm told.

It obviously wasn't, but what on earth was it?

The closer I looked, the more I found, there was piles of it, all over the cylinder head cover,and across the various engine ancillaries.

Looking at it closely, it looked plant based, but we had not parked under trees and were always moving - where had it come from?

I dusted the deposits away, and cleaned the top of the engine as best I could. It's still a mystery what it was, and we've never seen the problem again.

* * *

The Park4Night app proved again to be its weight in gold. It directed us to a small town called Montepoli di Sabina, just north of Rome.

Our Roof Top Tents are an obvious, and severe impediment to camping in towns.

In any event, the concept of urban camping is against our philosophy and ordinarily we would never camp in a built up area, but Montepoli di Sabina offered one of those ultra-rare opportunities to be proved thoroughly wrong.

As we made our way into the typically beautiful hill top town, the signs directing us to the Motorhome park took us right into the heart of the town.

It proved to be so well hidden, that we drove past it a couple of times before finding the tight and narrow entrance to the town car park, below which was the small tarmac motorhome campsite.

Not knowing what to expect, we were pleasantly surprised to find toilets, running water, and amazingly, free electricity hook-up that worked. The rare triple crown in free camping.

Our arrival did not go unnoticed, as car after car would make the unnecessary journey down the concrete ramp to the bottom level of the car park, where we were parked up, and make a three point turn and give us a slow drive by as they left.

Mostly they stared, we smiled back.

One or two, greeted us and complemented us in the 130.

It felt very odd to be so visible, yet camping entirely legally. The opportunity to walk into town and take a coffee or aperitivo whenever we wanted, was also a very welcome change.

Early in the evening, an Italian registered Motorhome pulled in and packed up a short distance from us. It was becoming more humid as each hour passed, and as a sure sign it was warm, Linda washed her hair in cold water without screaming.

It turned out that Mauro lived in the town, but some nights, he preferred to park in the camping area in his Motorhome. I didn't ask why, but I could well guess why he did it.

We chatted a while, before he got himself an early night.

***

We woke to wind and heavy rain.

We took a coffee in the town, and then packed up and headed in the general direction of Naples, where the weather looked to be slightly better, or so we thought.

Firstly staying at a lovely, but mosquito invested and difficult to find, spot by Lago di Fondi, south-west of Rome.

Fed up of dodging rain and mosquitoes, we trudged ever onward south.

***

With nowhere to sit inside, without the fuss of setting up the annex tents that can be located below our roof top tents, we must keep a keen eye on the weather.

Rule number one, if weather is bad, do not climb mountains.

Rule number two, if weather is **REALLY** bad, find a campsite.

You cannot underestimate the morale sapping misery of trying to camp in high winds and cold, driving rain. For the sake of 20 Euros or so for a basic campsite, I'll play that card every time. We spend enough nights under canvas, we have nothing to prove.

Options in the Park4Night app were few and far between, but I settled on a secluded woodland spot, some 4000 feet up in he mountains of Campagnia. Reviews were good and the photos looked epic.

At around 2000 feet, the weather quickly took a turn for the worse and soon became, what can only be described as, biblical.

I pulled over. You could barely stand up in the wind and driving rain that was battering the side of the mountain.

Fog and cloud were merging into an enormous grey soup that was swirling towards us.

I have a character flaw. A big one.

I hate turning back when I am driving others, even (*and sometimes especially*) if I know in my heart that it is the absolutely the right thing to do.

Its stupid and potentially dangerous, but I plough on, feeling that anything else is either failure or at the least, weakness.

It's easily the dumbest thing I do. A psychiatrist would have a field day, with it bound to be something to do with my relationship with my father, as most things appear to be.

Linda was, rightly, apoplectic with rage at my stubbornness.

Having reached the top, it was obvious to a blind man that even our renowned *'mountain goat'* would undoubtedly be blown off the roof, long before the tents would ever be erected.

* * *

Finally, after grudgingly admitting the idiocy of my intent, we headed back down the mountain, got hopelessly lost in the fog looking for hotels that turned out to be closed for the winter, and, to put a shiny tin lid on it, found ourselves on a tiny single track road, full of car sized potholes, and endless low hanging trees. We definitely hadn't come this way.

The farm road that we were in, ran parallel to the main SS 7 highway, but like an extended waking fever dream, I would see the main road on my right, just over the fence, but I just couldn't get to it. Mile after mile, after pot holed mile.

After 5 hours of driving and now, no cell coverage, the stuff of nightmares had begun. Linda was angry, Oliver was angry, and I was driving way too fast, crashing through water filled potholes, huge tree branches clattering the windscreen and roof tents.

Finally, after what seemed an hour, we found a connection with the main road, but still no mobile phone coverage. Bloody Italy!

I wasted no more time, and drove to the nearest town, and finally we had a Vodafone signal. Out of better options, Linda gave in and fired up Booking.com. on her phone.

They offered an Agriturismo a few KM away for a reasonable price.

We booked it and paid on line.

* * *

30 minutes later, we pull up to the iron gates of a dark, and deserted looking house on a hillside between Montefalcione and Lapio, in the Irpinian mountains.

A few minutes pass by and then a slightly concerning looking lady arrives, and explains that sadly, they are closed for the winter,

Our collective hearts sank.

We explained that we had paid on line, and we had nowhere else to go.

A short phone call, and then, Carmine came to the rescue - he had seen our 'beautiful' Land Rover pass the farm, and we should not worry, in 30 minutes they could be open again.

I could have kissed him, but thought better of it.

This is the Italy that I love.

As it happened, Carmine was the owner of the farm next door, and also the Bed and Breakfast that we had booked into.

The whole family were pressed into service. Beds were made and floors were swept. It was a military operation.

We asked if we could use the kitchen and let slip that we had not eaten all day - without another word he rushed to his farmhouse next door, and returned with hot home made beef stew, in a wonderful red wine and tomato sauce.

Turning his nose up at our cheap supermarket wine, he insisted that we drink a bottle of his own production red wine, from the fertile hills surrounding up.

As expected, it was beautiful and perfectly matched the beef.

'Would you like another bottle, and maybe some cheese from my farm?' he asked in Italian.

' Yes, of course' I said, *'Thank you, but we must pay you for all this.'*.

'**NO***, you are my friends."* he said quietly, but forcefully.

Not guests, but friends - barely 30 minutes together - the hospitality of southern Italian people is breathtaking and heart warming.

After a great sleep, a wonderful breakfast, and the purchase of a couple of bottles of Carmines wine, we bade farewell to him, his lovely family, and the Agriturismo Macchia dei

ALWAYS LOOK A GIFT HORSE IN THE MOUTH.

Briganti, but we will surely meet them again one day, that is for sure.

* * *

As we left, Carmine warned us that more severe weather was coming, and a farmer should know after all. Red sky at night, and all that.

Our next stop was the beautiful, magical Amalfi Coast. Part of the 'D*isney*' vision of Italy that I had, before we ever visited it.

Sorrento, Positano and the rest of what the locals call '*The Divine Coast*' is a bucket list dream for millions of people around the world.

The magical cliff top villages, the beach restaurants serving beautiful dishes of fish and pasta. Like meeting your heroes, I hoped that the reality would live up to my perception.

The impending weather was indeed getting serious, so I studied the apps for a cheap campsite where we could hold out for a few days, drop the annexes if necessary, and maybe visit the coastal villages, if we got a break in the weather.

I hit the jackpot with the magical world of the '*Ostello Campeggio- Beata Solitudo*' - a throwback hippy haven, a couple of hours drive from where we were, just north of Amalfi in a town called San Lazzaro.

* * *

Just three hours later, we wound our way through narrow car-lined streets, following a protracted one-way system, before arriving in the bustling cafe lined town square of San Lazzaro.

It couldn't be there, we were right in the centre of town, it must be wrong.

I reset the Sat Nav, drove through the town square and carried on through the endless one-way system.

10 minutes later, irritatingly, we had ended up exactly where we started, back at the town square.

To save further embarrassment, thankfully Paolo, the Kaftan wearing owner of the campsite ,had spotted us and was strolling over from the bar, guessing rightly that we were looking for him.

WE were mortified to learn that we were literally parked in front of a building, with a sign saying *'Beata Solitudo'*.

The camp was entered through the imposing archway of the former stables of the castle of General Avitabile, a fantastically colourful 19th Century Italian soldier, mercenary and adventurer, who, amongst other things, fought on the *'wrong side'* at Waterloo.

To make us feel better, he told us that everyone missed the entrance. I doubt it.

* * *

Driving slowly through the narrow archway, we had arrived into another world.

We drove up a gentle concrete slope, past an eclectic mixture of holiday chalets, shower blocks and a few dilapidated caravans, and finally arrived at the top terrace, an area dotted with beautiful shade giving trees.

The towns resident stray cats and dogs nervously circled us, looking for their next meal presumably, and the air was filled with the sound of wood being sawn and split for the impending winter.

We found the perfect spot, plugged in and set up camp, dropping both annexe's for the first time since we left the UK.

It felt like home already.

* * *

Paradoxically , despite the doom laden weather warnings from Carmine, the subsequent days provided some of the best weather we had had in a while.

We filled our days with reading, walking around the town, trying the many coffee bars and sampling the local restaurants.

On the 3rd day, the weather promised to be fantastic, so we take the bus to Amalfi, and hopefully, get a boat to Positano - out of season, possibly one of the most sensational places on earth.

* * *

The coast road to Amalfi has to be seen to be believed.

In places, the road clings to the side of the cliff in ways that seem to defy the laws of physics, and can narrow down to barely the width of a bus.

Buses ran every 20 minutes from just outside the campsite, so at 9.20 we jumped on a bus and hung on for the hair-raising 40 minute ride.

We had encountered the local SETA buses, and their fearless drivers, earlier in the week, so I was expecting the worst. They didn't disappoint.

The unwritten rule, it seemed to be, was that you stopped

for nothing.

Throttle had one position, flat to the floor, and forward progress was to be maintained at all times, with the single exception of meeting one of your colleagues in their identical blue bus, coming the either way.

Anything else in the way was to be met with flashing lights, and blaring horns.

I loved every single minute on it.

* * *

We arrived through a narrow archway, waved though by a policeman despite a red traffic light, and immediately lurched sharp right. In a cloud of brake dust and steam, we screeched to a halt at the Bus terminus of Amalfi.

The promise I made to Linda over 25 years before, had finally been honoured.

'Could we go home now', I joked. She punched me.

We were met by some classic Italian chaos.

The terminus was a short way from the harbour and immediately next to a large cobbled roundabout. A roundabout with traffic lights no less, that, despite a large police presence, had been recently converted into an impromptu car park by anyone and everyone.

The local police were playing their own version of vehicular Whack-A-Mole.

As they moved one vehicle on, another car would park up on the other side, and so on, and so forth. A game the whole constabulary can play. Hilarious to watch when you are in the happy position of being a bus passenger.

We joined the out of season crowds and walked around the

town.

Sadly, like so many tourist destinations, the shops were mostly selling generic gift products, but it was a beautiful day, and the town was pretty. Much smaller than we had imagined, but nice nonetheless.

I can imagine in August that it would become an overcrowded boiling hellhole of a place. Thankfully it was now the end of October.

We took a stroll down the harbour wall, and after Linda had performed her obligatory dip in the sea, we found our way to the boat taxis. We booked our tickets to Positano.

The midday sun was now at its strongest, we grabbed some cold drinks and waiting for our boat to dock.

* * *

As you will have worked out by now, if you have gamely waded through the sixty thousand plus words that it has taken you to get here, I'm no great writer.

This is about to become its most apparent, as I attempt, with my almost empty barrel of literary imagination, to adequately describe a very short boat trip from Amalfi to Positano.

Or more accurately, the boat trip back to Amalfi from Positano.

On the way there, I foolishly, and like the sheep that I am, followed the crowd. I sat in the upper deck seats on the wrong (*ocean facing*) side of the boat.

All I got for my trouble was a sunburnt head and the opportunity to admire a group of Malaysians who appeared to be trying to break the world selfie record.

Arriving around lunchtime, we did what every Englishman

should do, found a restaurant looking out over the sea, ordered a bottle of Sancerre (*sorry Italy*) and get stuck into the menu.

After lunch, we strolled through the narrow alleyways cut in to the cliffs, and checked out the tiny shops and bars. It was breathtaking, and, thankfully, easily lived up to our expectations.

Positano is even smaller then Amalfi, so after a brief walk around the art shops of the village, we headed back to the harbour to catch the next boat.

This time, me and Oliver stayed below.

We sat on the rear of the boat. I looked out the back at its wake, and watched Positano become smaller in the distance as we sped along the coast, made golden in the early evening sun, and Oliver, sitting next to the tricolour flag, with his back to the wake, basking in the sun as the wind blasted through both the flag, and his hair.

The sun was low in the sky, and if I shut my eyes, I am back there now, feeling the vibrations of the engines beneath me, hearing the roar of the water being thrust away from us, and all the time, staring at my son.

My brain had slipped into overdrive.

In a rush of conflicting and contradictory emotions, I felt thankful, regretful, elated, nostalgic and dejected all at the same time. Hard to achieve, but somehow I pulled it off.

It was as though the previous four years, all the stress and hardship, had all boiled down to just that one moment - that exact second.

I smiled at Oliver and mouthed '*You OK?*'.

He nodded and smiled. Coming up to 17 as we was, he was more OK than I think I will ever be.

ALWAYS LOOK A GIFT HORSE IN THE MOUTH.

* * *

Back in 2021, we were still reasonably new to the overlanding game and finding overnight camping spots is seldom easy.

The apps only tell you so much. It's a constant struggle for me, as I am someone who feels a compulsion to plan, and part of my anxiety problem is rooted in a perceived lack of control.

I like to know where I am going - I am a little in awe of those, like Felix whom we met in Tuscany, who can travel completely care free, just following their nose, and stopping when they get hungry.

I wish I could, but I can't,

Like life, camping is often a compromise. That unknown spot, secluded, safe, and with its own pristine sandy beach and drinking water supply doesn't exist - as if it did, it wouldn't be unknown for very long, now would it.

Our next stop after Amalfi was a beach side car park recommended by Park4Night - small but nice beach, plenty of space to park but by a fast/noisy road - good reviews though, what could go wrong?

For everything in life, the gut is a great barometer, and mine was telling me that this was not a great decision, but it was getting dark.

After some discussion, I bit the bullet and we got set up - dodging the ever present excrement (*human and canine this time*) and the prophylactic remains of many a *'romantic liaison' we cooked, ate and settled down to watch some TV.*

Just as it was getting dark, an old grotty looking car pulls into the otherwise empty car park and parks uncomfortably close to us. Its one male occupant sits in the car, engine running - not threatening as such, but weird.

Thirty minutes later a fellow traveller in full stealth mode (unmarked white panel van) pulls in and we have a chat. A Frenchman heading north.

Almost immediately, the other car, still with its engine running, leaves the car park - a coincidence you might think. Maybe, maybe not.

Anyway, spontaneity is all very well, but I feel a great responsibility for my family, so we are fast learning the compromises necessary for a stress free night - head for water (*lakes, reservoirs*) or mountains (*depending on the weather*) - try to be unseen from the roadside and above all, don't be afraid to up-sticks and move on if it doesn't quite feel right.

If all else fails, book a campsite.

We lasted the night, no additional condoms in the morning that I could see (*not that I was counting*), so we considered ourselves lucky, filled a bag of other peoples non condom related rubbish, and made our way further south again.

* * *

After the previous days shifty car park choice, I was a bit dubious about our next planned stop, a little further down the East coast of Italy in Diamante.

We camped in the deserted car park of the beautiful Teatro dei Ruderi (Theatre in the ruins) - a open air amphitheatre set amongst the ruins of the castle and the remains of the medieval town of Cirella.

Beautiful weather, no flies and not even a barking dog! Perfection.

Another first though, as not long after we had set up, we

got our first local police flyby on this trip, but we obviously didn't deserve any effort, as they took a look from a distance, turned around, and left straight away.

After a fun exploration of the ruins, the day ended with a stunning sunset and a nice glass of vino.

* * *

The south west coast of Italy is peppered with beautiful villages one after another. Our next stop, Tropea, was one of the very nicest. A beach town that is set high up above the coast, and entered by a very long and very winding road, or, in our case, a daunting amount of stone steps.

We parked on the beach front, checked out the almost deserted beach and caves before climbing the dreaded stairs and taking a closer look inside the walled village.

Linda had ticked the swimming box, and ice cream was taken.

Our camp for the night was in the ruins of Torre Marrana, a few miles inland, another *'romantic location'* that we selectively cleared up a bag of rubbish from.

The grim weather over the last few weeks had taken its toll, and we just wanted to get to Sicily. A quick call to Maltese Mark, and the deal was done.

The following morning, we broke up camp, and excitedly headed straight for the port of Villa San Giovanni, to get the first available ferry to Messina, Sicily.

* * *

We are now getting used to the disorderly nature of ferries

in Italy . Having booked on line on Saturday night, the ticket still hadn't arrived by email on the Monday morning.

It finally arrived as we were literally queueing in our vehicle at the self check-in machines. Predictably, despite this, the machine failed to accept our ticket, but for once, a human being was on hand to sort out our drama, and waved us through.

For reasons that still baffle me, the ferries are nowhere near the check in.

You are made to constantly doubt yourself, as the tiny signs direct you back into the town from where you came, and all the way around a long one way system before ending up almost back where you started. Only then, finally, are you led into the port and the ferries themselves.

We clattered up the loading ramp, parked up and headed for a viewpoint on the port side, the better to watch the brief, 20 minute, crossing of the Messina strait.

* * *

Ferry ports are more often than not, fairly grim industrial places, and Messina didn't dispel that prejudice.

Arriving in Sicily at midday, the traffic was heavy and chaotic. In what seemed to take forever, we crawled out of the industrial and commercial parts of this grimy city.

Despite a weather forecast that was pretty grim, and having clearly learnt nothing from our recent Calabrian adventure, we headed out of Messina to find a quiet and secluded spot for the night.

Ever the optimist, I had found an inviting camping spot high up in the mountains above Messina, offering the prospect of *'beautiful panoramic views of the Straights of Messina'*, forgetting that less than a week earlier, we had watched TV New reports of flash floods that had battered Sicily almost to death.

The recent *'medicane'*, a cyclone-like storm system that formed over the Mediterranean Sea, had dumped around one year's worth of rain over most of Sicily, in less than two days, killing a small number of people, and devastating a number of towns and villages.

* * *

The misgivings came early, as we left the highway and headed up through a series of ever smaller villages. It was starting to gently spit with rain.

The roads had deteriorated fast, and were now in an unbelievably shocking state, with huge slabs of tarmac missing and widespread subsidence. The worst that we had seen since Naples.

What tarmac that was left behind, had creating a giant *'crazy paving'* among the huge water filled potholes that pockmarked the surface.

The going was worryingly slow.

The further we went, the worse it got, the tarmac, such as it was, turning first into uneven gravel, and then into larger piles of rocks. The recent Cyclone had deeply rutted and washed out the upper portions of these farm tracks, leaving behind the sort of terrain that was more suitable for the King of the Hammers[26] off road rally .

Before I knew it, the road had become a steep and never ending rock strewn track, packed full of muddy switchback after muddy switchback, all of them too tight for the boat like turning circle of our Defender 130.

It was fast becoming a low gear technical rock crawl. Fine if you are in a lightweight 90 with buckets of flex, and a load of similarly equipped mates. Not so great in an overweight top heavy 130.

Despite my two days of driver training with Edd Cobley at Protrax, and the plummeting temperature, the sweat was beginning to form on my skin.

The rain was heavy, the mist and fog closing in. Passengers were getting restless.

All the while, the Sat Nav continued to ruthlessly mock me, by informing me that the remaining ten kilometres would take only 15 minutes. At our rate of progress, akin to walking by then, fifteen hours would have been more accurate.

We didn't have five hours, let along fifteen hours.

We slowly pushed, with Linda holding on to the grab handle above the passenger door like a limpet.

We occasionally passed a slightly bemused mountain man in his ubiquitous Panda 4x4, and managed to dodge the occasional intrepid off-road biker, coming bouncing towards us down the track.

Then the fog really arrived. We could no longer see the valley below, nor the next section of the track in the distance.

The passengers had had enough. Refusing to take photos or videos, they implored me to turn back.

Through stubbornness, and more than a little stupidity, I kept on going and then, the sage advice of Edd came to mind, *'don't be afraid to walk ahead'.*

I got out, and almost immediately regretted it.

The wind and rain was driving into me, soaking me head to foot in seconds.

I climbed the steepening incline and, rounding a corner, through the swirling fog, I saw a series of huge land slides and deep ruts, that were way beyond us, me and a top heavy 130. It was utterly impassable.

Much to the obvious relief of my passengers, I reluctantly admitted defeat and I agreed to head back down to Messina below.

The first problem was how to turn around a very heavy 130 on a steep rock strewn track, that was not much wider than our Defender itself. On the left was a steep rock face and bushes, and on my right, a flimsy sheep fence and a sheer drop down to the villages below.

I couldn't afford to get this even sightly wrong.

Edd came into my head again. *'Stay calm, walk the track, make a plan'*, he would say.

So off I set, and quickly found a spot around 100 meters back down the track that was just about wide enough for me to back into some bushes, and perform a multi point turn to get us pointing back down again.

I asked Linda and Oliver to get out. Ostensibly to help guide me, but in reality, if I was going over the edge, I wanted to be sure that it was me and me alone.

After a few gasp inducing moments from the crowd, I reversed her back over the rocks and made a 38 point turn to finally get her pointing downwards.

The drama, however, was far from over, as the next section down was some of the most challenging terrain that we had encountered going up - huge ruts with very acute angles and tricky see-saw tipping points.

Neither Linda nor Oliver felt able to spot me, so I began to descend the track, unguided.

In my limited experience, going down technical tracks is much harder than going up, and as we made our way through the trickiest sections, to prove my point, I got my right hand rear tyre stuck in a very deep rut. A lesson in the laws of gravity.

With the vehicle sitting up at an acute angle, pointed towards the sheer drop, I gingerly lifted my foot from the brake pedal, the brakes graunched, and I felt the weight above me start to shift dangerously further to the left.

In that split second, I felt sure that we were about to roll over, and right next to the sheer drop of the cliff edge. Only a few strands of barbed wire between the occasional wooden post stood between us almost certain tragedy.

Instinctively, I brought the steering to straight ahead, and floored her in low range second gear. I had absolutely no idea what I was doing.

A roar, a cloud of black smoke and our fantastic Falken MT Tyres bit hard into the rocks.

Like a scalded cat, Mandy shot up and over the rocks.

As the Defender rocked from side to side on the flat ground, I laughed nervously, and assured my passengers that this was all part of the plan.

It wasn't, it was the purest of luck that we were not barrel rolling, end over end, down the side of the mountain into oblivion.

Now completely drenched in sweat and gently steaming, I concentrated on getting us back down the rest of the track in one piece, and into a campsite.

The weather was horrific,and showed no sign of improving anytime soon.

An hour later, we're back in Messina, booking a campsite

ALWAYS LOOK A GIFT HORSE IN THE MOUTH.

before the next major storm was due to hit. I needed a shower and alcohol, lots of alcohol…

* * *

As the light faded, we stuck to the main highway heading south, toward Mount Etna, where we planned to visit the following day.

The campsite we found was run by the splendid Capitano Nino.

A giant of a man, his bearded face reminding one of Captain Nemo, rather than Captain Nino.

His English communication was faultless, so it was a little surprising to learn that he spoke no English at all, but clearly had a supreme command of WhatsApp and Google translate.

He greeted us with a bowl of fresh lemons grown on his farm, and was relieved to learn that Oliver spoke fluent Italian.

As it was out of season, we pretty much had the run of the place. The small campsite was well equipped and had direct access to the beach. As usual, the family swimmer was chomping at the bit to get into the sea again.

As Linda and Oliver headed to the beach, I busied myself finishing the set up of the camp.

As Linda was checking out the black sandy beach, the storm that had threatened all day, had finally arrived. The heavens duly opened.

Linda soon ran back, soaking wet, to find me dripping wet and swearing as I tried to complete the set up of our Darche awning. Rain was pouring down and insistently drumming on the canvas above me as I fought to get the last of the pegs in the ground.

The Captain, who appears to live on site in a motorhome, kindly offered to let us use the hut that housed his cooking and washing facilities. With the wind getting stronger, and the rain getting heavier, we gladly accepted

Poor Linda set about cooking a chicken stir-fry on the back of the Defender as the heavy rain turned into a full-blown thunder storm.

Once finished on the stove, we gladly retreated into Capitano Nino's hut, and opening a bottle of Carmine's wonderful Calabrian wine.

We felt blessed relief, as we ate our meal together, in the dry, listening to the incessant staccato drum beat of rain on the huts aluminium roof.

* * *

November the first, All Saints Day, began pretty much the same as most recent days.

Torrential rain.

Thankfully the temperature was higher and the wind wasn't so rough. Small blessings.

For reasons of comfort, and safety, we try not to set up or break down the tents in the rain. This is to prevent our *'Mounting Goat'* losing her footing and finding her self taking the quickest non-approved route from the roof. That would be a huge disaster for all concerned.

On this occasion, we had to move, so waiting until a slow down in the rain, we equipped the *'Goat'* with a set of waterproofs, and got on with it.

The weather forecast looked grim for the rest of the day, so it seemed pretty pointless going to Mount Etna, covered as she was in heavy rain, mist and fog.

I messaged our new friend Mark, further south east near Modica, and it seemed that the weather was not so bad there. He invited us to come a little earlier than planned, so we gratefully accepted, and set the Sat Nav for the South East of Sicily.

We were about to enter the land that time forgot.

* * *

Contrary to what you might believe, there are in fact at least two Italys, maybe more.

There is an Italy above Rome where, mostly speaking, the heavy industry and commerce resides. The Italy of the Dolomites, of Florence, of Venice. The glorious, incomparable food of Emilia-Romagna, and super reds of Tuscany.

Then there is an Italy below Rome. You can still find a very good meal, and a splendid glass of wine, but you soon realize that you are not in Kansas any more. There are undoubtedly beautiful pockets of southern Italian, and the people are as hospitable as their Northern brothers are rich. Wonderful people, but you cannot shut your eyes.

As you approach Naples along the main routes, the roads become steadily more broken and more dirty - apocalyptically huge piles of household refuse sacks, bulging at the seams, line the slip roads of many main roads. It has to be seen to be believed.

Literally thousands, upon thousands of bags of assorted household rubbish and industrial waste. I have never seen anything like it in Europe.

Derelict buildings are everywhere. Prostitutes perched on

kitchen chairs, sit patiently in the lay-bys for their next paying customer.

*　*　*

It's such a shocking contrast to the north.

Years ago, a colleague at Ferrari, who hailed from the North, told me that his fellow northerners routinely described someone born south of Rome as *'North African'*. 1970s racism is still alive and well in Italy.

For some northerners, all the problems seem to begin below the 42nd Parallel. They will tell you that Southerners are all thieves, they are lazy, they pay no tax. Blah, Bah, Blah.

My experience of the south, before visiting Sicily, was small but pertinent, as it completely contradicts the stereotype of the south.

I am blessed to be friends with a wonderful family in Molise[27]. Back in the mists of time, I interviewed a young Italian woman called Monica, for the role of a buyer.

She got the job, and less than 10 years later, I got a surrogate family.

Enzo, the larger than life patriarch of the Di Luozzo welcomed us to his home in December 2104.

Newly arrived as we were in Italy, he, and the rest of his beautiful extended family, treated us like we were **HIS** family. One of the most memorable nights of my life was the experience of seeing the band Toto, playing outdoors, in a piazza in Luca, accompanied by Enzo and his son Giovanni.

I will not hear anything against the people of the south.

Yes, the south has problems, but their kindness, generosity and open doored affection overwhelms any of the negative aspects of their surroundings. They rise above it.

However, you cannot deny, that the more south you go, the deeper the problems get, until you arrive, inevitably, in Sicily.

Sicily has a very long and chequered history, being conquered, subjugated and bartered numerous times between a succession of Princes, Kings and other regional strong men.

Even after Italian unification, Sicily was woefully neglected by the central government, and the island's economic and social problems were allowed to fester, until the 1990s when the federal government finally sent troops to deal with that running sore, La Cosa Nostra.

Having driven the final few miles of pristine new motorway down the coast to Noto, you would be forgiven for thinking that maybe the *'North African'* moniker was unjustified, but we were about to turn sharp right and head inland to our final destination, Frigintini.

It soon became clear that the south of Sicily is yet another Italy, one I knew absolutely nothing about. We were about to get a crash course with a Maltese twist.

* * *

Our kind host, Mark Attard, would meet us in the centre of the village of Frigintini at 5 pm, so we had an hour or so to kill.

The nearest large town, Modica, was a little further on from our destination, so we headed over and took a brief walk around the charming baroque buildings of the historic centre, enjoying the many shops that testified to the towns proud status as the famed home of Sicilian Chocolate.

The hour passed far too quickly, we grabbed some local

wine, some cakes and rushed back to Mandy.

The 15 minute drive to Frigintini took us deeper into the heart of rural Sicily. Long stretches of straight sun bleached tarmac, between kilometres of drystone walled terraces, scattered with Olive and Carob trees.

Everything was coating in the finest dusting of light brown, which despite the greeny, betrayed the arid nature of the soil below.

The further we got from Modica, the fewer cars we saw, and of those that we did, many looked like they considerably older than Olivers 17 years.

* * *

We pulled into the deserted centre of Frigintini, and waiting for Mark to arrive.

The village was one which seemed not to have a defined centre as such, but appeared to have developed around and along the main road to Modica, and a roundabout at one end of the village. The main buildings all seemed to be post second world war, and others much more recent.

Dusk was falling, so it would be a set up in the dark if he didn't arrive soon. We had no idea where Mark lived, but he had told us he was *'off-grid'*. We chatted as we waited.

A grey Land Rover Freelander arrived at high speed in the square, dropping a lazy cloud of dust behind it.

A beaming Mark walking over to us and warned us that it was a tricky road to his house, and we should follow up. He reminded me of someone, but I couldn't put my finger on it - after some discussion, we all exclaimed, *'It's the Meerkat from the advert!'.*

His small and slender statute and olive skin, coupled with short hair and a sharp nose, made him the spitting image of Sergei from the Comparethemarket.com adverts. I think he enjoyed the reference.

***

There is living '*off-grid*', and then there is living '***off-grid***'.

Over the next 10 days, we got to know that Mark doesn't do things by halves, but first, despite his advancing years, he proved that he drives like he is still the off road rally driver of his youth.

I did my best to keep up with the Freelander, as we swooped out of Frigintini and headed into the the countryside along wide, smooth, tarmac roads, with long sweeping bends. After a long day, this was all I needed.

After a few minutes, our Falken mud tyres shuddered us to a halt, we waiting for an oncoming car to pass, before crossing the carriageway, and following Mark up a narrow stone wall lined lane.

I had to take a few risks now to stay in sight of the Freelander. The road was getting narrower and rougher but thankfully, he had began to slow down a little.

We pulled up behind him outside some old farm buildings, the sun was setting, and a shadowy dusk was rapidly setting in. To my right, I could just see a car sized gap in the fence and the beginnings of a muddy track leading down a steep slope and disappearing into some trees.

Surely not. Surely yes!

He poked the Freelander nose through the gap, and he was off, bouncing down the track and into the trees. Linda was understandably nervous considering the mess that I had gotten us into recently, in the hills above Messina.

I popped it into low range, selected second gear, and followed Mark. As we entered the trees at the bottom if the slope, still no sign of the house, but at least it was relatively flat.

The track was mud, made slick and slimy by the recent rain, I noticed the occasional pot hole, particularly on the corners, had been filled will stones to add traction.

For once, our weight was a small advantage, we were sinking slightly into the track, and making our own ruts to drive through.

In the last light of the day, we sloshed and slipped our way along the middle section and waited, while Mark negotiated the last bit. I've seen enough YouTube videos to not sit directly behind someone attempting to climb a muddy hill.

In the darkness, the last section looked the most nerve wracking. It seemed to be a very steep section in two parts with a slight kink to the right in the middle as you passed through a gate to, what presumably was, his house.

I floored the accelerator and roared up the last section and landed with a bounce in the lower section of his tiered garden, but with low hanging trees where we were, and access needed to his farm machinery etc, we needed to get Mandy onto the next terrace.

Infinitely easier said than done, as I was about to prove beyond any doubt.

For reasons that still baffle me, I had taken her out of low range, so then spent 10 minuets cursing and sweating, as I tried to manoeuvrer our 3.5 tonne leviathan up and around his ancient olive trees, in the pitch dark, with everyone giving

ALWAYS LOOK A GIFT HORSE IN THE MOUTH.

advice about things I could not see. He must of thought I was a complete idiot.

Finally, we found our spot, and to to our great relief, we folded out the tents at last.

Mark was from Malta, a place I knew little about. Over the coming days, we would learn much more of this little island and meet the great and the good of his Maltese friends, some of whom had also made their home in Sicily.

Mark was a terrific host, and an honest one too.

His wife Barbara was in Malta and wouldn't return for a week or so. He told us with neither pride nor shame, that he doesn't cook and he has OCD. Linda laughed and offered to be the cook for the stay. At least we wouldn't starve.

That night we sat and talked over a simple meal of pasta

and a bottle of local wine. Mark was incredibly easy to talk to. We have a very similar sense of humour, and he is a born storyteller.

It turns out that he is steeped in the history of off-roading competition on the Island of Malta, and a life long Land Rover fanatic, even being part of the Camel Trophy judging team for the Maltese entrant of that most famous of off-road challenges.

After dinner, those that take coffee, took it, and we all sat outside on his beautiful verandah and stared up at a sky full of stars.

Stunning though the stars undoubted were, our breaths were about to be taken away but an entirely otherworldly phenomena.

Out of the corner of my eye, I caught a bright light, moving fast,

'Look!', whispered Mark excitedly, *'Did you see that? There it is again!'*

We all stared at the same section of sky, slightly dumbfounded - there were small bright lights in the sky, not much bigger than stars, but much brighter, and they were shooting through the sky, in and out of the clouds, in what appeared to be straight lines and at apparently incredible speeds.

This mesmerizing display lasted for a few minutes and then they were gone.

We speculated about the origin of these strange lights, but by now the wind had increased heavily and, unfortunately, Linda would have another disturbed night in the tent.

* * *

ALWAYS LOOK A GIFT HORSE IN THE MOUTH.

The following morning, over morning tea, Linda mentioned that, with North Africa still closed to Tourists, we were planning to spend the winter in Sicily.

We were thinking of trying to find some work, or at the very least some house sitting, should the weather get really bad.

Mark mentioned, unsurprisingly, that he had a couple of friends that maybe needed some help during the rest of the winter.

We left it that we would makes some calls, and see what he could come up with.

The lasting memories of travel are largely made up of the people that you meet along the way (*and sometimes the food that you eat...*).

Some of these people perform an additional function as a catalyst to lead you to meet and experience so much more. Mark Attard is definitely one of those people. Mark knows everyone, and everyone knows Mark.

* * *

On the main road, at the junction where we had turned to head to Marks house, sat the Frantoio Flamingo olive oil refinery.

Mark had a small amount of very old olive trees and had his oil produced there, though 2021 was a terrible year for Sicilian oil, with scorching temperatures leading to a very poor harvest.

He took us to buy some of the green liquid gold, direct from the factory, and having introduced us to the owner, we got the full guided tour, and the opportunity to purchase this most sublime of liquids, at a very agreeable price of 9 EURO per litre (*it sold for 15 Euro in local shops, and even more once bottled and exported*).

Across Sicily are many small scale oil processing businesses like this one, catering for all the small and medium sized olive producers based near them. We received a great welcome and it was fascinating to see the whole process.

It was enlightening to understand how this wonderful iconic product is produced. Local producers coming together to turn olives into oil, and chatting about their harvest - despite the machinery being modern, they have been producing oil here since 1939, you can imagine the same fundamental process being carried out for centuries before that.

Some of the trees remaining on the island were planted by the Saracen invaders over a thousand years ago, but others are believed to be much older still, with the very oldest estimated to have been planted when the island was a Roman province, over two thousand years ago.

The history of the land is all around you. It's absolutely intoxicating.

* * *

The following day, Mark had arranged for us to meet Anita, a Swiss friend of his, who lived around 30 minutes away. She was apparently very excited to meet us, and especially Linda, as she was experiencing some horse related problems, and she felt that Linda could very well have the perfect experience to be able to help her. (*If you have been wondering about the title of this chapter, congratulations on your stamina. So finally, here we go*).

Mark drove us to Anita's property just outside Rosolini. It was a stunning rural estate. 50 hectares of green pasture, terraced olive groves and carob trees, all criss-crossed with stony tracks, each of them lined with the traditional dry stone walls of the region.

Anita was in her mid sixties, and had lived for many years in Italy, and most recently Sicily, with her collection of wild cats and semi wild dogs, and, her recently departed Husbands prized, horses.

Behind her beautifully restored farmhouse, we met the horses in question, and Anita told us that whilst she loved the horses, she had no experience with them.

'Help me!' she implored, laughing freely and often.

She had a beautifully elegant jet black Friesian mare called Stella, but she wasn't the problem. Luna, the mother, and Siri, the foal, were the problem.

The youngster was essentially unbroken and wild, and had not been separated from the mother correctly. This made them both unpredictable to handle, and very dangerous to handle. Her Indian farmhand knew nothing of horses so they received next to no attention during the day.

Anita showed us around the rest of the property and seemed very excited that we might come and help her.

She enthusiastically showed us her empty apartments that she hoped to use in the future for bed and breakfast, and offered us the use of them if we wanted, in exchange for the horse work, and a few other things on the estate.

Whilst this seemed a reasonable win/win offer, I was at pains to say that we had the Defender and were happy to sleep in our tents, so as not to inconvenience her, or cost her too much money.

She insisted that it was not a problem, and they were empty anyway. She had an old Defender 90, and we could use that if we wanted. She had too many cars apparently.

It all seemed far too good to be true. Good for her, no doubt, but perfect for us.

We all agreed to think about it overnight, and Mark invited Anita to come to his house the following day for lunch, to discuss things first.

* * *

After an enjoyable lunch the following day, if anything, Anita was even more enthusiastic about the prospect of us coming to work at her estate.

She had friends staying at her property for a further week or so, but we were welcome to come any time after that. The deal was done.

Linda repeated her message that the horses were a complex problem, and would not be solved overnight. It could take many weeks to gain the confidence of the horses, before even trying to separate her from the mother.

We agreed to see how things would work out, and we told her that we could stay until maybe February or March, but no longer. *'No problem!'*, said Anita, *'We have lots of time'*.

We settled on a date and shook hands.

We finally had a plan for the winter. Linda was as excited as I had seen her for a very long time.

She thrived on having a purpose.

* * *

ALWAYS LOOK A GIFT HORSE IN THE MOUTH.

As Anita jumped into her Defender 90, and bounced down the track from Marks house, we thanked him for making the introduction.

He threw us a look, *'Be careful, she can be a funny one'*, he said. Barbara, his wife, who had retuned by now, nodded sagely in agreement.

'Really?', I said. She seemed a little scatterbrained maybe, but very open, relaxed and friendly from what I had seen.

*'Just make sure you are all working, and that she can **SEE** that you are busy all the time'*, Mark prophetically cautioned.

I milled this over. I've learnt in life to treat people as I find them, not as they are described to me.

Time would tell how wise those words would be.

* * *

We filled the following days with manual work around Marks property, and meeting up with some of his wonderfully interesting friends.

One such friend, Giuseppe 'Peppe' Mallia, was a fascinating character. A local teacher, he was also an amateur naturalist, organizer of local treks, and a long time grower of Olives for oil.

A very kind, welcoming, and laid back character greeted us in the centre of Frigintini, as we joined Mark and some other trekking regulars, ready for one of one of Peppe's Sunday morning hikes through the local countryside.

Earlier in the day, as we dressed to go on the walk, mischievous Mark had made no mention of our choice of T shirts and shorts for a walk in the countryside.

Conversely, he was prepared for an ascent of the north face.

I should have known.

After a 40 minute drive up the winding roads of the Sicilian interior, our convoy of trekkers arrived at the *'Bosco Della Contessa'*, a forest over 1000 metres above sea level, and despite being bathed in strong sunshine, the temperature had plummeted.

Everyone was very welcoming, and were even polite enough not to deride our somewhat inappropriate clothing selection, or our lack of tasty snacks (*a wide selection being vitally important, as we would soon find out*).

Italian trekking, if this is anything to go by, was made up of three equal parts - one part standing around talking, one part eating biscuits and fruit, and one part actually walking.

You know it's bad, when even I find the lack of walking an issue.

Once the biscotti were extinguished, we finally got going. The pay off was a truly spectacular climax to the walk as we gathered by a hunting tower and took in a breathtaking view across to Syracuse, and the Ionian sea beyond. Just reward for a few hours walking.

The following day, Mark took a phone call from Peppe, and, apparently, he needed some help with his olive harvest. We jumped at the opportunity.

Arriving at his stone walled groves of olive trees, Peppe's familiar red Freelander was parked just inside the gate, and he had begun laying the nets beneath the first few trees, nets into which the falling olives would be caught for collection.

His usual team of itinerant olive pickers had failed to arrive, and more importantly, their mechanised picking equipment was absent with them. Peppe had 200 trees to harvest, and he couldn't wait. He would start the harvest manually, and he needed all the help that he could get.

Much respect needs to go to those that are entrusted with gathering the olives of that many trees - it is back breaking work.

Using long poles, you must dislodge the olives by hand, and those at the very top of the larger trees, requires someone to climb up the trunk and along the larger branches, to dislodge them.

Just a couple of hours toiling was enough for this former desk jockey. We completed only two trees and filled 10 trays of olives. Enough for a few salad dressings maybe, but no more.

It was truly humbling to experience a traditional part of Sicilian life, even in such a small and outwardly insignificant way.

We left Peppe to his work and wished him a good harvest.

* * *

In the blink of an eye, it became time to bid farewell to Mark and Barbara.

The days spent with them in their *'hideaway'* in the hills called '**Mohba**' - an old Maltese word that refers to a secret place in a stone house where valuables are hidden from the bandits.

Bandits are, thankfully, much more scarce these days but the name still holds good - a wonderful tranquil place to hide away from a COVID filled world.

The hospitality offered by Mark and his wife Barbara was

humbling to say the least. They coped with our heavy 130 horribly cutting up the track to their simply beautiful off-grid house, and they put up with our incessant demands on their scarce supplies of water and electricity - when 3 people land on your doorstep, it's a very big deal when you live that far off the grid.

In time honoured fashion, on our last evening together, we treated them both to a meal in the centre of Modica.

Tomorrow, we would begin a whole new adventure.

***

As I drove Mandy through the imposing iron gates of Terre di Ritillini, I felt some apprehension at our new chapter, but the weather was amazing - we were in the middle of November, and it was better than an English summer. The property looked stunning

We pulled into the courtyard of the farm complex.

Anita was staying in a large apartment above the two empty smaller apartments. Mandy even had her own shelter, when Anita agreed that I could put her inside the unfinished barn, as she needed a good check over, after the many miles that we had done since leaving the UK in September.

Anita greeting us with a bottle of white wine, and a wonderful meal of self prepared fish pasta.

Linda was obviously contented, setting about transferring our food and belongings from Mandy to the apartments - she was noticeably relived that we had somewhere under cover for the wet winter that was surely coming.

So far, everything was going to plan.

BLOOD, SWEAT AND GEARS.

* * *

Morning came, accompanied by a beautiful sunrise that appeared over the old stone pig sty on the opposite side of the courtyard, now the home of a very noisy family of Goats.

Stepping out of the door, you were very often met by a a hoard of hungry ferile cats, fighting to get under your feet.

They numbered at least 20 adults and kittens, and we learnt, to our cost, just how ruthlessly they operated. Over the coming days, we learnt not to leave a door or window open, or a bag of shopping unattended outside the apartment. they were the polar opposites of escape artists, the little thieves would get in anywhere, and steal anything that was remotely edible.

We would come to realise over time, that Anita had some very odd attitudes to animal husbandry. The cats gave the first indication that we may be stepping into trouble.

The cats were acquired organically over time, if you understand my meaning, with the colony growing exponentially every year. She gave the impression of being concerned about this, but never so concerned as to actually do anything about the problem. She preferred 'natural' methods, whatever that meant.

They were becoming a serious pest and, it was plain to see that, her eccentric method of feeding them was not helping the situation - she would throw food from a sack, once a day, and leave the cats to fight over it themselves.

AS you would expect, the stronger cats got the majority of the food, and the smaller ones got next to nothing. The cats, having lost their ability to hunt themselves had, in effect, become ferile house cats.

None of the female cats were neutered, so 20 would soon be 30, and then 50 and then heaven knows how many.

Linda offered to round up the adult females so they could be neutered.

'Impossible', said Anita, they could never be caught. Linda, having extensive experience of working in a cattery, was confident that she could cage them over a short time.

Whether this was due to the cost, or some more esoteric *'natural'* reasoning, we could not be sure, but this was not the last example of Anita displayed her disinterest in doing what we felt was right for her animals.

* * *

Linda set about creating a routine.

Most mornings she rose early and accompanied Anita as she walked 3 of her 4 dogs Lana, Kiera, and Tigre. The final dog, Poopa, was deaf and blind, and largely stayed in her apartment.

Like the cats, it soon became obvious that the dogs were also pretty wild and largely untrained. Most were not lead trained, and had a poor recall, if any at all. She told us that she got complaints from the vineyard that bordering her land, unhappy with her dogs trespassing on their land, but seemed unbothered.

Each morning Linda would accompany Anita's live in worker, Gurdial, to put the horses out into the paddock.

Gurdial lived in the main farmhouse at the far end of the small courtyard, and at the beginning we saw very little of him, usually when he was moving the goats from the courtyard to their grazing and back. Oliver had found a way to communicate with him though, and would occasionally help Gurdial with chores concerning the goats.

Things slowly settled into a routine. Anita would come and go, and Linda would care for the horses, and we would busy ourselves pruning trees, cleaning vehicles and walking the dogs.

Anita enjoyed hosting parties and she very kindly arranged a birthday party for Olivers 18th. Mark and Barbara would come over, and Anita would invite some of her friends as well. It was a lovely evening and very appreciated by us all.

* * *

Everyting seemed to be going just fine, until suddenly, everything wasn't.

First of the month, Kick and a punch.

The morning of the first of December began as normal, with Linda walking the dogs with Anita, but out of the blue, Anita had bluntly informed Linda that she was very unhappy.

She said that there was not enough work for all three of us despite, three weeks earlier, saying clearly that anything that we did do was a bonus, and the priority was to help the horses.

She was very unhappy that we had told someone that we were staying until March. Apparently, her builder was coming in January, so we would need to leave by then.

It remains unclear who that someone was, but this was bizarre.

She either had a memory like a sieve, or she was playing a very weird game. We HAD told someone, that we could only stay UNTIL March… HER, several weeks earlier.

Furthermore, she said, we were using all of her things, and not paying anything. She was unhappy that we were using both apartments, using her car, her washing machine, her oven, her gas. The list was endless.

She had comprehensibly listed literally **every single thing** that she had offered to us in exchange for Linda dealing with the horses.

We had not specifically asked for any of them, and in every single case, she had offered them to us.

*   *   *

Linda was very upset, and then Anita began to cry. It was like kindergarten.

I was not crying, I was absolutely livid. I could see what she was up to. We had been led up the garden path.

She wanted the horses trained, but for less than free. She wanted us to pay for the privilege. The sheer neck if the woman amazed me.

I calmly explained that we were only using those things that **SHE** herself had proposed as the agreement, and incidently, I had filled her Defender fuel tank twice in the three weeks that we had been there - we used it almost exclusively for taking rubbish to the municipal bins, in the next village, and buying food once a week.

Regrettably, I restrained myself from commented about her recently rekindled love of driving her Defender. The love that seemed to conveniently coincide with me first filling the fuel tank. Coincidence I imagined.

I could see that Linda really enjoyed what she was doing with the horses, and we had all grown attached to the dogs, so, for the umpteenth time since we had met Anita, I offered the option for us to sleep in the Defender, and save her the trouble of providing the apartments.

Through tears, she waved her hands across her face *'No, No. this is not necessary. You stay in the apartments'*, she insisted.

I didn't know what to think. The woman changed her mind like the wind.

Exasperated, I suggested we buy a cylinder of cooking gas, around 50 Euro. She seemed content with that, for now. Linda less so.

I pushed again for a meeting with Gurdial. He was a Sikh and spoke only Punjabi. This made communication extremely difficult and much frustration and confusion ensued, particularly with the care of the horses. We needed a meeting with his son present, who spoke Italian fluently, as soon as possible to make the responsibilities clear. She agreed to arrange it.

Bizarrely, she finished the discussion by proposing a trip to a local wildlife reserve where it was possible to see wild flamingoes coming and going. I didn't hold out much hope after, given the previous 15 minutes. She'd probably forget all about it by the time her next wine bottle was open.

* * *

In the days following the discussion, things settled down to normal. We have the meeting with Gurdial and responsibilities were a little clearer, but worryingly, it was becoming obvious that Anita had no intention of doing what was necessary to sort out her horse problems.

ALWAYS LOOK A GIFT HORSE IN THE MOUTH.

* * *

Linda had repeatedly advised Anita that the mother and foal needed to be separated urgently. Not only Linda, but her farrier told her, her vet told her. But still. Anita took absolutely no action.

Progress with the horses would be impossible, until they were separated.

Four weeks had gone by now and with only four weeks left until January, there was next to no time to achieve anything at all.

They needed to be far enough apart that they could not call to each either. When pushed by Linda yet again to sort it out, Anita's reaction was to criticise what Linda had done with the horses. Anita felt that she wasn't spending enough time with them.

Linda pointed out bluntly that, until they were separated, she could spend 24 hours a day with them, and get precisely nowhere. This didn't go down well. Anita had watched a lot of YouTube videos, apparently, and was now a horse expert.

Linda spoke to her friend, Caroline Bowers in England, a horse expert, and she agreed with everyting that Linda was doing, and furthermore, suggested the possibility that foals aggression may be caused by a hormonal problem.

Anita dismissed this out if hand, she was heathy, and that's that. No Vet.

One wonders why, being such an expert that she is, Anita didn't manage to solve these problems herself. Easier all around, I would have thought.

* * *

Linda came back completely deflated, after speaking with Anita.

She was doing the best she could, but she was obviously wasting her time, and to make matters worse, Anita rarely visited the horses from one week to the next, despite them being 200 yards from her house.

I began looking for an exit plan.

I wanted to have my ducks in a row in case things deteriorated further.

Little did I know, just how well the gods of fate were preparing to care for us..

* * *

Linda had recently found a website called Trusted House Sitters, a portal to allow house owners to find someone to care for their home and their pets, whilst they are away.

Amazingly, the very day that we registered on the site, we received a message from a lady called Iris, who lived in Tuscany.

She needed help with her 5 rescue dogs for a few weeks, beginning in early January, but Anita was about to return to Switzerland for Christmas and new year and we had agreed to collect her from the airport on the same day that we would be required in Tuscany.

During a video call with Iris, she accepted us there and then. She understood that we would need a few days to get from Sicily, so we settled on the 12th of January as the prospective start date.

We agreed to keep in touch about the dates.

ALWAYS LOOK A GIFT HORSE IN THE MOUTH.

* * *

A week before Christmas, we helped Anita load the car with her baggage, ready to take her to the airport, for her Christmas holiday in Switzerland.

She seemed happy, jolly in fact, as we drove the hour or so to Catania Airport. Despite our ups and downs, Anita could be a very likeable and interesting character, and we were eager not to fall out with her in any way. Burnt bridges have no purpose, after all.

We pulled into the wonderfully named 10 minute drop-off point called, *'Kiss and Go'*, that every Italian Airport has.

Anita was exuberant, air kisses and *'Buon Natale'* for all.

We hugged and wished each other well, and Anita insisted that we should visit the centre of Catania, as it was very beautiful.

* * *

The bombshell arrived in digital form a several hours after dropping her off.

Anita was on the train to Switzerland, and seemed to have built up a head of steam, sending Linda a bizarre and rambling message accusing her of everything under the sun.

I was not entirely surprised, though she had said absolutely nothing in the car. According to her, Linda was ungrateful, never saying thank you for the perfect place that she had offered to us, and we had saved lots of money by not staying in a bed and breakfast for all these weeks.

Furthermore, we had used her washing machine - again, despite her offering its use freely, and as soon as she got back in January, she wanted us to leave.

I messaged her and said I would collect her from the airport myself, and we would leave the following day.

I told Linda not to reply to her messages.

* * *

Heading back from Catania, feeling very hard done by, her car broke down in the car park of a shopping centre. I tried bumping it, and for once, I didn't have my jumper cables.

Perfect end to a perfect day

Damn, I would have to contact Anita.

'Don't worry, I have breakdown insurance'. replies Anita to my message.

'Er', no you don't, I've checked your documents in the car', say I.

'Yes, I have them for all the cars', she insists.

I call the insurance company.

'She doesn't have breakdown insurance, it wasn't selected when the policy was renewed'. says the insurance company.

'Priceless', say I

At this point, I should have rolled it down to the exit ramp of the car park and let it go, but no, I'm better than that.

I use my own ACI breakdown insurance and 30 mins later, the car is started, but I am reliably informed that the battery is a complete goner, and under **NO** circumstances should I stop, **not even for fuel.**

Looks at gauge. Here we go… less than a quarter of a tank.

* * *

An hour or so later, we glided up the long drive on fumes

ALWAYS LOOK A GIFT HORSE IN THE MOUTH.

and parked the Fiat under the trees beside her apartment. I messaged her to get someone to sort out a new battery and stick some fuel in it.

We didn't touch it again. From the moment we got back, we used Mandy.

That night, Linda, having told Anita how upset she was about the message earlier that day, gets another rabid message from Anita.

Even worse this time, very personal abuse, falsely accusing Linda of being lazy by only spending two hours with the horses, questioning our parenting skills by taking Oliver on our travels. It went on and on.

I'd had enough. I contacted Iris in Tuscany, and told her that we would be able to arrive on the 8th January as originally requested.

I would tell Anita to make other arrangements for her collection from the airport, but only in the new year. I was seething inside.

* * *

Amazingly, after all her awful messages, Anita would continue send friendly emoji-full messages to me, all over Christmas, asking how the dogs were, were we OK.

She got one word answers.

She was puzzled why Linda didn't reply to her messages. An unbelievably lack of self awareness.

Whilst Anita was away, the change in Gurdial was staggering. He would come shopping with us, invite us to eat and drink with him in his apartment, he laughed and joked. He was an entirely different person.

I fear that there is a deeper story there, but one I sadly never got to discover.

* * *

Christmas came and went. Easily the worst since 2005, when the closure of the Terry's factory in York led to Chocolate Oranges being manufactured in continental Europe, of all places.

On Christmas day, we ate and stayed at an Agriturismo, up in the hills, recommended by Anita. As I should have expected, her recommendation was vastly overpriced and chronic value for money. The rooms were freezing cold, the owners dog hated me, and the food was weirdly fancy.

If it hadn't been for the wine, I would have slit my throat, there and then.

* * *

New year's eve came and went without even a pop.

One very clear highlight, however, was a fire pit BBQ with Mark and Barbara to say goodbye. It was great to see our lovely Maltese friends before we left.

I can't blame Mark, he did warn me, after all.

A lovely new years day, finished off with Jools Holland via VPN.

Before heading to Tuscany, we had one last important thing to do in Sicily.

Quite amazingly, I had managed to get on-line appointments for myself and Linda's COVID booster jab in the local town, despite us not being Sicilian residents, or indeed Italian for that matter.

Our appointments were 30 minutes apart on 4th January, but this is Italy, we'd go together and chance our arm.

We arrived at 3 pm and spent the first 10 minutes looking for the entrance. It seems that Sicilian vaccinations are secret. There were no signs whatsoever, but by a slow process of elimination, we finally found what appeared to be the entrance.

10 minutes now until the appointment, perfect.

We pushing through a small crowd loitering in the foyer, we had 2 options. Big room on the right, lots of people in it. Little room on the left, fewer people in it.

A small sign on the door to the big room read **Registration** in Italian. Worth a punt.

I knew enough about Italian bureaucracy, to know that just because I had completed a multitude of online forms, it certainly didn't mean that I would not have to do them all again, possibly more than once.

* * *

In possibly the least COVID secure method imaginable, we set about trying to register.

Everyone was milling around one small desk, manned by one very harassed looking medical volunteer, sweating profusely in his familiar fluorescent ambulance volunteer suit.

As more people arrived and squeezed through the lobby choked with people, the room began to fill up. With only a half a dozen seats, the rest of us stood around looking at each other.

You simply could not design a better way to transmit a disease amongst a group of people, if you tried. We both felt very uneasy. The locals were getting restless too. No one seemed to be getting a jab.

As I suspected, we would need to fill out lengthy paper forms for each of us, detailed exactly the same information that I had laboriously entered on line when I had booked the appointments weeks ago.

The place was a seething shambles by now.

After some investigation, the problem was revealed. Lots of people, but no vaccines.

Due to the short shelf life, the vaccines were due to arrive that day at 2 pm. They had not arrived. It was now 4 pm. They were due any moment, apparently.

The minutes ticked passed, and more people arrived all the time. We tried to move into the smaller room, but kept being sent back to the grossly overcrowded larger room.

Finally, lists of names were called and a few people went off for their jabs. A little after 6 pm, almost 3 hours after our appointments, we finally received our vaccinations.

To get them, we walked through closed corridors and climbed narrow flights of stairs, passing numerous of those people that had just received vaccinations, coming the other way to the entrance foyer.

The contrast between this experience, and the vaccinations that we received in UK could not have been more stark. It was unbelievable, and goes some way to explaining the continued high levels of infection in Italy.

* * *

ALWAYS LOOK A GIFT HORSE IN THE MOUTH.

The first week of January 2022 passed with Linda becoming more and more anxious to get moving, and the whole experience with Anita, other than meeting Gurdial, had left a very bitter taste in all our mouths.

The way that Anita was still treating her, sending wine fuelled, expletive laden messages for no apparent reason, was deeply affecting her, and in particular, the criticism of her parenting of Oliver had cut very deep.

It made her question everything we were doing, and why we we were doing it.

There's only one person to blame for that, and I will never forgive her.

The only way to fully wash that taste away, was to get to Tuscany, but I must admit to a little trepidation.

After such a negative experience with Anita, was Iris going to be friend or foe? Time would tell.

* * *

We spent our final morning at Terre di Ritillini packing Mandy, and with Linda, being Linda, scrupulously cleaning both apartments from top to bottom.

I made comprehensive videos to send to Anita as evidence that we had left them in a considerably better state than when we had found them.

A final goodbye with Gurdial, resulting in us taking lunch together, eating his wonderful, spicy, deep friend vegetables. He appeared as sad to see us go, as we were to leave him. He was a lovely, kind, gentle man, and we felt bad leaving him to his fate, he deserved a better life.

The sun shone, we waved goodbye. I messaged Anita with

the videos, and informed her that she would need to arrange her own collection from the airport.

As we drove toward Catania, heading for Mount Etna, we all blocked Anita on social media and messaging apps. She was finally history now.

From the high of meeting such nice, kind and friendly people like Mark and Barbara, in less than 2 months, we had had our faith in humanity completely destroyed, and caused us to question everything that we were doing. We were that fragile.

* * *

In early December, we had been invited via Facebook to visit another Maltese resident of Sicily. Moira and Philip owned Cirasala, a luxury B&B on the lower slopes of Mount Etna.

Driving back to Messina, was a perfect opportunity to take up Moira's very kind offer of hospitality. Sadly, by the time we arrived for our two night stay in January, Moira had contracted COVID, and was trapped in Malta under quarantine.

Despite Philip telling us that he was the businessman, and Moira was the social one, we were treated like honoured guests, staying in their two bedroom cabin in the grounds of the B&B.

ALWAYS LOOK A GIFT HORSE IN THE MOUTH.

On the second day, in stunning weather, we drove up the winding roads of a cloudless Mount Etna, arriving 6000 feet above sea level. Dust from her eruptions were evident at the sides of the road like black snow drifts after a bad winter.

Epic views in all directions. We walked on the black sandy slopes, despite the bright sunshine, thick coats and hats were necessary to combat the incredibly strong winds.

We were so blessed to be able to visit this beautiful place in such good weather. We bought a Buddha made from the black volcanic rock, and found a home for him on the dashboard. This is why we travel.

*　*　*

After the refreshing experience at Cirasala, it was great to leave Sicily with a clear reminder that, for every Anita in the world, there are thousands of people like Mark, Barbara, Peppe, Philip, Moira, and the rest of the people that you will find mentioned at the front of this book.

They represent all that is great about humanity, not her. Perspective is key.

＊＊

Now, we needed to get a real move on, as we had arranged to meet Iris in Tuscany in just a few days time, so we decided to take a longer ferry to the mainland, that would cut off a couple of days driving.

Whilst the crossing to Salerno was a more expensive option, ever one for a bargain, I found that the 2 am ferry was considerably less that the daylight crossing, and would gain us even more time as we would be moving while we were sleeping.

Oliver was horrified. His relationship to his bed was deep and long-standing.

It took a few goes for him to understand the gravity of the situation. Yes, we would be on a ferry all night. No, he would not have a bed. I lied and told him we could get on the ferry at 11pm.

I had no idea what time we could get on the ferry.

We left the B&B late in the evening and took a slow drive along the coast to Messina.

Add tiredness, darkness and the usual lack of signage, trying to find the ferry terminal turned into a frustrating 30 minute drive around the arse end of Messina, employing every swear word I could think of in two languages failed to help the situation.

ALWAYS LOOK A GIFT HORSE IN THE MOUTH.

Finally, after stopping and asking someone, we found the gate. Yes, it had gotten **THAT** serious, that I had to break the male drivers code of conduct, and ask for directions. I'll carry the shame to my grave.

* * *

As we drove through the unsigned gate, we drove towards a ship. Maybe ours, maybe not, it wasn't yet clear. Nothing was clear.

Sheep-like, I fell in behind a couple of cars parked in line a line before another gate, around which was a parked up police car, and some miserable looking security men, smoking cigarettes and staring at their mobile phones.

Even though we were not crossing an international border, since COVID, at Ferry Ports, they treated us in a much more secure way, in fact more so in many respects, than when we crossed the border between France and Italy, at the height of the pandemic.

Mirrors on sticks, passport checks, COVID certificates - apparently, it was easier to get into Buckingham Palace than getting on this ferry.

At midnight, sorry Oliver, we were ushered towards the ramp to join the ferry.

I drove on, no visible staff on the bottom deck until we reached the very end, where, unhelpfully, I was directed to turn 180 degrees back on my self and climb another ramp. Not easy in a 130.

As we crested the ramp, we were on an open air deck, deck number 5.

I stopped, waiting a few minutes, and with growing irritation, and minus any staff to tell me otherwise, I headed for a line of motorhomes and other high vehicles directly in front of me, with the intention of parking up next to them..

I could hear some bloke screaming *'Whoa, Whoa!'* from behind me, swearing a lot. Cazzo this, Fanculo that. Over and Over.

'I think he's talking to us', said Linda.

'Oh, he IS, is he?' I said

'Oi, Where the f**k have you been hiding?' I shouted at him, as I reversed Mandy a little to greet him.

Still shouting a mixture of swearing and unintelligible Sicilian gibberish, he was angrily pointing to the opposite end of the boat. It seems, I should have known where to go, and, by his estimation, I was some sort of raving idiot.

I was in my stride now, the switch had been thrown. He got the full Anglo Saxon hairdryer treatment, but sadly, he wasn't finished yet.

As we arrived near to the place that he wanted us to park, all the cars were pointing the other way. Baffled, in front of me was the massive structure of the ships funnel in the centre of the deck so, naturally, I went to drive around the back of it and park up in the line in the correct orientation.

'NON, NON, NON!', he screamed. He gesticulated madly that I needed to get on the front of the line but, seemingly, in the most awkward way possible.

Every tiny shunt of my 20 point turn in Mandy was accompanied with an expletive.

By this time, the mini Mussolini had wandered off to ruin someone else's night, so sadly he didn't get the full benefit, but it made me feel better.

Finally on board, and completely spent, we found some

ALWAYS LOOK A GIFT HORSE IN THE MOUTH.

seats in the bar, and settled down for a largely restless 10 hour crossing.

* * *

The morning dawned fresh and windy.

We were all still pretty knackered, but grateful that we would have a campsite that night to have some hot food and a shower.

Docking in Salerno was refreshingly simple and without incident, and more importantly, not far from our most favourite campsite, in San Lazzaro, just up the coast from Salerno. We needed no excuse to check in to the hippy paradise for one last night.

Driving the tiny coast road, from Salerno to San Lazzaro, was genuine bucket list stuff. Trying to feed Mandy through the eye of needle after needle was hugely rewarding.

We travelled the entire Amalfi coast, but the only thing missing was the weather. It was cold and grey. The coldest we had felt since we had arrived back in Italy.

The campsite was just as we left it. Just a colder version of paradise.

* * *

Leaving the campsite the next day, we encountered some very Scottish weather on the way to Tuscany. Sun, rain, hail and Snow were encountered in the few hours it took to drive the back roads to Montespertoli.

Letting someone into your home, and caring for your animals is a big thing. It's a genuine leap of faith, for both parties, that shouldn't be underestimated.

Still smarting from the painful experience we had endured with Anita, we warily arrived in the beautiful and tranquil Tuscan countryside to, hopefully, see out the rest of the winter.

We needn't have worried, as it soon became apparent that we had parachuted into the centre of the joyfully chaotic and colourful world of Iris, her lovely son, and her bonkers band of wonderfully eccentric rescue dogs.

Initially reticent, I soon warmed to both the situation and, especially, the dogs, which came in all sizes and shapes.

James, a deaf and blind eating machine of a truffle dog, followed by the joint heads of the barking department, Lucy and Reuben, and finally, the Italian white shepherding dogs of supermodel Syria, and the giant, mildly autistic Oscar.

Iris had recently bought a house in Turin, and would be travelling between the two properties as and when necessary. She would soon sub-let her property to Dominika and Jonathan, a local couple.

We soon settled into a routine of dog walking, and book writing.

We all felt instantly at home. Iris, made us feel valued and appreciated.

* * *

By late January, it was clear that we had eaten away any chance of getting to Canada within 2022, we were down to our last Twenty Thousand Euros that we held in contingency.

We had this in case the worst happened, and we needed to rent a property.

ALWAYS LOOK A GIFT HORSE IN THE MOUTH.

The combination of the COVID delays, and the unexpected rental costs, vehicle upgrades and repairs, had decimated the pot.

We had now lost over 12 months on the original plan.

Call it bad luck, or bad planning, or a combination of the two - the only way we were going to do the Pan American, was to raise some money, and fast.

* * *

The original plan was to spend a year in North America, and then write a book, before competing the final year of South America, and them publishing a further revision of the book including the whole journey, when we returned to the UK.

That plan was in complete tatters, screwed up and thrown in the bin.

I needed a new one, and fast.

9

Still in the Arena.

"Desperation can make a person do surprising things."
— ***Veronica Roth***

While in Sicily, I had decided, in a desperate attempt to raise some much needed cash, to write and publish a book about my life.

I may have a way with words, I grant you, but I am clearly no writer.

Not for the first time in my life though, I backed myself to dig the family out of the hole that I had firmly put us in.

* * *

I started to write. It proved itself a lot harder and much slower than I thought it would be.

In my mind, as I would write a sentence , I would hear my words in the voices of great intellectuals, and they often sounded clumsily simplistic, or even plain dumb.

I persevered, but it was difficult, with a house full of noise to contend with, and the voice of Hitchens, Dawkins or Chomsky goading me in my head.

Some days were better than others, but time was running out. Without the mechanism to sell books on line efficiently, particularly as I live in a Land Rover, I needed to find a way to raise the money up front.

I settled on a crowdfunding but made the cardinal mistake of over-stretching. I set the target such that I could print a 1000 softback and 1000 hardback books. The economies of scale were massive. Who was I kidding though? In retrospect, how are earth would I have sold 2000 books? Pure hubris.

Despite a valiant effort to piss off literally everyone that I had ever come into contact with in my life, I fell short. I had pledges of fourteen thousand Euros against a ridiculously ambitious target of Twenty One Thousand Euros.

I was gutted. Was I greedy? Maybe a little. Was I stupid? Almost certainly.

Another plan was needed, yet again.

* * *

Lightbulb moment. I figured, that if I could get everyone that had pledged, to pre-order the book instead, I could then order just enough books to satisfy the initial demand, and still make it work somehow. The individual books would cost considerably more, but I would have to swallow that. This still might work, maybe.

Over 10 days, I set about pissing off everybody again, by repeatedly asking/begging them to convert their pledge.

Despite my campaign of gentle harassment, only roughly

50% of those that had pledged support, converted it into an order.

I was crestfallen.

Any last dream of Canada was flattened and dead again.

* * *

I carried on writing, but enthusiasm was thin on the ground.

I found it increasingly hard to focus. Yet again I had proved the truism of my life. I was not worthy of a project of this magnitude. So I had dared greatly, so what? I had let down my family, and much more painfully, I had let down all the sponsors who had believed in me, and believed in my ability to deliver this expedition.

What little self belief still remaining, crawled back inside me, out of shame and ignominy. As usual, I kept this hidden away inside me, festering away.

It's still there, gathering figurative dust.

* * *

After happily agreeing to a date few extensions, to help Iris, we would to stay in Tuscany until the third week of March.

Before leaving, we had the great joy of meeting some old friends, as they were passing through on the way to Greece from the UK.

Graeme and Laura Thompson had stayed with us briefly when we lived in Monteombraro, but this time we would get to spend a few days with them in Tuscany.

They are simply two of the nicest people we have ever met. Wise and compassionate beyond their years, they teach play based therapy for children in traumatic situations. I cant think if anything more noble. We broke bread, and talked of music, art, literature, comedy. Despite having spent less than a handful of days in each others company, I know we will be friends for life. That's why we travel. It was great sadness, that we wished them well and waved them off.

It's clear that Linda would have stayed in Tuscany forever. She would still be there now, I imagine, without my mill-stone around her neck.

We needed to keep moving as both Oliver's and Linda's passport would expire in June, and we were never anywhere long enough to risk posting them abroad. So, we had a target, to be back in UK for June.

Whenever we had reasonable Wi-Fi and somewhere to sit, I was writing.

I had the same target for the book - Eighty Thousand words to be published by the end of June.

* * *

We came up with a plan.

We would head back to our old stomping ground of Monteombraro first, for one last sift through our things we had in storage with our beautiful friend Elisa at the Hairdressers, and then book a few more house sittings, so that I could continue to write during April and into May.

In between we would informally camp as normal, sleeping in our tents.

Finally, in early May, we would take a slow drive through the south and east of France before arriving back in the UK towards the end of the month, perfectly timed to finish the book, and finally publish the damn thing.

* * *

In our time in Italy, we met many people, and in particular in Monteombraro, we met people that will doubtless remain great friends for life.

One such person is Elisa, a woman for all times.

She is the woman that has come the closest to getting my beard, at its crusty fisherman longest, into a 'Jack Sparrow' like beard pony-tale. Close, but currently, no cigar.

STILL IN THE ARENA.

After spending a few days in the hills near Bologna, informally camping in a municipal car park in Savigno, we contacted Elisa, and we cheekily invited ourselves to camp in the car park of her other business, the village's famous water park. It was still out of season, but they lived on-site, and we were welcome to come and stay as long as we wanted.

Elisa is a beautiful soul, and with her husband Roberto and daughter Celeste, just one third of a family of beautiful souls. She has cut our hair, and she has stored what remains of our possessions, but, much more importantly, she had welcomed us wholeheartedly into her life.

But before we could go to see them, we had visitors expected. It can be a lonely life on the road, and some people like it that way, but it's also nice to hook up with a fellow traveller every now and then.

Lawrence & Rachel are British vets, who travel as The Overlanding Ambulance, and were attempting the world's longest journey by Ambulance, in their ex-military Land Rover Defender Ambulance.

Proper overlanding, it has to be said. I was very jealous, if truth be told.

It was lovely to break bread with them and camp together for one night, despite their arrival attracted the local police to come a have a look at what was going down.

As usual, they were curious more than anything and left contented that we were the good guys.

* * *

Those few short days we spent with Elisa and her family were some of the best days we had experienced in our whole time in Italy. Elisa shares my interest in spirituality and Buddhism. She welcomed us in wholeheartedly.

We laughed together, cooked together, ate together, and all cared for the beautiful, bubbly Celeste. We each helped out wherever it was needed. It was a wonderful happy, incomparably hippy time.

Half jokingly, she invited us to stay for the summer and work in the swimming pool. I was half-jokingly seriously tempted, but regrettably, we just had to move on.

* * *

We had agreed to be in Turin on 12th April, as Iris asked us to sit for her in her new property, whilst she went to Morocco for a week or so.

I would get to spend time with my lovely, though slightly autistic, friend Oscar, the strangest, saddest dog that I have ever had the pleasure to meet.

It fitted with the plan, and the plan revolved around having Wi-Fi to be able to write. The next few weeks would be a blur of house sits, and long days of writing, rewriting and editing, until it was time to leave Italy, enter France and meander our way to England.

***

We crossed into France on the 3rd of May through the tiny unmanned border crossing of Breil-Sur-Roya, the narrow road rising high up along the escarpments, adjacent to the river's gorge.

So many times we had rushed through France to get to Italy, full of mind-numbing days driving along dead straight Autoroutes, and negotiating the dreaded Boulevard Périphérique, Paris's answer to the equally grim M25 in London.

This time, we HAD time. We slowly drove along the Riviera, taking in Cannes, Monaco and the rest. The weather, for once, was fully on our side.

We had some adventures, including almost getting the Defender wedged into a narrow street in Monaco, twice. Yes, the same street. We followed this up by being locked into some French Forestry land overnight, and having to get a little 'creative' to get out in the morning. Low range paid for itself that day.

We camped in some truly beautiful places as we made our

way through the south of France, some of the most memorable ever.

Sadly not all were memorable for the right reasons. One such, concerned the beautiful town of Collobrières, a village in Provence that had barely changed since 1939. Change a few shops fronts, drop a few road signs, and you are back there in pre war France.

***

It's a rare day when you get something for nothing. Free lunch anyone?

STILL IN THE ARENA.

On the outskirts of the village, an incredibly nice human being owned a field, and he allowed anyone to camp on it, and for as long as they wanted.

   He had guests who had been there for the over three months. He was a man of his word, and, as we would find out, a man of the world.

He would visit all of his guests each morning and each evening, just for a chat. He told us that he had travelled a lot in his life, even marrying a woman from Peru, no less.

We spoke about our plans, and we fussed his lovely playful young dog, who excitedly followed him everywhere. He told us where to go in the village to get what we needed.

He wanted absolutely nothing in return.

Seeing him the next morning without his dog, we enquired after him.

'Ah, he is dead, I am sorry to say', he intoned sadly.

Did he say dead?

Yes. He had run after a truck, barking at the wheels, slipped on the grass, got caught by his collar and was pulled under the wheels and crushed.

He was crushed, I was crushed.

The young represent hope, even dogs.

We were stunned. Offering condolences was insufficient, but that's all we had.

We left with a heavy heart.

* * *

We continued our way north with the target of a ferry from Cherbourg on the 18th of May. The intervening week was spent leapfrogging from mostly one charming municipal campsite to another.

Unlike Italy, France is blessed with a superb network of small municipal campsites, the vast majority of which are free, and those with reasonable facilities are a third of the price of what you would pay in a UK campsite.

STILL IN THE ARENA.

It's so hard to live the way we want to live, in the UK.

We have taken a little criticism in the past for appearing to *'travel from one friend to another'*. Our life is Illegal for one thing, and all land is owned by somebody. Unless you spend your entire time in the wilds of Scotland or North Wales, or maybe Yorkshire, so often, your only chance of a stress-free night, is to camp at a friend.

That's the country we live in.

* * *

Anyway, well done, you've nearly made it.

We set out in 2016 to live a very different life. I guess we can say, in some respects at least, we have achieved that. I don't get up each day, dreading my work.

Has it providing the spiritual renewal that I needed? Hardly. I have a long way to go to slow down my mind, but at least my left eye doesn't twitch the way that it used to do, but it's clear that I still have the same underlying problems of self doubt and inferiority.

The greatest thing about the process of writing this book, is that it has brought into much sharper relief, the many issues that I have been carrying within me for a very long time, and it has granted me the opportunity to look at my character from a distance, and realise that, as a personality that allegedly represents less than 1% of the population, I have spent far too many years ploughing a very long lonely furrow, in completely the wrong field. I should have been looking for galaxies.

Try not to make the same mistake.

Conclusion

"Do or do not. There is no try."
- Yoda

* * *

If you take anything away from the book, **take this...**

1. Live a life that **YOU** want to live, in the way **YOU** want to live it.
2. Hurt no one, and trust everyone, until proven wrong.
3. Understand exactly who you are inside, and be **THAT** person, and not the person you **THINK** you want to be on the outside.
4. Continue to build the very best version of **YOU**.
5. Never turn down an opportunity, but have the courage to walk away from anything that is not 100% of what **YOU** want, or what **YOU** need.
6. **NEVER** be afraid to fail at anything, large or small.

CONCLUSION

Finally, as a parting gift, I'll leave you with these immortal, inspirational words…

> *It is not the critic who counts; not the man who points out how the strong man stumbles, or where the doer of deeds could have done them better.* **The credit belongs to the man who is actually in the arena**, *whose face is marred by dust and sweat and blood; who strives valiantly; who errs, who comes short again and again, because there is no effort without error and shortcoming; but who does actually strive to do the deeds; who knows great enthusiasms, the great devotions; who spends himself in a worthy cause; who at the best knows in the end the triumph of high achievement, and who at the worst, if he fails, at least fails while daring greatly, so that his place shall never be with those cold and timid souls who neither know victory nor defeat. -* **Theodore Roosevelt, April 23, 1910.**

Currently, I am still to be found in the Arena, and only fate will decide when I leave.

Sicily December 2021

Notes

AVOIDING MISERY HANDED DOWN.

1. *If you are dying to find out - maybe start here with an interview with the former head of Astrophysics at Oxford University. You would like to think he would have a fair idea. https://www.esa.int/Science_Exploration/Space_Science/Is_the_Universe_finite_or_infinite_An_interview_with_Joseph_Silk*

2. *Peter Lorimer was a legendary Scottish Footballer who played for Leeds United Football club in the English First Division from 1962 to 1979 and finally in 1983–1985, and held the club record for highest goalscorer with 238 goals in all competitions. He died in March 2021 https://en.wikipedia.org/wiki/Peter_Lorimer*

3. *It seems that the infinite nature of the cosmos is, as with most things these days, far from certain. The observable universe is still expanding, maybe, so who knows? Further reading...https://theconversation.com/is-space-infinite-we-asked-5-experts-165742*

4. *Asthma is a major non-communicable disease (NCD), affecting both children and adults, and is the most common chronic disease among children. Inflammation and narrowing of the small airways in the lungs cause asthma symptoms, which can be any combination of cough, wheeze, shortness of breath and chest tightness. -* **WHO** *website.*

5. *Yes, it's a thing. Cherophobia is also known as an Aversion to happiness and has been academically studied - further reading in the Journal of Cross-Cultural Psychology.*

6. *This is the test that I took, but there are many others.*
   https://www.16personalities.com/

7. *Henry "Harry" Patterson, commonly known by his pen name Jack Higgins, was a British author. He was a best-selling author of popular thrillers and espionage novels. His novel The Eagle Has Landed sold more than 50 million copies and was adapted into a successful 1976 film of the same title. Wikipedia*

8. *Whicker's World was a British television documentary series that ran*

from 1958 to 1994, presented by journalist and broadcaster Alan Whicker. Originally a segment on the BBC's Tonight programme in 1958, Whicker's World became a fully-fledged television series in its own right in the 1960s. Wikipedia

LIFE AS A FLIGHTLESS BIRD.

9   *"It's absolutely true that some brain functions occur in one or the other side of the brain," Anderson says. "Language tends to be on the left, attention more on the right. But people don't tend to have a stronger left- or right-sided brain network." https://www.apa.org/monitor/2013/11/right-brained*

PUNISHMENT OF ANSWERED PRAYERS.

10 *Until the much anticipated 1988 Licensing act, which extended the permissible opening hours for public houses to 11am to 11pm, the most enthusiastic drinkers were unable to continue their imbibement between 3:00pm and 5:30pm.*

11 *Luton Town FC beat Arsenal in the Littlewoods Cup final at Wembley 3–2. The match was won in the 92nd minute with a goal by Brian Stein, after Luton had come back from being 2–1 down and goalkeeper Andy Dibble saving a penalty in the 79th minute. Luton scorers were Brian Stein (2) and Danny Wilson. 96,000 fans were in attendance, including my brother-in-law.*

12 *Claude Littner is an American-born British business executive, made famous for his involvement with the Apprentice TV show in the UK. Renowned as the most fearsome interviewer, among a panel of aggressive interviewers utilized in the last stages of the reality show, he would often reduce the candidates to tears as he shreds their half-baked business cases before their eyes.*

13 *The sobriquet 'Woody' was earned very early in the McLaren career of Dave Bradley. It makes reference to an incident, just a few days into his role as a team van driver, when he was despatched in a flatbed truck to collect a consignment of wooden planks. Specifically, whilst returning to the McLaren factory, he managed to close the entire southbound carriageway of the M25 motorway, when his poorly secured load was jettisoned across all three lanes.*

14 *The Young Ones is a British sitcom first shown in 1982 and 1984. The show focused on the lives of four dissimilar students and their landlord's family on different plots that often included anarchic, offbeat, surreal humour. https://en.wikipedia.org/wiki/The_Young_Ones_(TV_series)*

15 *Gordon Murray, is a South African born, but British domiciled, Automotive Engineer. After a long career in F1, he was the mastermind behind, what*

NOTES

many believe to be, the world's first Hyper car, the McLaren F1, launched in 1992.

16   The BTCC or British Touring Car Championship is a touring car racing series held each year in the United Kingdom, currently organized and administered by TOCA. It was established in 1958 as the British Saloon Car Championship and was renamed as the British Touring Car Championship for the 1987 season. Wikipedia

17   Some years after my Interview, Colin shared with me the amusing story of an interview that he carried out the day prior to mine. Another interview for the role that I was ultimately offered, it was conducted with an old acquaintance of mine. She shall remain nameless, but her explosive reaction to my name being mentioned was apparently startling to the point of not being unlike a sufferer of Tourette's syndrome. Whilst we had crossed paths in my career in Touring Cars, what Colin didn't know was that she felt perennially pipped at the post for jobs, roles that were ultimately taken by me!

18   Goodbye, Mr. Chips is a novella about the life of a school teacher, Mr. Chipping, written by English writer James Hilton and first published in 1934. It has been adapted into two feature films and two television presentations.

19   Christian was employed as Sporting Director as Pitchforth was still, in effect, the Team Principle, until such time as his contract was settled.

PAIN WITHOUT PURPOSE.

20   Jock Clear is an English senior performance engineer working for Scuderia Ferrari, where he is currently the Driver Coach for Charles Leclerc, alongside Calum MacDonald for Carlos Sainz Jr. Wikipedia

21   Adam Offord Buxton is an English actor, comedian, podcaster and writer. With the film-maker Joe Cornish, he is part of the comedy duo Adam and Joe. They presented the Channel 4 television series The Adam and Joe Show and the BBC Radio 6 Music series Adam and Joe. Wikipedia

22   David Peter Meads, known professionally and personally as Scroobius Pip, is an English actor and podcaster as well as a former spoken word poet and hip hop recording artist from Stanford-le-Hope, Essex. Wikipedia

PLANS AND PANDEMICS.

23   The never ending road trip, was an article that was published by the BBC in the Autos section of their website, that sadly, has recently been swept under the digital carpet.

24 Jeremy Charles Robert Clarkson is an English broadcaster, journalist, farmer, game show host and writer who specializes in motoring. He is best known for the motoring programmes Top Gear and The Grand Tour alongside Richard Hammond and James May. Wikipedia

ALWAYS LOOK A GIFT HORSE IN THE MOUTH.

25 Michelangelo Merisi da Caravaggio, known as simply Caravaggio, was an Italian painter active in Rome for most of his artistic life. During the final four years of his life he moved between Naples, Malta, and Sicily until his death. Wikipedia

26 King of the Hammers is an off-road race that combines desert racing and rock crawling. This race is held in February on Means Dry Lake at Johnson Valley, California, United States. Wikipedia

27 Molise is a mountainous Italian region with a stretch of coastline on the Adriatic Sea. It encompasses part of the National Park of Abruzzo in the Apennines mountain range, with rich wildlife and trails. The regional capital, Campobasso, is known for its mountaintop Monforte Castle and Romanesque churches. Northerners like to joke that it doesn't exist. https://www.bbc.com/travel/article/20191023-the-italian-region-that-doesnt-exist

About the Author

Nigel Betts was born and raised in Northamptonshire, England. He began writing in 2022, with his first publication 'Blood, Sweat and Gears - a memoir.'

He spent over 30 years working in the high stress environment of the Motor Sport Industry, including 26 years in the very pinnacle of the sport, Formula One, in 2019, he would suffer a monumental midlife crisis.

To combat this mental and physical crisis, and his mounting disaffection with the modern way of working and living, he set out to make radical and lasting change, by leaving work, and sinking the family's life savings into becoming a full time vehicle based overlander and author.

Married, with one son, he now lives at the side of the road, in a rooftop tent above a Land Rover Defender 130, unless the weather is particularly terrible, then you will find him scrounging a bed from one old friend or another.

You can connect with me on:

- https://itchyfeetoverland.com
- https://twitter.com/ItchyFeetOvrld
- https://www.facebook.com/itchyfeetoverland

Printed in Poland
by Amazon Fulfillment
Poland Sp. z o.o., Wrocław
29 July 2022